The Village Hall by Jon Wilmot, 1995

CHARTHAM HATCH

From Village School to Village Hall

The story of a building and life in a small village near Canterbury in Kent

Written and published by the History Project Group of the Chartham Hatch Village Hall Society

ACKNOWLEDGEMENTS

We are extremely grateful to all those we have spoken with during the research for this book - for their willingness to share their memories, to lend or donate their photographs and postcards and to contribute to our oral history recordings. Photographs, postcards and documents reproduced in this book have been acknowledged wherever possible. Where we have been unable to ascertain the original source, we have indicated this accordingly. We have collected far more memories than we have been able to include here and these will be archived for the future.

Many people have been involved in many different ways and we would like to thank you all. We would like especially to thank Veronica Litten, without whose initial account of the history of the hall this project would have never started, and Jim Sanders for his painstaking help in preparing the images.

We would also like to thank the Local Heritage Initiative*, without whose financial support the project would not have been possible.

We have tried to record faithfully what we have been told and hope that this book will give an insight into the changes involving one specific building and into the life of a village community in general.

Published by Chartham Hatch Village Hall Society 2007

Copyright © Chartham Hatch Village Hall Society

All rights reserved. No part of this publication may be reproduced, stored in a retrieval system, or transmitted, in any form or by any means, electronic, mechanical, photocopying, recording or otherwise, without the prior permission of the publisher.

ISBN 978-0-9556146-0-6

Printed by The Press on the Lake, Stonar, Sandwich, Kent

* The Local Heritage Initiative is a national grant scheme that helps local groups to investigate, explain and care for their local landscape, landmarks, traditions and cultures. The Heritage Lottery Fund (HLF) provides the grant but the scheme is a partnership, administered by the Countryside Agency with additional funding from Nationwide Building Society.

CONTENTS

Introduction	1
Gateway through the Woods – A Brief History	3
The Village School – The First Fifty Years	17
The Village School – The Remaining Years	41
Memories of the School	59
School House	75
The Social Club	79
The Village Hall – A Factual History	83
Village Hall Activities	105
The Tower	141
Appendix – List of committee members	145

Chartham Hatch

There is a hamlet they call Chartham Hatch
Of which in England there's no match,
Does not lay claim to village green
Or Tudor scenes and ghosts unseen.
For tired nerves it's nature's pill
Just two small streets on brow of hill.
Five roads lead off through orchards fair
Through which as you walk you breathe fresh air.
Small tits, bullfinch, jays and greenfinch,
Blackbirds, chaffinch, thrush and goldfinch
Dip through hedge entwined with bramble
As you daily take a ramble.
Unspoilt, unmentioned, unpretentious,
It reigns in silence, pertinacious,
Protective, proud towards the seat
Of England's history at its feet.
Two thousand years of power and change,
Of people, bustle and counterchange
Have been observed from this skyline
O'erlooking Thomas Becket's shrine.
This Chartham Hatch, this Kentish perch
That stands three miles from England's Church
Still gives to pilgrims who pass this way
Renewal of Faith in God's natural way.

Author and date unknown

Jill Simmons, 2006

Introduction

Photo: Ann Sanders

Chartham Hatch Village Hall, January 2005

Chartham Hatch is a small hamlet of around 200 households in the parish of Chartham, Kent. It is just over three miles slightly south of west of Canterbury and one and a half miles north of Chartham itself. Surrounded by woodland and orchards and situated between the A28 and the A2, it is on high ground approached from all four points of the compass by roads which converge at the crossroads by the village hall (the former school). The Pilgrims Way and the North Downs Way cut through the village on their way to Canterbury.

In 1998 Veronica Litten, a keen local historian and environmentalist, wrote an unpublished account of how the Chartham Hatch village school became the village hall after the school's closure in 1966. She delved into the village hall Minute Books and established how the idea of a village hall came about. She described how shares were issued and bought by several of the villagers, how a management committee was set up to run the hall and how, after various ups and downs, it became used regularly for social events and gatherings.

Several members of the current village hall committee thought it was important to carry out further research to build on this account, to find out the history of the school and to talk to those who remembered the school and the early days of the hall. They applied for Lottery funding, without success. However, a second application in July 2004 proved successful and it was with funding from the Local Heritage Initiative that this book has been produced as part of the "Chartham Hatch - From Village School to Village Hall" project.

To set the scene, we have written a short first chapter on the early history and the development of Chartham Hatch, including Chartham's early beginnings. It was because of the ability to grow 'typically Kentish' crops such as hops, coppice woodland, soft fruit and top fruit that the village developed in the first place, and we hope this first chapter gives an insight into how the village grew as it did, why there was a need for a school and where the children lived. We have also mentioned more recent changes in the village which we hope will be useful to future historians. There is a map of the village and its outlying areas on the inside front cover, with an enlarged map of the village itself on the inside back cover.

There is also a short section on the first Social Club to run in the village. It was formed at the end of World War II and ran for around twenty years. Along with the school and the chapel, it was at the centre of many village activities. The school and the chapel both closed in the mid-1960s and, as a result of a vigorous campaign, the school building became the village hall. Many events have taken place in the hall over the years and these, together with a more factual history of the hall itself, are described in additional sections. The Appendix lists the hall committee members from the first meeting in 1967 to the present time.

We have visited many archives, spoken to many people, recorded many memories and read many Minute Books. The meetings recorded in the school Minute Books covered both the Chartham and Chartham Hatch schools, which was initially a little confusing, but we believe we have managed to unravel them, extracting the entries relevant to the Chartham Hatch school. There have also been some conflicting memories among the people we have spoken with – again, we hope we have been able to unravel most of them but, if there are any inaccuracies, we apologise !

It is obviously impossible to include in this book all the material we have gathered. However, it will be available for future generations as all our documentation has now been donated to the archives of the Chartham Society, a local environmental and historical organization.

We are grateful to have had this opportunity to visit the past and hope that there is something here for everybody – from factual history to personal memories.

Valerie Elvidge, Ruth Harling, Jenny Harries, Ann Sanders
History Project Group
Chartham Hatch Village Hall Society

Source: Out of copyright – photo courtesy of Alma Hill
Chartham Hatch in 1988 looking north – the village hall is at the crossroads top left, partially hidden by the large oak trees

Gateway through the Woods – A Brief History

An interesting discovery

Little is known about the very early history of Chartham Hatch, although the remarkable discovery of a polished flint axe in 2002 by a local smallholder, Bill Bean, in a field at the end of Primrose Hill indicates that the area was occupied as far back as 3,000 to 2,500 BC.[i]

Other early occupancy

There is much more evidence of very early occupancy in Chartham than in Chartham Hatch itself. Examples include:-

'fire pits' dating back to over 4,000 years ago found at the bottom of Howfield Lane on the site of Motorway Sports Cars (now Brownhills Motorhomes);[ii]

a large quarry pit of Roman date with a Roman burial and large quantities of material from the middle of the fourth century in the grounds of the former St. Augustine's Hospital;[iii]

six graves and grave goods typical of the early Anglo-Saxon period at Horton.[iv]

Bigbury Camp

We do know that, within half a mile of the village in what is now the neighbouring parish of Harbledown, a Celtic British settlement was established on the northern side of Bigbury Road, just over 2 miles west of Canterbury. This settlement is now called Bigbury Camp. It was established initially in ca. 450 BC and renewed some 250 years later with defence systems forming a stronghold, or hilltop fort.[v] There is little to see now of the earthworks that made up this fort. Probably most people driving beside the woods along Bigbury Road are unaware that, close by, there was once a settlement where families lived, worked and fought during what is now known as the Iron Age. Excavations have been confined to the Bigbury Camp site but we can imagine how there might have been groups of huts in clearings in the surrounding woodland with trackways leading to the area which, much later, became known as Chartham Hatch.

The Romans attack

It is believed that the fort at Bigbury was attacked by the invading Roman army in 54 BC when Julius Caesar and his Seventh Legion made a second foray into Britain, crossing the River Stour (most likely at Tonford). His armies made camp and attacked the fortified hill top,

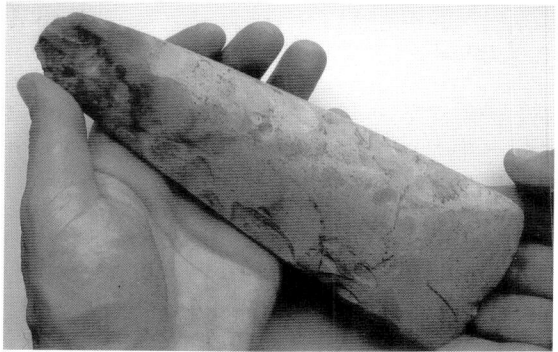

Photo: Courtesy of Bill Bean
Neolithic polished flint axe, 21 cm long and weighing 585 g, believed to be for ceremonial use

driving its occupants away. After Caesar left, the main centre of local settlement switched to the Stour-side Canterbury location, and Bigbury was abandoned in ca. 20 BC.[v]

Slave chains

Many artifacts, including pottery shards and iron tools, have been excavated at this site and are now located in museums at Canterbury, Maidstone and Manchester. F.H. Thompson in his article "Excavations at Bigberry, near Canterbury, 1978-80"[vi], includes a detailed account of all the items found, the most famous of which is a chain for six slaves from ca. 50 BC, now in The Manchester Museum.

Slaves were one of the main exports from Britain, along with hunting dogs, hides, grain, cattle, gold, silver and iron.[vii]

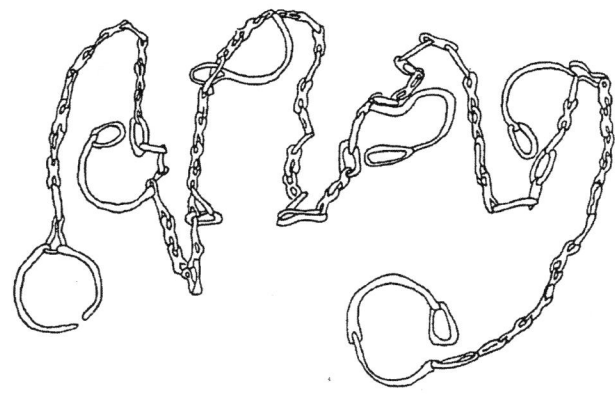

Slave chains from a drawing in The Antiquaries Journal, 1983, Vol.LXIII, Part II, p.271

Photo: Jenny Harries
Sickles excavated from Bigbury now held in the Museum of Canterbury

The hill fort is sold

The hill fort, part of a larger area of woodland, was in private ownership until March 2004 when Bigbury Hill and the 60 acre woods in which it sits were bought by the Kent Wildlife Trust. The Trust plans to return the hilltop to heathland, with native oak, silver birch, poplar, beech and other more traditional types of tree replacing the sweet chestnut coppice plantation.

The name Bigbury is derived from the Old English *Bycge burh* meaning a stronghold on a bulge.[ix] However, the alternative 'Bigberry' is sometimes used.

A brief history of Chartham

In contrast to Chartham Hatch, the history of Chartham is well documented. In 871 the land later known as the Manor of Chartham is said to have been given by Alfred, Duke of Kent, to Ethelred, Archbishop of Canterbury, and the monks of Christ Church "towards their clothing".

In those days a manor was a clearing in rough land where a certain tribe, or number of families related to each other, built themselves dwelling places and tilled the land in common for the good of the community. They kept a certain amount of sheep, cattle, pigs, poultry and sometimes horses on common meadow land and waste land.

Kent was at this time part of the kingdom of Wessex, governed by a practically independent Duke of Kent.[viii] Chartham was called Certham (Old English *Cert ham*, settlement on rough commonland).[ix] This became Certeham in 874[x] and Chartham in 1610.[ix]

The Domesday Book

At the time of the Domesday Book in 1084 the area now known as Chartham Hatch would probably still have been mainly woodland. What we now know as the parish of Chartham (then called Certeham) was made up of six manors – Chartham, Horton, Howfield, Denstead, Shalmsford Bridge and Shalmsford Street – and was in the administrative district of the Hundred of Felborough. A modern translation[xi] of the Domesday Book states that Chartham

> "answers for 4 sulungs. Land for 14 ploughs. In lordship 2. 60 villagers with 15 cottagers have 15½ ploughs. A church; 1 slave; 5½ mills at 70s; meadow, 30 acres; woodland, 25 pigs. Value before 1066 when acquired £12; now £25; however, it pays £30".

Its glossary of technical terms states that

a cottager was the inhabitant of a cottage often without land;

a villager would have had some land;

a sulung was a Kentish unit of land measurement, usually reckoned at 200 acres.

Chartham Hatch is formed

An inquisition into the tenant land of the manor of Chartham and its tenants, probably drawn up in the early decades of the 13th century, indicates that tenant land had been extended since the date of the Domesday Book through the clearance of new land. It is likely, therefore, that the hamlet of Chartham Hatch, which in medieval times was known as Bovehacch, was created in the period of land clearance which took place between the late 11th century and the early 13th century.[xii] It would have continued to develop where the hatch, or gateway, to the woods was crossed by ancient trackways used by traders, travellers and pilgrims following the ridge of the North Downs to Canterbury.

The Manor of Denstead

Ireland's History of Kent records that the Manor of Denstead was owned by the Crevequer (or Crèvecoeur) family, who also owned Leeds Castle near Maidstone. It was given in 1263 by Hamo de Crevequer to the Priory of Leeds, founded by one of his ancestors. It remained in its possession until the reign of Henry VIII when it devolved to the crown and later passed into private ownership. The manor consisted of 400 acres, of which seven acres at Highwood were titheable. The remainder was subject to a yearly contribution to the rector of Chartham. Denstead Farmhouse, the timber-framed manor house, was built in the 16th century or earlier.

Bow Hatch

The 18th century historian, Edward Hasted, refers to both the hamlet of Chartham hatch (*sic*) and the hamlet of Bove-hatch (vulgarly Bowhatch), although the map of the Felborough Hundred in his History and Topographical Survey of the County of Kent of 1798 shows only Bow Hatch. (The name Bow Hatch comes from the Old English meaning "above the hatch"[x]).

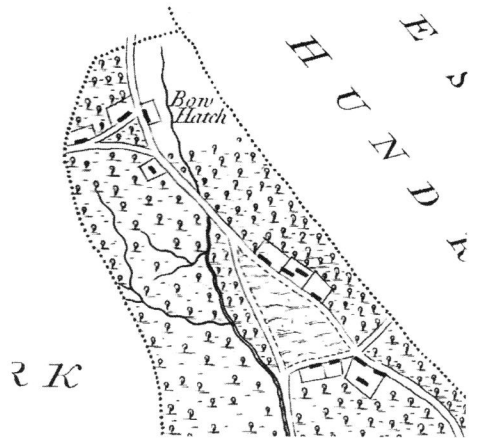

Extract from Edward Hasted's map of the Felborough Hundred showing the location of Bow Hatch. The area to the west of the hamlet was the Ville of Dunkirk, containing "the king's ancient forest of Blean", and the area to the east was the Westgate Hundred. Hasted describes the land to the north of the parish as "mostly high ground, and covered with woods, extending almost up to the high Boughton road to London, through which the boundaries of it are very uncertain, from the different growths of the high wood in them".

He describes Bow Hatch as being near a poor, sandy area of soil leading to Highwood. At that time, the nucleus of the village appears to have been around the former Royal Oak public house and Hatch Farm House; the name Bow Hatch would, therefore, appear to be very apt. Robert Morden's 1695 map of Kent, one hundred years earlier, also shows Bow Hatch.

Hatch Green

Later maps refer to the lower, more populated, area as Hatch Green or The Hatch. A map of the parish of Chartham produced by J. Grist of Canterbury in 1823 does, however, call this area Chartham Hatch. The map below shows how the village would probably have been when the rector of Chartham, the Reverend Henry Moody, recorded in 1859 that he visited approximately 40 families in Chartham Hatch, and in 1870 approximately 60 families. Many of these families would have been farm workers living in tied cottages, with possibly three generations living in the same house.

Early dwellings

In Hatch Lane, the Royal Oak public house, now a private dwelling following its sale in 2004, still has medieval timbers. Other very early dwellings in this area include Rose Cottage, which was built in the 1600s or earlier, and Hatch Farm House in the late 1600s or 1700s. Hatch House was built in the 1700s; a Georgian façade was later built onto its south side, and the property was divided into two dwellings in 1962. The dwelling with the façade retained the name Hatch House, while the other dwelling was named Sayes Court in 1965. Mount Cottages, the last pair of cottages at the top of Hatch Lane, and The Mount at the top of Primrose Hill (formerly three cottages but now one house called Orchard Mount) were built in the 1700s.[xiii] Further down Primrose Hill, an examination of the timbers in the house named Broadview has revealed that some date back to 1594.

To the west, the cottages at Puddledock (now Puddledock House and Puddledock Cottage) were built in 1723, reputedly on the site of a former Priory.

In New Town Street, the building that is now the Chapter Arms public house was part of Primrose Farm, once owned by the Dean and Chapter.

Extract from the Ordnance Survey map originally published by Col. Mudge on 1st January, 1819. This edition was first published in 1970 with a second impression in 1980 for David & Charles (Publishers) Ltd., Devon, ISBN 0 7153 4433 1

Close inspection shows a windmill in the field opposite Orchard Mount (above the words "Hatch Green"). This field is, naturally enough, called Millfield.

White Wall and Fishponds

At the end of Primrose Hill there was a cluster of cottages at White Wall; further on, towards the village of Dunkirk, there was another group of cottages at Fishponds. According to Hasted, the house and grounds which once stood at Fishponds "though now gone to ruin, were formerly made and kept at a large expense by Samuel Parker, gent., the grandson of Dr. Parker, Bishop of Oxford, and rector of this church, who resided there." Samuel Parker was the rector of Chartham from 1667 to 1686 when he was consecrated Bishop of Oxford. Probably the cottages in this area dated from the late 1600s or early 1700s.

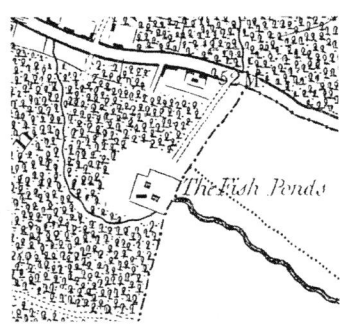

Edward Hasted's 1798 map of the Ville of Dunkirk shows Fishponds on its boundary with the Felborough Hundred. The stream is the Cranburne which still flows today, rising in Court Wood in the parish of Dunkirk just under a mile south of the A2 and joining the River Stour between Tonford and Whitehall, to the west of Canterbury. It was described by Hasted as "a strong chalybeate", i.e. full of iron or minerals

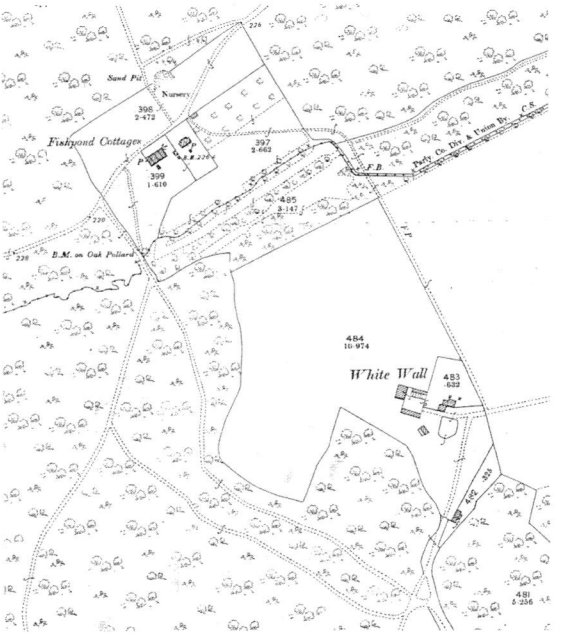

Extract from the Ordnance Survey map surveyed in 1871 and revised in 1896 showing the cottages at White Wall and Fishponds. The cottages, which were demolished in the late 1950s/early 1960s, never had electricity, mains water or drainage.

The seed mill

The seed mill which once stood in the dip in Primrose Hill was described by the *Kentish Gazette* in 1819 as a "water, seed and corn mill". It would have provided some employment, though how long this lasted is not clear. It is believed to have been built in 1704. What it was used for at that time is not certain, but we do know that the *Kentish Gazette* described the mill as "Mr. Hambrook's intended water-mill" when it reported on a "shocking accident" in 1791 when labourers were sinking a drain and one man was "entirely buried, standing upright in the drain". However, by 1819 the mill had been twice advertised for sale and in 1820 the gear work was subsequently put up for sale, as the flour mill "for want of sufficient power has never been put in motion". The mill was again put up for sale in 1826, together with three acres of hop ground and a double cockle oast, though this time it was described as being "in good repair, fit for immediate work". A map of 1841 shows it belonging to a Mr. Chandler with a Mr. Kelcey as tenant. By 1859 it appears to have been turned into cottages as several families were living there.

Seed Mill Cottages from a watercolour by Leslie T. Hopper, 1949

Villagers remember the cottages being used to house evacuees during World War II and being lived in until the early 1950s.

As with many outlying agricultural cottages, they had minimal facilities – in January 1950 the

Kentish Gazette reported that the owner was asked by the Parish Council to provide another water pipe as the eleven occupiers had only one tap, from which some of them had to carry water 75 yards.

The cottages were finally demolished in the mid 1950s by Bert Groombridge, an agricultural contractor, who with his wife also ran the Royal Oak public house in Hatch Lane from ca. 1949-1960. Many of the bricks from the seed mill were used in the foundations of his bungalow in Bigbury Road.

'Little Hell' and a primitive chapel

There were more houses in Primrose Hill than there are now, with most of the occupants working either on the land or at the seed mill. For many years this area was known as 'Little 'Ell' because, it is said, of the numerous arguments and fights among the residents. Many older people today still remember it by this name! At the end of Chapel Row there was a Primitive Methodist chapel, which was probably built in the early to mid-1800s when the Primitive Methodist movement spread into the villages from Canterbury.[xiv] The chapel was already in a poor state of repair and being used for storage when it was badly damaged by a flying bomb (doodlebug) in World War II. The site was cleared and the bricks used to repair the houses in Chapel Row which had also been damaged.

More dwellings

Cottages in Hatch Lane (now Nos. 1-5) were built on the site of previous dwellings. An Indenture for their sale in 1888 from Edwin Colthup of Nickhill to Stephen Baldock, grocer and baker, Chartham, describes them as being erected and built some years ago by John Fagg Harvey (the owner of Hatch Farm) on the site of "two messuages or tenements". These cottages changed hands many times from 1800 onwards, and were probably rebuilt in the early 1900s. Amongst the deeds for these cottages, there is also a receipt for rent payable in 1751 to the Dean and Chapter.

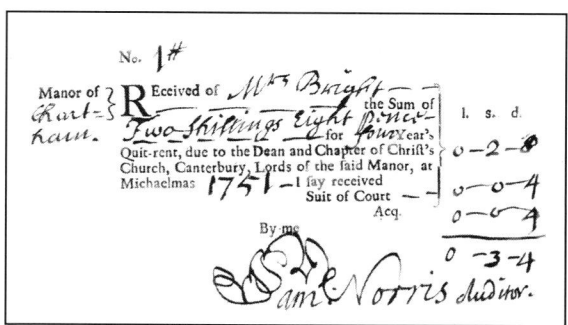

Courtesy of Judith Hattaway

Cottages in Primrose Hill and Howfield Lane also appear on early maps.

Today's village

Most of Chartham Hatch as we now know it was built from the late 1800s, starting with the school in 1873 (now the village hall). School House followed shortly afterwards in 1874. The cottages on the west side of New Town Street (previously known as Primrose Road and then later locally called New Town, Coombs Row or New Street) were built, from the mid-1890s, by the Coombs family who ran the Chapter Arms. These ten cottages were called Primrose Cottages and were most likely the farm cottages for the nearby Primrose Farm. They were put up for auction in 1898 in three groups of lots.

Extract from map of Lots 1-17 to be sold at auction by Mr. Edwin L. Gardiner at the Auction Mart, St. Margaret's Street, Canterbury, on 23rd March 1898. The Chapter Arms is described as being "close to a good road and in a rapidly growing neighbourhood".

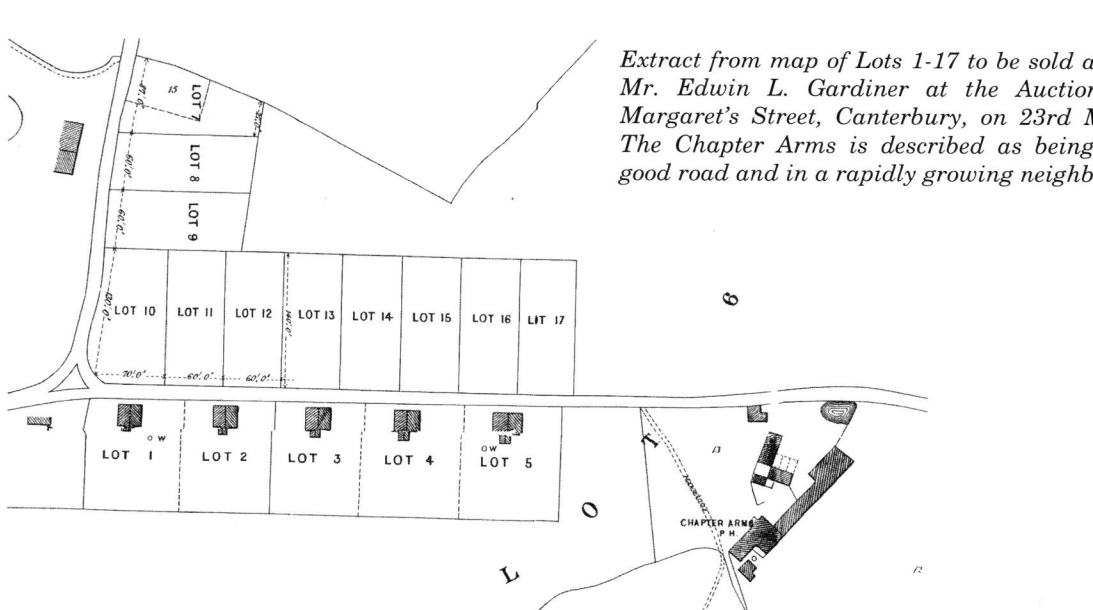

- Lots 1-5 were described as "newly erected semi-detached cottages, each with tenants"
- Lot 6 was The Chapter Arms public house, Primrose Farm and cottage
- Lots 7-17 were plots of land on the east side of Primrose Road and on Howfield Lane.

When these cottages were built, the total number of dwellings in the village increased by almost half.

The Coombs family was a large one, with several members living in New Town Street over the years. Mrs. Ann Coombs, the widow of the late Williams Coombs, who had been for a period of 38 years the owner of the Chapter Arms, died in 1912. Her obituary records that the funeral took place on 13th May "at the residence of her grandson, 2 Primrose Cottages, Chartham Hatch, where she had resided since retiring from business sixteen years ago......She leaves five sons and daughters, forty-three grandchildren and thirty-seven great- grandchildren".

School Cottages in Town Lane were built in 1899. No link between School Cottages and the school has been found; this pair of farm cottages was probably given this name as they were the only other houses apart from School House near the school. Very early cottages in the current centre of the village are Yew Tree Cottage and the adjoining Folly Cottage in Howfield Lane; these were once a single dwelling, listed in the 1891 census as Sparrow Court. It is said that Cherry Ridge, opposite, was built around 1860 as two cottages (Cherry Ridge and Rose Cottage) using old materials from a previous house in Chartham. Steed Cottages, also in Howfield Lane, were probably built towards the end of the century.

Who owned the land?

A map of 1841 lists the owners, tenants, area and use for each plot of land in and around the village. There are many different owners but several names appear many times – Mesdames Lane (Denstead), Richard Ambrook, John Stupperfield, George Finch and George Gipps. Much of the land on the south-west side of the village belonged to the Ecclesiastical Commissioners and was sold in 1895 to Henry William Arnold, "of the county of Middlesex and Nickle, Chartham".[xv] The Arnold family also owned several plots to the south of Howfield Lane. Much of the land to the north-east of the village and in the village itself belonged to Mr. George Bowdler Gipps of Howletts, near Bekesbourne, and was put up for sale in 1906 with the rest of the Howletts Estate.

The majority of the land and cottages to the north and north-west were part of the Denstead estate.

The strip of land behind Yew Tree Cottage and the houses in Town Lane which had originally belonged to George Gipps was subsequently owned for many years by the Butcher family, who also owned the shop on the corner of New Town Street and Howfield Lane (now No.11 New Town Street). They had a smallholding with pigs, strawberries, raspberries and cherries. The land opposite was sold to a draper called Baldwin, whose shop was at 32-33 High Street, Canterbury, and several terraces of houses, the majority with flat roofs, were built in Bigbury Road and Howfield Lane in 1937. There was a gravel pit on the east side of Bigbury Road owned by the F.H. Hooker Group.

More development

There was another spurt of development (mainly bungalows) in the 1950s and 1960s along Howfield Lane and Bigbury Road. Nightingale Close was built in the mid-1960s where there were once apple trees, cherries and blackcurrants backing onto woodland and the gravel pit. It was so called because of the nightingales that used to sing in the woods. Since then, however, new housing has been mostly 'infilling'.

Other changes

Several old dwellings have been replaced by modern buildings. These include Tin Tops in Hatch Lane, so called because it originally had a corrugated iron roof (now Brackenside), and, in Howfield Lane, The Bungalow - a wooden bungalow originally occupied by members of the Butcher family - and the thatched cottage on the site of the current Bove End. The Colt bungalow (Sunnyside) and The Woodlands, also in Howfield Lane, have replaced a dairy and a galvanized tin bungalow. In Bigbury Road, there used to be several single storey buildings which were replaced by the current houses and bungalows from the 1960s onwards. Several houses have also disappeared – among them Yew Tree Cottage, Primrose Cottages and Seed Mill Cottages in Primrose Hill, and the cottages at White Wall and Fishponds.

Over the last century, buildings and activities having a social importance have also come and gone.

Local shops

In New Town Street there was a shop in a wooden hut in the front garden of No. 7 run by Fred Philpott who was trained as a tailor after returning wounded from the First World War. Villagers remember buying haberdashery and shoes. Best remembered of all was 'Pout's sweet shop', run from the front room of No.14 in the late 1930s to the early 1940s by Aggie Pout and Vi Carter.

Village shop and post office

The main village shop was originally in New Town Street, at its junction with Howfield Lane. Built in the late 1890s, No. 11 was owned by Mr. and Mrs. Swinford Butcher who ran the shop from an extension built on to the side of the house. It was owned in succession by Mr. and Mrs. Sidney Butcher (brother of Swinford Butcher), Mr. and Mrs. Jim Lowman and Mr. and Mrs. Jack Downs until it was finally bought in 1968 by Mr. and Mrs. David Kemp.

For several years this shop had been in competition with another grocery shop in a prefabricated building close by in Howfield Lane, built by a Mr. Delo from Canterbury. We believe the first people to run the shop were Mr. and Mrs. Delo, followed by Mr. and Mrs. Jim Mummery. There were several owners until, in the autumn of 1971, Mr. and Mrs. Kemp bought it and transferred their business to it.

The sub-post office was originally in the Howfield Lane shop and was transferred to Mr. Downs' shop in New Town Street around 1964/65. In 1968, it attracted unwanted visitors when, on 3rd October, two men with stockings masking their faces rushed into the shop. Both Mr. Downs and Mr. William (Bill) Faulkner, who was collecting his pension, were half-blinded by ammonia thrown into their faces and then clubbed to the ground. The thieves escaped with £260 in postal orders. Mr. and Mrs. Downs had just sold the business to Mr. Kemp and were to have left the following week. When Mr. Kemp bought the Howfield Lane shop in 1971, the post office was transferred back.

In 1985, Mr. Kemp resigned his duties of sub-postmaster and the village no longer had a post office. The telephone kiosk and post box were transferred to their present sites near the village hall. The shop was put on the market in the same year, finally closing in 1986 without a buyer. It was demolished, the land sold and two detached houses built on the site.

Photo: *Courtesy of Peter Tong*
Mr. Frank Ross, milkman, in Howfield Lane with Steed Cottages in the background. Both he and Mrs. Ross used to deliver milk round the village. Initially, the delivery was by horse and float. The above photograph shows him with his later mode of delivery – motorbike and sidecar.

Photo: *Courtesy of Peter Tong*
'Sunnyside' in Howfield Lane where Mr. and Mrs. Ross lived (out of view to the right of Mr. Ross in the top photograph). Mr. Ross used to collect the milk from Belsey's Farm, Horton, and get it ready for delivery in the dairy at the back of the house.

Source: *Kentish Gazette*
Detectives and reporters gather outside The Stores and sub-post office in New Town Street following the raid the previous day

The village was without a shop until 1990 when Lesley Larrigan, with the help of Valerie Elvidge, ran "The Shoppe" in the village hall every Tuesday and Thursday afternoon. Offering refreshments (served by Mary Cox and Mabel Sparks) as well as groceries, fresh fruit and vegetables and frozen food, it was a welcome amenity and rendezvous for residents and visitors alike. It closed in 1992 when Hatch Stores opened at Little Oaks in Bigbury Road. This shop was open for less than two years and now the village is once again without a general store, although eggs, fruit and vegetables can be bought from the farm shop off Town Lane opened by Lil Bean in 1996.

Primitive Methodist Chapel

There was also a Primitive Methodist Chapel directly opposite the school in Town Lane, with a Sunday School for the children. It was demolished in 1968, and a pair of semi-detached houses was built on the plot a few years later.

Photo: Courtesy of Philippa Bennett
The Primitive Methodist Chapel in Town Lane looking from the Village Hall, taken at the first Easter Monday Pram Race in 1967

Local employment

Traditionally, farming has been the main source of employment, the largest farms being Nickle (originally Nickhill) Farm, Howfield Farm, Denstead Farm and Hatch Farm. Although the main farmhouses and buildings of both Nickle and Howfield Farms are in Chartham, both farms own a substantial amount of land in Chartham Hatch. Nickle Farm was in the hands of the Arnold family from 1895, when Henry William Arnold bought it from the Ecclesiastical Commissioners, until it was taken over in 1997 by the present owners, F.W. Mansfield and Son. The Mount family lived at both Howfield Farm and Denstead Farm until 1970 when both farms (part of the Mount Estate) were bought by Jack Scott. These farms traded as Scott and Griggs, and Scott and Knowles until 1988. Since then, both Howfield and Denstead Farms have been in the hands of Newmafruit Farms Ltd., and some of the orchards in the Denstead area have been sold to private owners for grazing horses. The farmhouses were sold to private owners; the farmhouse at Howfield became Howfield Manor Hotel. The hotel later became part of the Swallow chain which went into liquidation in 2006 and is currently home to several tenants until a buyer is found.

The farms grew mainly top fruit (apples, pears, plums and cherries), soft fruit (strawberries, raspberries, blackcurrants and blackberries) and hops, all of which were very labour intensive. There were sheep and hens and, before the advent of modern tractors, horses for drawing the farm machinery. Currently, the orchards are mainly apple, some pear and some recently re-introduced plum. Sweet chestnut trees were coppiced by woodmen to supply fence posts, palings for chestnut spile fencing and hop poles. There were also charcoal-makers who worked kilns in the woods. This traditional coppicing of the sweet chestnut still continues, albeit on a much smaller scale. Until 2006, villagers Maurice and Ron Port supplied fence posts from the sweet chestnut they had coppiced. A new fencing business, Wells and Sons, has recently moved into the woodland to the north of the village. Most of the woodland in Chartham Hatch has now been sold to the Kent Wildlife Trust or in small parcels of land to private individuals.

Whole families, living in tied cottages, worked on the farms, and up until World War II it was expected by the farmer that the wife of a farm labourer in a tied cottage would also work in some way on the farm - for example, weeding the crop fields, picking the fruit and, in the hop gardens, stringing the bines in April and then pulling them down and picking off the hops into bins at harvest time.

Although the number of local farm workers decreased after World War II, many women from Chartham Hatch worked either full-time on the farm or at fruit-picking time right up until the 1990s. Nowadays, most of the seasonal work is carried out by workers from the European Union who live on-site in caravans.

There are no longer any hop gardens in the village. Denstead Farm continued growing hops until the late 1950s. The oast belonging to the farm was sold for private housing in the early 1970s.

There were also several smallholdings. Chartham Raspberries, a small business run by Alfred Bird in New Town Street, provided employment in the 1940s, not only in picking the raspberries, but also in packing and sending by rail the canes to other growers, some as far away as Scotland. Mr. Bird's workforce included German prisoners of war. There is currently a smallholding in Primrose Hill which David O'Meara has worked for nearly thirty years, sending his crops to Covent Garden in London. In winter he makes chestnut paling fencing.

With the arrival of the railway in Canterbury in the 19th century, Chartham Hatch was also home to 'plate-layers' and 'gangers' who laid and repaired the railway lines which passed through Chartham.

Others went to Chartham for employment – to the paper mill, which has made paper since 1738 and which still provides employment although on a much reduced scale, to St. Augustine's Hospital (or the Lunatic Asylum as it was called when it was built in 1875), which closed in 1993 and has since been developed for residential housing, and, more recently, to Mixconcrete Pipes Ltd., which closed in 1983.

In 1979, Hoppers Farmhouse Bakeries relocated from Wincheap in Canterbury into the oast in Hatch Lane. The oast had been used by Nickle Farm as a cold store for apples since it stopped being used for drying hops at the end of the 1920s. David Hopper's workforce was largely local. The bakery used the new premises to concentrate on a range of cakes and to develop ready-to-fill pastry cases, the first to be produced in England. It no longer produced bread. When business expanded still more, Hoppers Farmhouse Bakeries moved to larger premises in Herne Bay in 1993 and the building was converted into four private houses.

Most of today's workers commute to local towns or even to London, which has greatly changed the character of the village.

In conclusion

The development of the village as we know it today would certainly have been influenced by the building of the school in 1873. The village at this time consisted mainly of isolated, small clusters of rural cottages and the school was built for the children who lived in these cottages. Gradually, more houses were built and the village started to take shape. Over the years growth has been mainly confined to within the village itself, leaving the surrounding woodland and orchards relatively untouched. The original 'hatch' or 'gateway' would have led the traveller on foot or horseback through the woods and beyond. Today's modern traveller still uses the 'gateway' but, it has to be said, at a much greater speed and frequency!

Photo: John Harling, 2000

Maurice and Ron Port making sweet chestnut fencing

Images of the past

Photo: Courtesy of the Chartham Society
Mr. Swinford and Mrs. Emma Butcher outside their shop in New Town Street

Photo: Courtesy of the Chartham Society
Mr. William and Mrs. Ann Coombs of the Chapter Arms

Postcard above: Courtesy of the Chartham Society
Time for tea and a photograph – Mrs. Polly Hubbard fifth picker from left

Photo right: Courtesy of Bernard Moat
Mr. Hugh Arnold inspecting the apples with Mrs. Kennett to his right, Jack Dixon to his left and Charlie Hubbard on the cart

Apple picking at Arnold's farm

Photo: Courtesy of Peter Tong

Jim Ross, son of Mr. and Mrs. Frank Ross, outside the school

Photo: Courtesy of Sylvia Adams

Hop picking at Denstead Farm in 1943. The tractor driver is Walter Coleman and standing closest to the tractor is Albert "Punch" Hills.

Photo: Courtesy of Pat Amos

Cherry pickers, Chartham Hatch in the 1930s
Lewis Butcher, Jess Moat, Sid Butcher, Hilda Arman (née Butcher), Dave ?, Harry ?
Fred Butcher, John Letson (with guns)

Photos: Left - Courtesy of Pat Amos / Lena Elvidge
Below - Jim Sanders

Left: Mr. Swinford Butcher (right) with his brother, Sidney, outside the Chapter Arms in the 1920s. Swinford Butcher used to take villagers into Canterbury by horse and cart for a shilling.

Below: The Chapter Arms, 2006

Photos: Right - Courtesy of Mel and John Martin
Below - Jim Sanders

Right: The Quoits Team at the Royal Oak in the early 1900s. The landlord, pictured with his wife, was Mr. William Horton.

Below: The Royal Oak converted into a private dwelling, 2007

Photos: Courtesy of the Chartham Society

The barn at Denstead Farm before and after its conversion in 1995

Brief History

Postcard: Courtesy of Bernard Moat

Left: Mr. and Mrs. Butcher's shop at the junction of New Town Street and Howfield Lane.

Photo: Jim Sanders

Below: No.11 New Town Street in 2006

Photos: Ann and Jim Sanders

The village shop and post office owned by Mr. and Mrs. Kemp. It was demolished in 1986 and a pair of detached houses (below) erected.

Photos: Ann and Jim Sanders

The last village shop was at Little Oaks, Bigbury Road from 1992-1994. It is now two dwellings (below).

Photos: Left - Norton Harries
Below - Jim Sanders

Originally a wooden bungalow belonging to the Butcher family, 'The Bungalow' in Howfield Lane was replaced by the modern bungalow below in 2001.

Photos: Right - Courtesy of Bill Bean
Below - Jim Sanders

This half brick and half galvanized tin bungalow in Howfield Lane was replaced by The Woodlands below in 2005

---

[i] Report by John Willson, Senior Site Director of the Canterbury Archaeological Trust, dated 5.6.02 (unpublished)
[ii] *21st Annual Report of the Canterbury Archaeological Trust*, 1996-7, Article 11, Tim Allen
[iii] *21st Annual Report of the Canterbury Archaeological Trust*, 1996-7, Article 12, Jonathan Rady
[iv] *Archaeological Cantiana*, Vol. CXXIV, 2004, pp, 369-370. Published by the Kent Archaeological Society
[v] R.W. Pepper, "Bigbury", *Harbledown Heritage*, Harbledown Conservation Association, 2000
[vi] F.H. Thompson, "Excavations at Bigberry, Near Canterbury, 1978-80", *The Antiquaries Journal*, Vol. LXIII, Part II, 1983
[vii] *The Geography of Strabo*, Book IV, Chapter V, Loeb Classical Library, 1923
[viii] Selena Randolph, *Chartham in Days of Old,* 1911
[ix] Judith Glover, *The Place Names of Kent*, B.T. Batsford, London, 1976, p.40
[x] J.K. Wallenberg, *The Place-Names of Kent*, Appelbergs Boktryckeriartiebolag, Uppsala 1934, p. 369
[xi] *Domesday Book, Kent*, edited by Philip Morgan, Phillimore, Chichester, 1983
[xii] Angela M. Langridge, "The Population of Chartham from 1086 to 1600", *Archaeologia Cantiana*, Vol. CI, 1984, pp.217-244. Published by the Kent Archaeological Society
[xiii] Chartham Parish Design Statement, published by Canterbury City Council in conjunction with the Chartham Society and Chartham Parish Council, March 2005
[xiv] John A. Vickers, *The Story of Canterbury Methodism in 1750-1961*, 1961, pp. 24-25

The Village School – The First Fifty Years

I, Alice Colman, commenced my duties here January 11th 1875, but have only just received the Log Book. There were 44 names on the Register when I came. There is a great deal of sickness about and the weather is very bad, in consequence of which the average has been low. I entered one little girl on Monday February 1st and last Monday three more girls. Today, a little girl died suddenly – was at school two days ago. Average attendance for the week – 34.

Postcard: Courtesy of Bernard Moat
Earliest known photo of the Chartham Hatch village school

Thus reads the first entry in the Chartham Hatch Board School Log Book. The story of the school, however, does not start in 1875; we must go back to what is probably the most important education act ever to be passed – the 1870 Education Act. Schooling had been very haphazard up until this time, with the majority of children, particularly in the poorer rural and industrial areas, receiving very little, if any, education. In Chartham Hatch most would have been needed to help their parents in the surrounding farms, orchards and hop gardens.

Schools

Until the 1870s, instruction had been provided by the various Voluntary Schools funded by charitable organisations such as the National Society, which aimed to teach the Anglican religion to the poor, and the British and Foreign School Society, which promoted education that was not centred on any particular denomination. There were also Wesleyan and Roman Catholic schools, mainly in towns, and small private schools, often known as Dame Schools, for which a charge was made. These were run by men or women with no real teaching qualifications. However, the only schooling provided in the parish of Chartham was by small private schools, including schools in Chartham Hatch at Denstead and in Seed Mill Cottages.

Education for the Poor

The introduction of the 1870 Elementary Education Act drafted by William Forster to provide 'Education for the Poor' was a turning point in educational history. For the first time children were expected to attend school on a full-time basis for a minimum of five years although, in reality, attendance was not always enforced. (It wasn't until ten years later, with Mundella's Education Act of 1880, that the enforcement of attendance up to the age of ten became a statutory requirement.)

School Boards

School Boards, elected by ratepayers, were set up to examine the provision of elementary education in their district and were empowered to build and run schools out of the rates in areas where there were no National or British and Foreign Society Schools. These schools were known as Board Schools. The country was divided into about 2,500 school districts. School Boards were given the authority to make their own bye-laws, both to enforce attendance and to charge fees if they so desired. The 1870 Act also allowed women to vote for the School Boards and granted them the right to be candidates to serve on the Boards.

X. In what part (or parts) of the District is such accommodation required? How many children ought to be provided for in each of the schools required?

The proposed new schools (not very far from the church) are for 50 B, 40 G, 60 Inf⁰ — Classrooms might be added to these for (altogether) 30 ch., and a mixed school be built at Chartham Hatch for 40 children

XI. Do you recommend that the District be dealt with *by itself*, and a notice issued accordingly, for the supply of the above mentioned deficiency? *If not—*

Yes

Signed this 7 day of November 1871,

P. F. Routledge, H.M. Inspector of Schools.

Source: National Archives, Kew
Extracts from the Inspector of Schools' report on the Parish of Chartham, 1871

The provision of schooling in the parish of Chartham was duly 'examined', and the resulting inspection report dated 7th November 1871 by Mr. P. Routledge, H.M. Inspector of Schools, stated that

> "the Parish of Chartham in the County of Kent is estimated, in 1870, to contain 1,250 inhabitants of whom 1100 are the class whose children may be expected to attend elementary schools. School accommodation ought to be provided for 220 children – boys, girls and infants, but only 37 children were being accommodated at the already existing small private schools in the district".

Plans for a school at Chartham

However, plans were already underway for a new school in Chartham. The rector, the Reverend Henry Moody, had approached the National Society on 25th October 1870 asking for aid towards building a Church School at Chartham, and the appropriate form had been sent to the National Society on 25th February 1871. By the time of the Inspector's report, the Draft Conveyance of the school site had already been approved and a grant of £35 promised (about 5% of the final building costs).

The Inspector's report continued:-

> "the proposed new schools (at Chartham) are for 50 boys, 40 girls and 60 infants. Classrooms might be added to these for 30 extra children and a mixed school be built at Chartham Hatch for 40 children".

At that time, a child was classed as an infant until it became seven, when it 'became' either a boy or a girl. The very youngest were classed as 'babies'.

The Inspector also recommended that the Chartham District should continue with its current arrangements with the National Society to provide the school accommodation required, i.e. the school would not be a Board School with government funding. In fact, these arrangements were almost complete, with final approval from the National Society for the school at Chartham being given on 23rd February 1872.

….. and at Chartham Hatch

Chartham Hatch was to be a mixed school for Girls and Infants and was for a long time referred to as the Chartham Hatch schools. It should perhaps be remembered that, in 1872, Chartham Hatch was a very small hamlet, consisting mainly of isolated groups of cottages whose inhabitants were nearly all labourers on the nearby farms and it was for these children that the school was built. Boys at the Chartham Hatch school had to transfer at the age of seven to the Chartham school, where they stayed until they reached the leaving age of ten. It wasn't until 1927 that boys remained at Chartham Hatch until the age of eleven, by which time the final school leaving age had been raised to fourteen.

Although still a village, Chartham was considerably larger and wealthier – it had its own church, village green, industries, shops, tradesmen, railway station and landowners. Its school was also much larger and had been built to take 170 children.

School Management Committee

Consequently, on Easter Monday, 1st April 1872 at a vestry meeting "pursuant to the Trust Deed of the 9th March 1872", members were elected to form a School Management Committee to serve the new schools at Chartham and the proposed schools at Chartham Hatch. In addition to the rector, Henry Moody, and the churchwardens, Messrs. William Finch Harvey and William Weatherley (*ex officio* members), the Reverend John Hulke Dixson, the licensed curate, was also appointed. Together with Messrs. Charles Thomas Drew, John Homersham and Frederic Beard, they would serve on the committee which would be elected yearly.

These were all notable gentlemen in Chartham –

- Mr. Harvey was a farmer at Thruxted
- Both Mr. Weatherley and Mr. Drew were associated with the Chartham Paper Mill
- Mr. Homersham owned a shop by Shalmsford Railway Bridge
- Mr. Beard was a landowner living at Horton Manor.

All were present at the first meeting of this new School Management Committee held in the Boys' School Room on Saturday, 13th April 1872. This may have been in the private school on The Green in Chartham. Mr. Evan Lake was unanimously elected Secretary and Correspondent to the Committee. Mr. Lake was the son of Milton landowner, Robert Lake, and was the younger brother of Mary Lake who had run the private school at Denstead. He read to the Committee the Deed of Grant and Declaration of Grants of the schools' new buildings which was then duly executed by the Reverend Henry Moody and the churchwardens.

Source: Centre for Kentish Studies, Maidstone
Cover of the first School Management Committee Minute Book

The list of probable subscribers who would pay an annual contribution towards the cost of running the schools was then taken, and it was found that "the following might be relied on".

The Rector	£10	0s	0d
Mr. Hardy	£5	0s	0d
Mr. Kershaw	£5	0s	0d
Mr. Hammond	£2	0s	0d
Mr. R. Lake	£2	2s	0d
Mr. Bell	£1	0s	0d
Mr. Beard	£3	3s	0d
Mr. W.F. Harvey	£3	0s	0d
Mr. Drew	£1	1s	0d
Mr. Weatherley	£2	2s	0d
Mr. Dixson	£2	2s	0d
Mr. E. Lake	£1	1s	0d
Mr. Homersham	£1	0s	0d
TOTAL	£38	11s	0d

It was also thought that the Dean and Chapter, Mr. G. Gipps, Mr. Thomson and others might be "reckoned as subscribers if applied to".

The First Master and Mistress at Chartham

It was decided to place an advertisement for a new Schoolmaster at Chartham in the National Society Monthly Paper. "A man and wife" were required, at a salary of £140. The Managers' Minutes record that Mr. A.G. Martin and his wife, from Gulval, Penzance, were appointed as the first Master and Mistress of the Chartham schools, to come on 3rd October 1872.

Village School to Village Hall

Postcard: Courtesy of Bernard Moat
Chartham schools in the early 1900s

Inauguration of the Chartham schools

The schools at the Box Trees in Chartham (now known as Bolts Hill) cost £761 to build. The money was raised mainly by fund-raising, together with subscriptions from landowners and land occupiers in the village and from the government and other sources. The *Kentish Gazette* of 2nd July 1872 reported the inauguration of the new schools which had taken the form of a church service with the Bishop of Dover on the previous Thursday. The report, which went into great detail on the structure of the new buildings, concluded with the reply to the rector by Mr. Evan Lake, Honorary Secretary of the Fund-Raising Committee, that "the outstanding deficit of £15 would be wiped off by the £17 church collection that had taken place that day" and that this meant they could "commence with a good nucleus towards the fund for erecting their contemplated schools at Chartham Hatch."

School accommodation had been provided for 170 children at Chartham but the Government Inspector had recommended that, for the entire parish, accommodation for not less than 220 should be provided. Therefore, they had still to provide schools for 50 children at Chartham Hatch and to do that would, it was estimated, cost £250. He hoped that, having made so good a commencement in the erection of the main schools in the parish, the erection of the supplementary schools would be a "matter of hardly any appreciable difficulty."

On 31st July 1872, a notice was received from the Education Department confirming the Inspector's recommendations for the provision of a National Society school at Chartham, but it also stated that "if the private school kept up by Miss Lake at Chartham Hatch, which was visited by H.M. Inspector in November last, is continued, no further accommodation will be required". However, the Committee was able to confirm that Mary Lake had discontinued her school at Denstead during midsummer 1872.

Fund-raising for Chartham Hatch

Following the inauguration of the Chartham schools, fund-raising continued for the erection of the new schools at Chartham Hatch. One such event, an amateur concert in the School Room, Chartham, was given on Wednesday, 9th October, 1872. According to the *Kentish Gazette*, "there was a fair audience". The concert opened with an overture from Rossini's *Il Gazza Ladra* most efficiently performed by Mr. Winterbotham, Mr. P. Heinery and Messrs. Tench, J. White, G. Nicholson, Penn and R. Kempton, with an aria performed by Miss Lake. Several visitors were present from Canterbury, among them the Very Reverend the Dean of Canterbury with his family. A collection was also made in aid of the National Schools at the Harvest Thanksgiving Service on 23rd October.

Mr. Gipps donates land

The new schools at Chartham Hatch were to be built on land donated by Mr. George Gipps of Howletts in Bekesbourne. Mr. Gipps owned much land in and around Chartham Hatch and had been on the Chartham School Fund-Raising Committee. The National Society was informed on 20th October of the Management Committee's intention to provide another school and teacher's residence, and was sent a draft Conveyance of the site.

The proposed Church of England schools at Chartham Hatch were united with the Canterbury Diocesan Education Society at the Quarterly Meeting of the Diocesan Board held on Thursday, November 14th 1872 at Canterbury in the presence of Henry R. Moody, Rector, John Hulke Dixson, Curate, Frederic Beard and Evan Lake, Honorary Secretary.

The site was officially transferred on 2nd December 1872 when, under the School Sites Acts 1841 and 1844, George Gipps "freely and voluntarily and without valuable consideration, granted and conveyed property to and unto the use of the Minister and Churchwardens of the Parish of Chartham". This property was "a piece of woodland, measuring 1 rood, at a corner on the North West side of a Bridle Road from Chartham to Harbledown where the Denstead Road and the Road to Howfield Farm and Canterbury respectively meet". The land was to be used to erect "a school for the education of Children and Adults or Children only of the labouring, manufacturing and other poorer classes in the Parish of Chartham, and as a Residence for a Teacher or Teachers of the said school." Education committees in the 19th century recommended providing free accommodation near schools "to provide a degree of respect for the teacher".

[For those of a mathematical inclination, a 'rood' is defined by the *Oxford English Dictionary* as "a superficial measure of land, properly containing 40 square poles or perches, but varying locally". A 'pole' or 'perch' is defined as "a linear measure varying from 6 to 8 yards". As we all should know, a 'yard' is approximately 0.9 metres!]

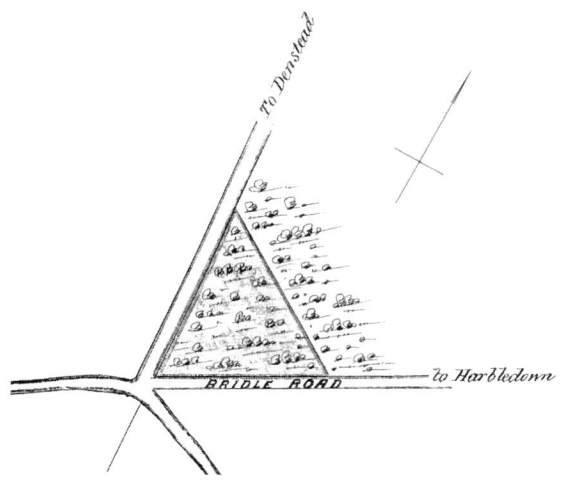

Source: Canterbury Cathedral Archives
Drawing of the transferred land taken from the official transfer document

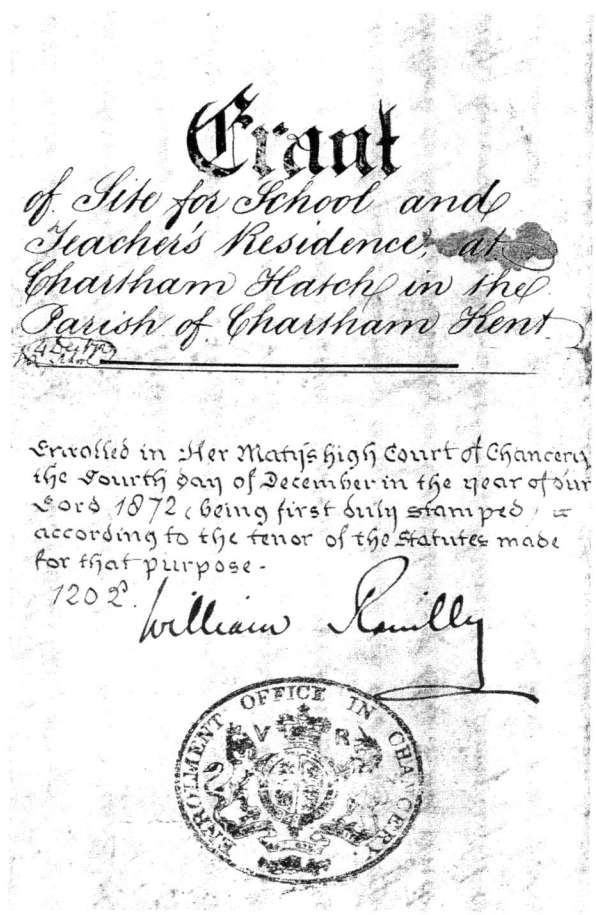

Source: Canterbury Cathedral Archives
Official Transfer document

Village School to Village Hall

What price education?

Schooling at that time was not free (it did not become free until 1891), and school pence had to be paid weekly. Fees for both schools were agreed at the meeting of 11th October 1872 and, as there had been "some feeling in the Parish that a fee of 3d would be too much for large families", these were set at:-

> 3d for the first child, 2d for the second and 1d for all others

Under the Order of the Poor Law Board dated 6th July 1871 it was the duty of the School Mistress to record "punctually and accurately in a book" the fees received and to "set forth therein how she had disposed of the monies received". She had to balance the book weekly and pay over the fees to the Treasurer of the Board "at the close of every week".

Aid is requested

The Management Committee applied to the National Society for aid in January 1873 towards "building one schoolroom to accommodate 67 children". These children would have lived mainly on the outskirts of what is now the current village – down Primrose Hill and beyond at White Wall and possibly at neighbouring Fishponds (most children from Fishponds would have gone to the nearer school at Dunkirk), and at Denstead, Puddledock and Hatch Green. There were very few houses in the village at this time. The Managers said that the schoolroom was needed as it was too far for the children to go to the school and the church or Sunday School in Chartham. A grant of £31 was promised - £16 for the school and £15 for a teacher's residence. In the event, only £16 was received as the Managers were unable through lack of funds to go ahead with the residence.

A Ladies' Committee was set up in January 1873 to assist the main Management Committee. Mrs. Beard, Mrs. Drew, Mrs. Wildash, Miss Alice Lake (sister of Evan and Mary Lake) and Miss Homersham were all elected. (It is interesting how the same names keep appearing!)

School building

At the same meeting, it was proposed that an advertisement should go out inviting tenders for the erection of the Hatch school. Four tenders were subsequently received and were discussed when the Management Committee met again on Monday, 3rd March 1873. Tenders had been requested for (a) School, Residence and Offices (toilets) and (b) School only and Offices and had resulted in the following quotes:-

Mr. W. Gentry	(a) £495 0s 0d	(b) £281 0s 0d
Mr. C. Foad	(a) £487 0s 0d	(b) £272 0s 0d
Mr. Wiltshire	(a) £515 0s 0d	(b) £287 0s 0d
Mr. John Cozens	(a) £499 0s 0d	(b) £280 0s 0d

The Secretary reported that £280 was available if the School and Residence were built and £250 if the School only was built. It was agreed that only the school should be built and that Mr. Foad's tender of £272 be accepted.

We have not been able to find the architect's plans of the school (though these are referred to in correspondence between the Management Committee and the National Society) but we have learned from the application to the National Society that the schoolroom was to be 30 feet long, 18 feet wide and 24 feet high to the underside ridge, i.e. the width of the present building but only approximately half as long (the half next to School House), with walls of brick 14 inches thick, a roof of tiles and floor of wood. It was to accommodate 67 children, at 8 square feet per child as prescribed by the Education Department.

Although there have of necessity been changes over the years, the current building retains hints of how it used to be. The tiles on the roof are still the original ones and are of a distinctive pattern, which was repeated when School House was built approximately a year later. It is interesting to note that schools at Davington, near Faversham, Chilham and Wickhambreaux have tiles in a similar (though not identical) pattern, as do two other former schools in Canterbury – in London Road and in Rhodaus Town. There may also be others!

Photo: Jim Sanders

School - The First Fifty Years

The original windows were much smaller, and the buttresses on the front of the present building were not part of the original construction. The latter may have been added following the Log Book entry on 12th April 1918 that "the wall to the south-east appears to be sinking".

Top - Postcard: Courtesy of Bernard Moat
Bottom - Photo: Jim Sanders, 2006

The small round window high on the end wall nearest School House would have added light to a somewhat dark schoolroom. However, it is no longer visible from the inside, as a ceiling was put in at a later date.

Photo: Jim Sanders, 2006

The entrance to the schoolroom was at the back of the building. Luckily, the archways above the former windows and door can still be seen in the brickwork on the inside wall opposite the windows and, from these, it can be deduced that there was a door and a window to the side of the fire nearest School House, and another window to the other side of the fire. The outside wall also shows where the door would have been. The fire was initially an open coal fire. Rainwater was collected in a tank which a builder had been instructed to build in August 1874 (there is no evidence to show whether this was above or below ground).

Water supply problems

There had obviously been problems with the water supply as a surveyor had been instructed to investigate. He reported that the well was dry and that he had found it impossible to find a source of water by boring. Whether there had been enough water from the well previously and whether this had been the reason for siting the school there in the first place, we can only speculate. We believe the pump currently in front of the building to be the original one, although it has been repaired and renovated several times. Whether the pump drew water directly from the tank or whether the pump was over the well and the tank water went into the well, again we do not know.

The toilets were outside by the boundary wall at the back (referred to in the Minutes and Log Book as the "offices").

The playground was originally unfenced. It is not until November 1900 that we learn from the Log Book that it was "railed in". The Head Mistress, Miss Mills, had in fact written to the School Board in June 1887 asking if they would erect a fence "round the school ground" but her request had been refused.

An interesting discovery

One of the most interesting facts to come to light from the Log Book is that there was originally a 'gallery'. In Victorian schools, children often sat on long benches or had their desks on the 'steps' of a tiered, wooden platform, known as a gallery, that rose to the back of the classroom, presumably to make sure that they could all see the teacher or, more likely, that they were all clearly visible to the teacher. A gallery also meant that a large number of children could be taught at the same time by one mistress. We do not know whether the gallery was installed when the school was built (the first mention of a gallery is in the Log Book of 1878 when the Mistress recorded "gave gallery lesson on Goat"), what type of gallery it was or in which direction it faced. It appears that it was the Infants who occupied the gallery, with the Log Book recording in 1899 that "desks have been fixed on the gallery for the Infants". The gallery was eventually removed in 1907.

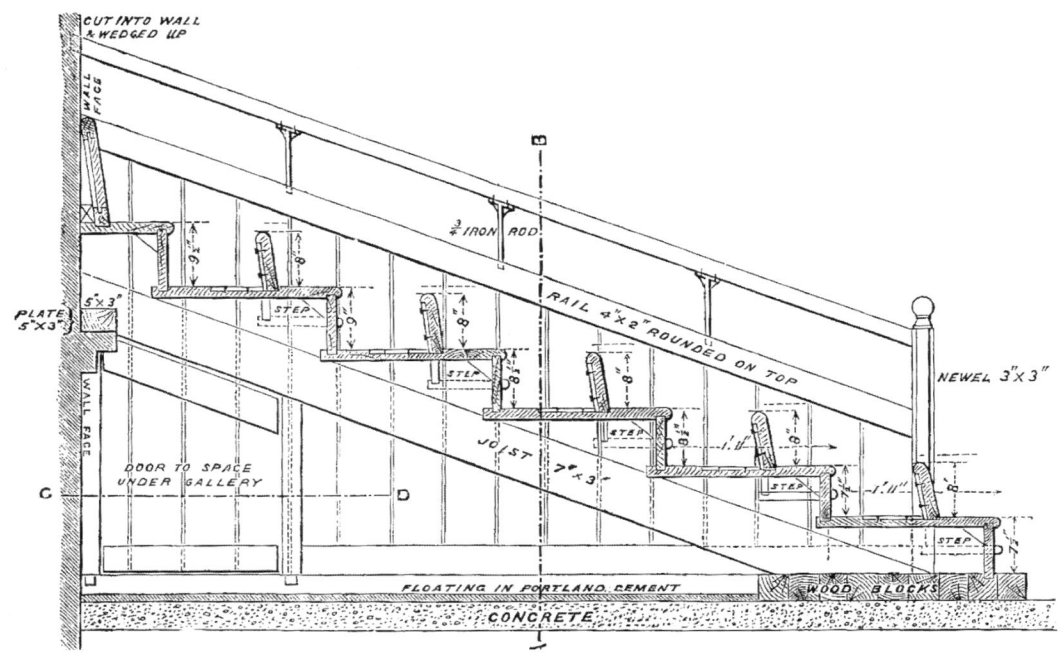

Source: "School Architecture" by E.R. Robson, Leicester University Press
This type of gallery was officially recommended for Infants but it is not known whether this design was used at Chartham Hatch

The diagram above, taken from "School Architecture" (Leicester University Press, 1972) written by E.R. Robson and first published in 1874, shows the cross-section of a gallery recommended for Infants. The one in Chartham Hatch may have been similar to this but, of course, much smaller.

Completion at last!

On 5th September 1873 the Management Committee wrote to the National Society to tell them that the school was finished and asked for "the necessary papers for claiming the Grant".

The very first Mistress

On Monday, 13th October, the Chairman and Secretary of the Management Committee reported "the election of Miss Annie Dyason, late of Selling School, to the post of Mistress of the Hatch School. She would take up her duties as soon as she was able to come having been prevented hitherto by her sister's illness".

Books were ordered to be obtained according to the Inspector's requirements and Mr. Homersham was directed to send two tons of coal and some wood.

Financial worries

However, on 17th November, it is evident that both National Schools, in common with many other church schools throughout the country, were running into financial difficulties. The capital account showed a deficit of £84 2s 2d on the Hatch school and £46 11s 9d on the Chartham school. It was decided to borrow £90 for the Hatch school and £50 for Chartham.

The financial situation was obviously causing concern, as at the December meeting the Chairman "made a few comments as to the advisability of having a School Board with a view to clearing the school from debt and getting the children to attend". Board Schools received an annual government grant based on examination and attendance, an annual grant from the Overseer of the Poor out of rates paid to the Poor Law Board and had the services of an Attendance Officer to deal with absenteeism. A special Committee meeting was held on Monday, 22nd December 1873 where it was unanimously proposed that

> "having regard to there being no prospect of the funds for the present year meeting the expenses, and with a view to preventing the stoppage of the Education of the Poor in the Parish it is desirable to form a School Board for the same".

It was also agreed that
> "a meeting of the subscribers be called, a copy of the said Resolution be forwarded to every subscriber and the state of the finances placed before them with a view to ascertain their views as to the future carrying on of the school".

Following the meeting of the subscribers, the Chairman, Frederic Beard, sent the following letter on 25th February 1874 to the Secretary of the Education Department, Whitehall, London SW:-

"Sir – I beg to inform you that at a meeting of Ratepayers of the Parish of Chartham, held at the National School Room on 23rd inst., it was unanimously resolved 'that it is expedient that a School Board should be formed for the Parish of Chartham'. I also beg to forward a copy of the Notice which I have duly published."

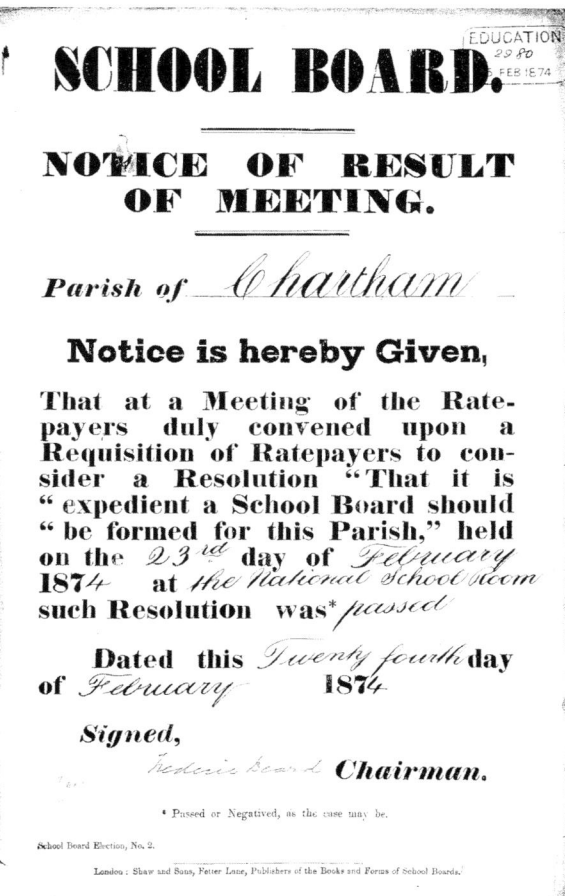

Source: The National Archives, Kew

A School Board is formed

The Secretary of the Education Department presumably had no objection as a School Board was formed, holding its first meeting at the School Room on Thursday, 16th April 1874. Present were Messrs. W.F. Harvey, G. Holloway, Alfred Foreman, Joseph Stubberfield and Frederic Beard. The following Officers were elected:-

Mr. Frederic Beard	Chairman
Mr. George Holloway	Vice Chairman
Mr. G. Furley	To be appointed Treasurer
Mr. F.S. Cloke	To be appointed Clerk at a salary of £15 per annum

It was also proposed that the Board attend a conference with the School Committee on the following Saturday at the School Room.

Difficult times

The Board and the School Committee duly met to discuss the proposed transfer but "no resolution was agreed to". However, at the next School Committee meeting, a draft Deed of Transfer was drawn up to include both schools and it was directed that this should be sent to the National Society and the Diocesan Board for approval. A letter was also to be written to all the original subscribers. The Treasurer, Mr. Drew, was instructed to pay the accounts as far as the funds would provide – this would leave a balance in hand of just over £14 for Chartham and 1s 2d at Chartham Hatch. Hard times indeed!

Over the next few months there were several School Managers' and Board Meetings relating to the transfer. A Draft Lease was sent to the Education Department pointing out that the Managers were at present "without funds" and that there was a possibility of the schools being closed for a time unless some arrangements could be made whereby the Board could take over the schools provisionally, pending the final transfer. There were various provisions in the lease, including the Managers' retaining possession of the schools from 9.00 to 9.45 every morning to enable the teaching of religious instruction and also for three evenings in the week.

The Education Department replied that there was nothing in the Draft to which they would refuse to give their consent, provided the conditions of Section 23 of the 1870 Elementary Education Act were first satisfied (that two-thirds of the original subscribers, as well as any other contributory body such as the National Society, were in favour of the transfer). The letter also stated that any provisional arrangements between the Board and other parties would be taken by the Board at their own risk. It would be for the Authorities thereafter to decide whether any expenditure by the Board in consequence of their taking charge of the school under such arrangement was legal, and pointed out that, until a satisfactory transfer under Section 23 was effected, the Department would not recognize the School as a Board School or pay any Annual School Grant to the Board on its behalf.

The Board unanimously agreed to the proposed terms subject to a few minor alterations which were subsequently agreed with the Managers, and the Clerk was directed to ask Mr. Lake to act as Solicitor to the Board.

The transfer is agreed

A few days later, on 20th May, at the Managers' Committee Meeting held at the Chartham school, the Draft Transfer of the schools was approved and the rector, Cyril Randolph (now the Chairman), and Messrs. Harvey and Weatherley signed the agreement on behalf of the Managers. Mr. Lake sent a circular to subscribers on 23rd May 1874 requesting their attendance at a meeting the following Wednesday where a resolution would be proposed approving of the Draft Transfer. All present at the meeting consented to the proposed transfer.

The leases

The leases were approved and engrossed for execution by the Education Department on 27th June. All that was needed now were the signatures of the Managers and the Counterparts to be executed by the Board. The Board's term of 21 years would commence on 1st August 1874.

At the Board Meeting of 9th July, the Common Seal of the Board was affixed to the Counterpart Leases and sealed and signed by the Chairman. The seal had been chosen at a previous meeting and a die cut. A box had been bought for 12s 6d in which to keep the die, together with an ebony handle to enable it to be used with sealing wax.

Terms of the lease

The Counterpart Lease, dated 8th July 1874, was a "Memorandum of Agreement between the Reverend Cyril Randolph of Chartham in Kent, William Finch Harvey of Thruxted in the Parish of Chartham aforesaid Farmer and William Weatherley of Chartham aforesaid Miller, three of the Managers of Chartham Hatch National School in union with the National Society for promoting the Education of the Poor in the principles of the Established Church, and the Chartham School Board."

It goes on to say:- "The Managers agree to 'let' and the Board agree to 'hire' the School House, playground and premises at or near Chartham Hatch, in the parish of Chartham, for a term of 21 years from 1st August 1874." The yearly rent would be 10s 0d – payable on 1st August in every year – and would be "free and clear of all charges and deductions whatsoever". The premises had to be kept "in good and tenantable repair and condition" and also "kept insured from loss or damage by fire to the sum of £300 in the County Fire Office or some other respectable Office of Fire Insurance to be approved by the Managers".

Source: Canterbury Cathedral Archives
Counterpart Lease

School - The First Fifty Years

School Mistress and School House

The Board had already started to think about how the school should be run under the new system. At their meeting on 29th June, it had been unanimously resolved

(a) that a cottage be built for the Mistress upon land belonging to the Managers, and the clerk was directed to see Mr. Ellsmore to ask him to prepare the plans and estimate the cost;

(b) that a Certificated Mistress would be appointed from 29th September at a salary of £35 per annum and two-thirds of the Government Grant, together with a partly furnished house, and an advertisement should be inserted in the National Society's Paper;

(c) that a fee of one penny per week be charged for each child.

It should be mentioned here that an agreed portion of the Government Grant went to the Head Teacher. This grant, however, depended on attendances and on the children passing an examination at the annual inspection. Children were only eligible for presentation at the examination if they had attended school 250 times, morning or afternoon, during the school year. The Infants were only tested by the number of attendances; the Juniors were graded into "Standards" and were examined at the end of each year, starting when they went into Standard I at the age of seven or eight. Chartham Hatch school never received the highest grant: its children passed only a "fair" or "good" examination. The grant was paid annually and was recorded in the School Board Ledger. The grant received in 1878 was £32 2s 0d, of which the Mistress received half. By comparison, a reflection of its larger size and "excellent" examination, the grant for the school at Chartham for the same period was £140 12s 0d.

There are many mentions of School House in both the Managers' and Board Meeting Minutes and, as we have also learned about the house from our interviews with those who attended the school, a separate section has been devoted to it later in this book.

A Mistress is sought

An advertisement for a Mistress had been duly placed in the National Society's Paper with duties to start on 29th September 1874. There were no enquiries and the advert was inserted again. This time there was one applicant, a Miss Helen Brooker of Waltham Cross but, by the time the Clerk had written to her to make arrangements for an interview with the Board, he had received a letter from her stating that she had had a more advantageous offer and had accepted it. It wasn't until a fourth advert had been placed with a different payment scheme – from £35 and two-thirds grant to £45 and half grant – that any more applications were received. However, at a meeting of the Board on 17th December it transpired that, of the four applicants, three had already obtained other situations. Unfortunately, as the fourth did not propose to reside in the house, the Board could not appoint her and the position had to be re-advertised. The Chairman was therefore empowered, in the event of any applications, to peruse the testimonials and make the appointment (presumably to save time).

The children had not been without schooling during this time. At the beginning of October, the Board had agreed that the Chairman should ask Miss Lake (it is not known whether this was Mary or Alice Lake) to "assist in the matter" regarding arrangements for opening the Hatch school. It appears that Miss Lake engaged a Miss Goble as Mistress from week to week, at a salary of 15s 0d with fuel and lodging. Miss Goble started in mid-October and she continued until 11th January, when the School Mistress was finally appointed. Miss Goble may have come from Sittingbourne for her interview as there is also an entry in the Ledger for 1s 5d being reimbursed to Miss Lake for Miss Goble's rail fare from Sittingbourne.

A Mistress is appointed

At the Board Meeting of 14th January 1875 we learn that the school had a new Mistress. The Chairman had appointed a Miss Alice Colman, who had had temporary charge of Bekesbourne School. She was not Certificated as required (this was to cause problems later) but would sit for a Certificate at Christmas. She would be paid £45 per annum and half grant, with a partially furnished house with coals. Her office was determinable on three months' notice on either side.

School Log Book

Alice Colman wrote the first entry in the Chartham Hatch Board School Log Book on Friday, 19th February 1875 as follows:-

I, Alice Colman, commenced my duties here January 11th 1875, but have only just received the Log Book. There were 44 names on the Register when I came. There is a great deal of sickness about and the weather is very bad, in consequence of which the average has been low. I entered one little girl on Monday February 1st and last Monday three more girls. Today, a little girl died suddenly – was at school two days ago. Average attendance for the week – 34.

All schools receiving Annual Grants had to have a Log Book provided by the Managers out of school funds. Instructions were issued by the Board of Education on how to keep a Log Book and these were printed at the front of the book. Entries had to be made by the Principal Teacher at least once a week specifying ordinary progress and other facts concerning the school or its teachers, such as the dates of withdrawals, commencement of duties, cautions, illnesses, etc. The Log Book had to contain statements of fact only, and no expressions of opinion on conduct or as to the efficiency of the school were to be entered in it. It also had to contain verbatim copies of the summary of the Inspector's reports and was regularly inspected and signed by the Chairman of the Management Committee. Even though most of the entries did comply with these regulations, the Log Books do gradually reveal a picture of life in a small, rural school.

The Mistress also kept a Register together with a record of punishments handed out. Unfortunately, because of the sensitive nature of their content, we have not been allowed access to these books.

Duties of a Monitress

Miss Colman requested a Monitor to help her. The Board agreed to allow one shilling a week. It wasn't until this was increased to two shillings a week that anyone was appointed.

The first Monitress mentioned in the records is A. Hubbard. The duties of the Monitress at the Chartham school, Lydia Cook, were listed in 1873 as "teaching infants in aid of the Mistress, cleaning out the school, lighting fires and taking charge of the school during dinner hours".

The duties of the Monitress at Chartham Hatch would have been similar. It wasn't until several years later that we see the wages for a cleaner recorded in the School Ledger.

Attendance and non-attendance

The Board arranged for Mr. George Moore to carry out a census of the children in the district in January 1875 so that the bye-laws governing attendance could be enforced. As the grant received by the school depended partly on attendance (until the Code of 1890 was introduced which abolished attendance grants and gave schools a grant depending on how many pupils were registered), the number of children attending was crucial.

There were many reasons why children did not attend. In rural areas children were often absent to work in the orchards and hop gardens:-

August 2nd 1876 : Several children kept from school to go harvesting.

July 25th 1877: Many children away from school today to go picking fruit, only 17 present.

May 15th 1891: Several girls absent helping their mothers in the hop gardens.

Postcard: Courtesy of Norton Harries
Hop picking in East Kent, postmarked Canterbury 1904

October was the traditional time when farm workers were hired and often families would move to another village. An annual Michaelmas Fair was held at the Cattle Market by St. George's Gate in Canterbury, with many attractions that proved difficult to resist:-

October 16th 1891: Have lost several children by the Michaelmas removals.

October 18th 1878: Attendance low as children have been attending a fair in Canterbury.

In November 1878 many farm labourers in Kent and Sussex took part in a strike against a reduction in their wages imposed by their employers because of the low prices fetched by corn and wheat. By December most labourers had gone back to work but not without hardship:-

November 25th 1878: One child withdrawn, the parents having to leave their house on account of the strike among the labourers.

Sickness, weather and poverty

There were many absences through illness; scarlatina, measles, whooping cough, rubella, typhoid fever and diphtheria all feature in the Log Book. The school was closed on several occasions as a result of illness. It was ordered to close from 6th-20th May 1886 by the Sanitary Inspector; between 2nd-16th May 1887 owing to "so much illness amongst the children"; in January/February 1898 owing to an outbreak of measles and between 8th-22nd May 1916 owing to rubella. It appears that there were also many children affected by the influenza epidemic of 1918 as the Managers closed the school between 28th October and 11th November 1918 because of 'flu'.

Rather poignant entries in 1893 and 1910 tell us:-

November 10th 1893: A great deal of sickness about just now – a little girl died this week rather suddenly, only being away from school a week.

July 25th 1910: Standard I girl died yesterday after being absent only a week from school.

The weather also affected attendance. Staying at home would certainly have been much more attractive than struggling in wet clothes along muddy dirt tracks and unmade roads! The Log Book records:-

July 16th 1875: Wet all week. Attendance very low. One day only 15.

March 1st 1876: Very wet and windy – only 9 present.

November 12th 1886: Weather very rough all the week. Thursday morning only 6 children came so closed school.

May 18th 1915: Very wet morning. Only 20 children came to school and as three of these were very wet we could not open. 17 children this afternoon – also wet. 7 very wet – sent home.

There were many instances of the school having to be closed because of wet weather or heavy snow and this affected the amount of grant received by the school. In 1891 the Head Mistress had to open the school on several Saturdays in March and April to make up for closures during the winter.

Children were also absent because their parents could not pay the school fee (this was not abolished in most elementary schools until 1891) and needed them to work. The Poor Law Guardians were supposed to pay the fees of children receiving parish relief or where parents could not pay, but this did not always happen.

The Attendance Officer

Notices were issued to parents whose children did not attend. Initially this task was carried out by the Clerk to the Board (Mr. Fred Cloke) but in 1876 an Attendance Officer was appointed - Mr. George Moore. He was succeeded in 1888 by Mr. George Norris who also held the post of Assistant Overseer of the Parish. He, in turn, was succeeded by Mr. C.J. Carr in 1899, at a salary of £10 per annum, when the posts of Clerk and School Attendance Officer were combined. The Attendance Officer visited the school regularly, reported at every Managers' meeting and issued notices on parents whose children were not attending. In extreme cases final notices were issued, and the Attendance Officer was directed "to take proceedings before the Justices in the event of such notices not being complied with". Indeed, the *Kentish Gazette* of November 1878 reports two parents from Chartham being fined at the St. Augustine's Petty Sessions for "neglecting to send their children to school".

School fees raised and class distinction

The fees which had been set at a penny a week when the school opened were increased by the School Board in June 1876 because, according to the "Report of the Work of the Board from its Election in 1874 to the Triennial Election in 1883", they had found "that the fees charged at their Schools were much lower than those in any of the Schools in the surrounding districts, and that there was nothing in the circumstances of the population to render it necessary that an exceptionally low fee should be charged". The following scale was therefore adopted:-

Class I Labourers' Children: 2d for the first Child and 1d for all others
Class II Artisans' and Mechanics' Children: 3d for the first Child and 2d for all others
Class III Tradesmen's and Farmers' Children: 6d for each child.

The children were "classified" by the Board and cards given to them stating into which class they had been placed. Until September 1891 when fees were abolished and the Board received a 10 shilling grant per child based on average attendance instead, all newly admitted children were classified at School Board meetings to determine how much they should pay.

The same report states that "this raised income by a very considerable extent and had resulted in a saving in the amount required from Rates of nearly one penny in the pound per annum". The School Ledger for Chartham Hatch shows an increase in the amount received by the school from £1 17s 8d at the end of the quarter in May 1876 to £2 12s 2d at the end of the August quarter for around 58 registered children. There was a significant drop at the end of the December quarter but we learn from the log books that "the Head was informed of cases of scarlatina" in November and in December "there was no attendance all week because of deep snow", thus showing how the weekly attendance money could fluctuate.

Too tired to concentrate

Sometimes, when the children did attend, they were too tired to concentrate. In May 1917 the Head Mistress wrote:-

The children are beginning to suffer again from the parents going to agricultural work. Many children by 9 am have had breakfast and been playing since 6 am. By schooltime they are tired and sleepy.

There had been a similar comment the previous summer when "the majority of mothers" had started fruit picking and were leaving their children in the playground as early as 6.30 am.

Bars, medals and certificates were given to the children for good attendance.

School leaving age

The minimum school leaving age was raised from 10 to 11 in 1893 and amended to 12 in 1899. In rural areas, certain children could have part-time exemption as shown by this Log Book entry:-

7th April 1916: Owing to the granting of licenses to children over 12 years of age for agricultural work, several girls left till October 11th.

They were, however, expected to stay at school until 13 to compensate. The leaving age was raised to 14 with the Education Act of 1918. At Chartham Hatch, the girls stayed on until the leaving age and the boys went to Chartham school at the age of 8. From the mid-1920s, the girls went to Chartham at the age of 11; the boys still transferred at the age of 8.

More Mistresses!

The Education Board had never been happy that Miss Colman did not possess the necessary qualifications – she was an Uncertificated teacher. Even though she wanted to sit the Certificate examination, the Board was told that "she was not qualified for examination under any of the Clauses of Article 47 of the New Code" and they were forced to ask her to resign at Christmas 1875 and to advertise the position.

Miss Harriet E. Jefferies of 44 Wheeler Street, Maidstone, started as Mistress on 10th January, 1876. She handed in her resignation in March 1878, to be followed by H.E. Letchford for three months, before Mrs. Laura Jenette Barker started in June. This time twenty-two applications had been received for the post! Unfortunately, with the death of her husband on 1st October, Mrs. Barker resigned in November. The next Mistress was a Miss Caroline Mills who taught from 30th December 1878 to 31st July 1894. She gave as her reasons for leaving that the work had increased so much in the last few years and that she had a great difficulty in teaching the Standards in the same room with the Infants. (She had, in fact, requested a curtain in August 1889 to divide the classes, though it is not known whether this was granted.) These were to become the first of many references to overcrowding. Miss Mills' salary started at £45 per annum but, at her request, it was increased to £50 per annum in August 1885. She also lived in School House and received half the grant. Miss Mills was unhappy with the state of the house and many repairs had to be carried out, including the installation of a new stove. Her sister, who also lived in School House, helped out in the school on several occasions.

Miss Mills was followed in October 1894 by Miss Helen Mary Haslam, whose first entry in the log book read "I find the school in rather bad order and some of the scholars very backward. There is much apparatus and materials required." Miss Haslam made many requests of the Board for improvements to the school (books, apparatus, blackboard and easel, bell) and to School House (additional furniture) and had also stated that "she could not retain her position unless some alteration could be made to enable her to have a companion to live with her." It is not known whether this request was met but her salary was increased to £60 per annum. The final straw appears to have been that the furniture she had requested for School House which had been "absolutely necessary if she was to remain" was unsatisfactory and she handed in her resignation on June 1897. From the Log Book entries she did appear to try to encourage the children to do better – from letting those leave early on a Friday afternoon who got four sums right the first time, to having some ground dug up for the children to cultivate themselves to encourage them to take pride in the appearance of the school, and to giving extra attention to some "exceptionally dull" new children who had never been to school before. Maybe her expectations were too high for a simple village school?

The next Mistress was Ella Mary Letchford from Harwich who started on 24th June 1897 and whose sister, Isabella G.M. Letchford, started as an Assistant on 5th July.

Photo: Courtesy of Ella Willmott
Miss Ella Mary Letchford

Ella Mary Letchford left the school in 1911 because of ill health. E.S. Mount took temporary charge of the school during her absence from 9th October 1911 until Miss Marion Mugford was appointed in January 1912. Miss Letchford died in December 1911 of typhoid fever and is buried in Chartham Cemetery. Her sister continued at the school until March 1920.

Miss Mugford was followed by Amy E. Allen from October 1915 to May 1917, when Mrs. Helena H.J.W. Wood was appointed. She reverted to her maiden name of Wallis after the death of her husband and taught until August 1944. She is well remembered by many of her former pupils.

Photo: Courtesy of Rhoda Wills
Mrs. Helena Wood

Up until 1917 it had been customary for rent and coal to be deducted from the Head Teacher's salary. This was changed in 1917 when Kent Education Committee decided that the Head Teacher would pay a quarterly rent to the committee and provide his/her own coal.

What did the children learn?

Lessons in Victorian times were strictly prescribed by the Education Department, starting with the obligatory, "essential" subjects of reading, writing and arithmetic – the three Rs. Singing and needlework for the girls were also essential subjects, though we learn from the Log Book that in October 1882 the boys had also started to learn needlework and knitting and there are many references to the children knitting "the cuffs" and "the strips". The needlework was regularly sold to parents and the income paid into school funds. Drawing was taught only to boys over the age of seven following an Education Department directive in 1891, so would not have been taught at Chartham Hatch.

Other subjects were introduced into the curriculum such as Object (or Collective) lessons, where the children were required to talk about the picture of an object (e.g. a cow, a forge, paper, the Bookbinder) or the object itself (e.g. apple, glass, coal, salt), and Suitable Occupations. Subjects such as Geography, History, Grammar, were classed as "specific" subjects and were taught to the older children who would have been graded as Standards V, VI and VII. If children passed the examination in any of these subjects, extra grant money was received by the school. The Log Book records Miss Haslam wanting to try for the extra grant for needlework with the children taking it as a Second Class subject; the garments made would be examined at an inspection.

Suitable Occupations and Object Lessons were, in today's parlance, Education Department initiatives. Both were aimed at getting pupils to act spontaneously and to be stimulated to think for themselves rather than just to learn from text books and the teacher. A Circular in 1894 expressed concern that, when pupils moved from the Infants to the Juniors, the conventional methods for teaching Juniors lacked the stimulus for observation and reasoning, and recommended Suitable Occupations such as drawing with coloured chalks, modelling in clay, embroidery of outlines, the formation of geometrical patterns and models and building with cubes. Inspectors were urged "to explain to Managers how very interesting, inexpensive and educational all these methods were". Object Lessons, according to a Circular on Rural Schools in 1900, were not to be mere descriptions from text books but "the practising ground for observation and inference, illustrated by simple experiments and practical work".

There are many references in the Log Books to singing and the children learned songs such as "Coo Coo Pretty Pigeon Coo Coo", "Hop, Hop, Hop", "Where's the Old Grey Goose?", "The Clock", "The Rain is Falling Fast" and "Being Useful". Songs were also presented to the Inspectors at examination. Poetry for the older children in 1898/99 included selections from "The Merchant of Venice" (Shakespeare) and "Poor Fisher Folk" (Victor Hugo). The children would have learned to recite these by heart but what they made of them we can only guess.

School timetable

The timetable, which was "necessary to secure order and regularity", had to be followed strictly and it was agreed at the beginning of the school year between the Inspector and the Managers. A copy had to be displayed in every classroom. Minor deviations from the timetable were allowed but had to be noted in the Log Book – if not, money could be deducted from the grant. There was also a winter timetable when school started and finished earlier in the afternoon and lessons were rearranged to take advantage of the light. The small windows did not help.

December 15th 1908: Needlework will be taken first and the nature study lesson last on Tuesdays and Thursdays for a few weeks during the dark days.

The school year started after Easter; it was not until 1913 that the year started after the summer break, on 1st October.

Swedish drill

Organised team games did not feature in the early Government school system – these were for people of a higher social class in public schools. In order to instil discipline and to improve physical fitness in the working classes, children in government schools practised drill according to a prescribed syllabus. This was initially a military-style drill, later to be replaced 'Swedish drill' (so named because it originated in Sweden), which still had the prescribed elements of repetition but with additional emphasis on graceful movement. The Infants practised marching. Several of the people who attended the Hatch school in the 1920s still remember these exercises. It was not until much later that organised team games were introduced nationally into Government schools.

In January 1905 the Log Book records "Received dumbbells for use throughout the school".

Religious instruction was taught every morning between 9.00 am and 9.45 am under the special provision that the Managers had included in the lease.

We know from the Log Books and the Minute Books that slates and books came from Canterbury in 1876 and that the children sat at seven foot long parallel desks, several of which were provided by a Mr. James Martin, who was also asked to provide three dozen hat pegs in 1893. (This was probably James Martin, who was a builder, carpenter and undertaker on the Green at Chartham.) Sand trays were also used by the children to practice their letters – they would write in the sand in a shallow tray with a stick and then smooth the sand when they wanted to start again. The trays were kept under the children's chairs when not being used.

Monitresses

The School Mistress was often assisted by a Monitress, who was usually a young girl who passed on what she had learned from the teacher to the younger pupils. Records show that the following were Monitresses at the Hatch school:-

> A. Hubbard (1875), Sophia Hubbard and Amy Coombes (1876), Jane Lawes (1880), Lucy Finch (1882), Matilda

School - The First Fifty Years

Finch (1886), Emma Hall (1889), Emma Moat (1890), Ellen Wildlark (1890), Miss Tumber (1890), Mary Hoare (1892), Amy Johnson (1896), E. Penfold (1896) and Ellen Oldfield (monitoress 1906-08, supplementary teacher 1910).

Ellen Oldfield married in 1912 and became Mrs. Whitcombe, remaining at the school as an Assistant Teacher until 1933.

Photo: Courtesy of Hazel Lewis
Mr. and Mrs. Whitcombe in their retirement

Photo: Copyright unknown

Photo: Courtesy of Colin Wood

Two early school photos

A pupil teacher

Given the swift succession of Monitresses in 1890, the Board became unhappy with the teaching arrangements at the school and the Vice-Chairman, Mr. Watson, proposed that a pupil-teacher be appointed. A pupil-teacher was generally an older girl who wanted to become a teacher. She would serve a kind of apprenticeship, teaching the children while at the same time receiving tuition from the Mistress, before sitting an examination to enter training college for training for a Certificate. If she did not sit the examination or was not successful, she could continue as an "uncertificated assistant".

In June 1892 Mary Hoare, aged 16, was appointed as a pupil-teacher at the rate of four shillings per week and was to receive instruction from Miss Mills. From census records, it would appear that this was the Mary Hoare who lived with the Spillet family in Shalmsford Street (she was called Miss Spillet in the Log Book in 1895). On 3rd June, 1897 Mary Hoare was recognised as an Assistant under Article 68 (upon production of a medical certificate). However in July, she resigned owing to the ill-health of her mother.

Her place was taken by Isabella G.M. Letchford, the sister of the Mistress at the time, Ella Mary Letchford, at the same salary that Mary was receiving when she left of £20 per annum. By comparison, a Monitress was still paid very little; in November 1896 Amy Johnson was hired at one shilling per week.

The first inspections

Schools were inspected annually by Her Majesty's Inspectors and books given as prizes to the children for good attendance.

The first inspection was carried out by the Reverend C.F. Routledge on 4th June 1876. Miss Jefferies recorded in the Log Book:-

This school was inspected for the first time. The children have passed very fairly. Some more picture cards, reading cards and a comparative sheet of animals should be got. There is an offensive smell in the offices [toilets].

A. Horton, S. Baldock, G. Tappenden, J. Allard, M. Moat and D.(or A.) Baldock were not qualified for presentation not having made five-twelfths of 250 attendances.

Harriet E. Jefferies – Certificated Mistress – 2nd Class
Fred S. Cloke – Clerk of the School Board.

Following the inspection, the Board received a report from the Education Department saying that it appeared that the children had passed very fairly and that the amount of grant for the five months was £11 11s 8d. The Board, however, were not particularly quick to act on "the offensive smell" as it took until November to obtain a supply of Calvert's Carbolic Powder!

Inspections were carried out annually, from which we learn that the school was usually awarded the "good" grant. Comments from the Inspector included: "The working of the Infants is not quite up to the mark and the arithmetic of the First Standard is rather weak, otherwise the children have passed a very fair examination" (1877) and "The children in the First and Second Standards passed a creditable examination in Elementary subjects. Their English is also very fair, but Geography not up to the mark. The children are in satisfactory order and the Infants are fairly well taught" (1883).

Surprise inspections

There were also occasional surprise visits – one by the Reverend Canon Routledge in March 1881 brought to light that the schoolroom had not been whitewashed as recommended in the previous year's report and that the offices required attention. Another surprise visit by Mr. Rapson, his assistant, in February 1888 revealed that the Attendance Register had not been marked for eight or nine days. Miss Mill's letter of explanation to the Board gave as the reason the fact that the roads were almost impassable on account of snow and few children had come to school.

Concerns

School numbers had been rising steadily ever since the school had opened. In 1901 there were seventy-four children on the register in one classroom. This had not gone unnoticed by the Inspector. In 1899 he had expressed concern at the size of the classroom for the number of children, reporting in June "there is urgent need of a classroom". He also wrote in 1904: "The enlargement of the school should no longer be delayed. Infants and older scholars suffer from always being taught at the same time in one room". However, it was not until 1906 that the enlargement was carried out.

Photo: Courtesy of Ella Willmott
A Jubilee Celebration at Chartham – probably the Diamond Jubilee as some of the children appear to be wearing brooches and medals

Jubilees

It wasn't all lessons and inspections. The children were given holidays to celebrate Royal occasions. The first such event recorded in the Log Book, to celebrate Queen Victoria's Golden Jubilee on 24th June 1887, reads:-

Took the children down to a fete at Chartham – tea, games, fireworks, illuminations. Saw some of the beacon fires. 'God save the Queen'.

The *Kentish Gazette* is much more eloquent and describes the event, organised by a committee of the Reverend C. Randolph, Messrs. F. Beard, P. Platten, G. Holloway, E. Colthup, J. Wood and W. Harvey, as follows:-

"The programme was carried out most successfully by the committee organised for that purpose. The tea for the aged, poor and children was excellent; in fact after all those for whom it was provided had finished, such an abundance of the good things remained that the committee were enabled to give a good meal to a great number of the poor who had assembled in the fields for the purpose of viewing the sports. Owing to the excellent arrangements made by the Sports Committee (consisting of J. Howard Esq., Captain Marten, Messrs. Holloway, Beard and Colthup) the part of the day's amusements, coming under their especial management, was carried out most satisfactorily without a single hitch. The day's rejoicings were brought to a close by a good display of fireworks. The City Band was in attendance."

There were also other organised events in Chartham reported by the *Kentish Gazette*:-

"With characteristic liberality Mr. William Harvey of Thruxted and Burnt House Farms entertained forty of his work people with roast and boiled beef and plum puddings. During the evening 'God Save the Queen' and 'Rule Britannia' were sung, and hearty cheers given for the Queen. Benjamin Day proposed a vote of thanks to Mr. Harvey for the bountiful supply placed on the board, with fine nut brown ale added. Mr. Harvey remarked to the young folk that most likely they would never live to see the like again.

"At Shalmsford Mr. and Mrs. Foreman gave a garden party to lasses and lads from 14 to 25 years of age. Fifty-five sat down to tea and twenty seven of the tenants came at nine in the evening to sing the National Anthem with the whole force of their vocal powers, which was done amid a display of fireworks. Dancing on the lawn kept up until past eleven; other friends coming in, the party numbered upwards of 200. Mr. Williams Epps of Rentain Farm proposed a vote of thanks to Mr. and Mrs. Foreman, which was given with musical honours. In returning thanks, Mr. Foreman said he and his wife were amply repaid for what they had done by the loyalty the whole company had shown to Her Majesty the Queen".

The school also celebrated Queen Victoria's Diamond Jubilee on Tuesday, 24th June 1897, closing for the week.

The *Kentish Gazette* reporting on the ceremony in London described how "Some thirty or forty English and foreign princes preceded the Royal Carriage as a guard of honour, thus typifying the alliance of the Royal family with the dynasties of Europe. Representatives of every important nation or nationality upon the globe joined in honouring the Queen on her Commemoration Day. Every colony and dependency sent typical examples of its forces to exemplify to the world the unity and the joy of the whole wide-spreading British Empire".

There were rejoicings all over the country with beacon fires in the evening. Chartham was no exception, the splendid celebrations being described in great detail in two separate reports in the *Kentish Gazette*. The first report had only briefly described the celebrations, concentrating instead on the garden party given by Mr. and Mrs. Foreman at Shalmsford.

"At Shalmsford, Mr. and Mrs. Foreman gave a garden party on their lawn to lasses and lads from 14 to 20 years of age, and about 49 accepted the invitation and sat down to tea. Tenants and friends came in the evening, making a goodly party. Croquet and other games, interspersed with harmony, were kept up till eleven o'clock, Miss Jessie Nash presiding at the piano. A vote of thanks to Mr. and Mrs. Foreman and Miss Miles for their kind hospitality was passed with musical honours and, in reply, Mr. Foreman said that he and his wife were amply repaid for what they had done by the loyalty shown by all present to her Most Gracious Majesty – the Queen."

A week later, the second report goes into much more detail.

"The festivities in this village were worthy in some points of rather more extensive notice than could be given in our condensed report of a week ago. The scene on the village green where the children (to the number of 460) assembled, was an extremely gay one, largely owing to the decorative work of Mr. C. Richardson. Thanks, too, are due to Miss Randolph, whose decorations were much admired. Also to Messrs. Shrubsole, Terry and Horton, whose places of business were quite gay with bunting, flowers, Chinese lanterns and coloured lamps. Mention should be made also of the entrance to the residence of Mr. Drew, where an arch of evergreens and flowers had been constructed, and the gates were hung with pretty little flags and devices in coloured lamps, which, when lit at night, looked very pretty. The gardens of Mr. Cremer's house were also illuminated in the evening with numberless Chinese lanterns, and the night being calm, the whole green was hung with lanterns of all hues, shapes and sizes, which, together with the 200 flags, presented a most charming and animated appearance.

"The presentation of brooches and medals to children by Mrs. Pomfret was a very interesting function, and it should be mentioned that in addition to the entertainment of children during the day, about 60 aged persons sat down to a substantial meat tea in the schoolroom, which was prettily decorated, while upwards of 20 were provided for at their own homes.

"The bonfire at night was observable for many miles around. The St. Stephen's Drum and Fife Band was in attendance and played the National Anthem, in which all present heartily joined, at the finish of a day of memorable rejoicing. A word of praise is due to the Committee, and especially to Mr. Hayward (treasurer) and Mr. H.W. Taylor (hon.sec.) who had laboured hard to make a day a pleasurable one for the children, among whom over 200 prizes were distributed. The other members of the Committee were:- Reverend Cyril Randolph (Chairman), Mr. W.P. Pomfret, J.P., Mr. C.T. Drew, Dr. L.A. Winter, Reverend Neville A. Holt, Messrs. J. Wood, J. Jordan, W. Hoare and H.A. Horton."

Other holidays and celebrations

There were school holidays at Christmas, Easter and in summer which were agreed between the Mistress and the Board. In rural areas the summer holidays were determined by the harvest and varied in length. In the summer of 1885, the Log Book records the school closing on 7th August and not reopening until 9th October; in 1894 the new Mistress, Miss Haslam, records that the school had been closed for eleven weeks for the 'harvest holiday', as the summer holiday was then called, and in 1913 the Log Book records that the holiday had been extended until 1st October as hop-picking was not finished.

Other public holidays and days off recorded in the early Log Books were:-

Thursday July 6th 1893: The marriage of the Duke of York and Princess Mary – of course gave the children holiday.

July 13th 1899: School closed to enable children to attend Band of Hope outing.

School - The First Fifty Years

August 15th 1901: School closed for day on account of Chartham Flower Show.

June 25th 1902: Closed school for two days for coronation of King Edward VII.

July 13th 1905: Holiday for the Band of Hope treat.

January 15th 1909: School closed this afternoon for the children to have a tea given by Mrs. Pomfret of Mystole.

The Band of Hope was a temperance organisation for working class children and outings were often organised for the children.

There were several times when the children left school early to attend a "tea party". We have no further details so can only assume these were charitable treats given to the children by the more affluent members of the parish.

Empire Day, to mark Queen Victoria's birthday, was celebrated in schools every 24th May from 1903 until 1958, when its name was changed to British Commonwealth Day. The Log Book records:-

May 24th 1905: Empire Day. The pupils practised saluting the flag and a half holiday was given.

May 24th 1909: Empire Day. The children were given lessons on Empire, sang an Empire song and after saluting the flag sang the National Anthem. A half-holiday given in the afternoon.

May 24th 1916: Short address by Head Teacher, then "Flag of Britain", "God of our Fathers", saluting the flag and National Anthem.

What facilities were there?

In the early days of the school there were oil lamps, an open coal fire, water from a pump in the playground and outside toilets (the 'offices'). Very little changed over the first fifty years. Both the classroom and the toilets were whitewashed, though not always on a regular basis, as the Managers often had to be reminded by the teacher that they needed to be done – the Managers did make sure, however, that they were done before an inspection! Most of the general repairs, whitewashing and cleaning out of the toilets was carried out by Mr. Wood.

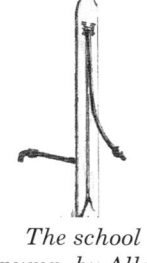

The school pump by Allan Colledge

Scavengers and cleaners

The original 'offices' (probably earth closets) were substituted in 1897 by 'pail closets' and the old privy vault was filled in. The pails were emptied overnight by Mr. Percy Harvey, who had the unenviable job title of 'Scavenger'. There were several complaints, both at the Chartham Hatch and the Chartham schools, about the way he did this; the Managers' Minutes record that, instead of taking away the contents of the Chartham school closets every evening, he was in the habit of putting the contents of the pails into a tub behind the school and emptying it twice a week! Around this time there were also improvements made to the water supply which took several years to complete and the Managers in the meantime paid Mr. and Mrs. Reynolds for water to be delivered - most probably the Mr. and Mrs. Reynolds listed in the 1891 census as living at Sparrow Court, Howfield Lane.

Initially, the Monitress was also responsible for cleaning the school and lighting the fire. The first cleaner to be mentioned is Mrs. Hoare in 1890, followed by M. Godden, Mrs. E. Sims and Mrs. Reynolds. It is recorded that both Mrs. Sims and Mrs. Reynolds were paid £1 0s 0d per quarter. The longest serving cleaner was another Mrs. Hoare, who lived at 2 School Cottages; she retired in 1945 and, according to the Log Book, was presented with a subscription of £7 by the Reverend Gore-Brown "in recognition of her many years at the school (34)".

Overcrowding

As far back as 1899 the Inspector had expressed his concern that the school was overcrowded and that this was affecting the teaching. His report of 8th June 1903 stated: "Mixed School – The enlargement of the school should be no longer delayed. Infants and older scholars suffer from always being taught at the same time in one room. Infants Class – The Infant class is still taught in the same room with the older scholars and the teaching is of course carried on under difficulties with the work of the upper part of the school". The Log Book also recorded the difficulties:-

October 13th 1905: Children suffered from overcrowded state of the school, it really being impossible to do good work.

Plans for enlargement

The School Board and the Managers had in fact been discussing the enlargement of the school since 1902. The first set of plans submitted by the Board to the Managers in 1902 were turned down because "they included virtually the substitution of new schools for the present ones as only a very small portion of the existing building would be left". Revised plans were accepted in February 1903 but it wasn't until May 1904 that "notice was given that the Kent Education Committee propose to enlarge the Chartham Hatch Council School".

Board School to Council School

It should be noted that the school was now no longer a Board School. The 1902 Balfour Education Act had created Local Education Authorities (LEAs) who had taken over responsibility for Board Schools, though it wasn't until 1st August 1906 that the formal transfer was made and the school would officially be known as the Chartham Hatch Council School. There had been some confusion over the lease – in 1895 the premises had reverted to the Managers as the original lease had expired, although the School Board continued to run a school. The Managers were in the process of consenting to a new lease for a term of 30 years when the 1902 Education Act meant that the school was transferred to the County Council. However, after much correspondence, the lease was finally agreed in 1906.

Enlargement completed

The plans were approved on 28th April 1906 and the enlargement completed on 12th January 1907. The Log Book records the disruption:-

October 5th: School is carried on at a little disadvantage owing to work of enlarging school being in progress.

December 14th: School closed today for four weeks to allow for the alterations to premises being completed.

Again, we have been unable to locate any plans but we do know from correspondence in the summer of 1906 and from the Architect's Certificate signed by M. Jennings of 4, St. Margaret's Street, Canterbury, on 28th January 1907 that:-

(a) the new classroom measured 23 ft by 18 ft which, when added to the existing classroom, gave a total area of 954 square feet;
(b) the length of the existing classroom was increased by one foot;
(c) a cloakroom was added ridged north-west to south-east but a wall separating the boys from the girls and infants was refused;
(d) the request for a larger window was refused, instead its obscure glass was to be replaced by clear glass. However, it was agreed that if this proved insufficient, then the window would be enlarged;
(e) the request for additional offices and stores was refused.

Nine square feet per child

Chol. Harrison, Assistant Secretary, Kent Education reported on 11th July 1907:-

"I have visited this school and seen the enlargement. The accommodation is sufficient for 60 older children and 44 Infants. The old room has been lengthened by 1 foot and is now 31 ft x 18 ft and can very well accommodate 60 older children, giving each 9 sq.ft, the children being visibly small, the boys after Standard I going to Chartham Council School. The new room is 23 ft x 18 ft and can hold 44 Infants. It has always been the custom to send away the Boys leaving Standard I and the LEA seem to wish to continue it. It works well, and indeed the school is full without the big Boys."

In fact, these numbers were never reached. The highest number of children recorded on the roll was 77 in 1908, two years after the enlargement had been carried out, and from that time on numbers gradually declined each year.

Loans were taken out by Kent County Council to pay for the enlargement of the school (£648) and the new furniture needed to fill it (£25) over periods of 30 and 10 years respectively.

One can only imagine what an event this must have been for the village! The Log Book records some of the changes:-

January 14th: School re-opened. Alterations completed but rooms not yet furnished.

March 1st: The new furniture has been arriving during the week. Some of it is in use but until the desks for the Infants are filled the new room cannot be used.

March 11th: The Infants have taken possession of their new room today and are working according to the new timetable.

March 18th: The gallery has been removed and the room entirely filled with new desks.

The cloakroom had two entrances; the one nearest School House (the present entrance) was for the School Mistress and the other on the opposite side was for the children. This continued until the school closed.

The Infants were taught in the Gravel Hill side of the building and the Juniors in the School House side. Again, this remained unchanged throughout the life of the school.

Postcard: Courtesy of Bernard Moat

The above photograph clearly shows how the school was enlarged and was probably taken shortly after the alterations.

The interior of the building also gives clues to the changes that took place as no attempt appears to have been made to match the two halves! The photograph below clearly shows the differences between the original (back) half and the new (front) half - the dado rails are at different heights and the construction of the walls and ceiling is different.

We can only assume that the partition which is still in the hall today, although a little too unstable to be used, was put in at the time of the alterations.

A tower on the roof

The new half was built with a tower on the roof – whether this was a bell tower, a ventilation tower or was purely decorative, we do not know. We know, however, that ventilation was provided in the new half by means of air vents. Air came in through a grating in the outside wall and up a channel in the wall to a vent on the inside wall. Turning the handle 90° on the vent opened a flap at the top and let the air into the room. This handle was in the shape of a small hand. There are still three such vents in the room, although only one has its handle. Unfortunately, the mechanism no longer works. Ventilation would certainly have been necessary - a crowded schoolroom heated by coal and lit by oil lamps would not have produced a healthy atmosphere.

Photo: Jim Sanders, 2006

Photo: Jim Sanders, 2006

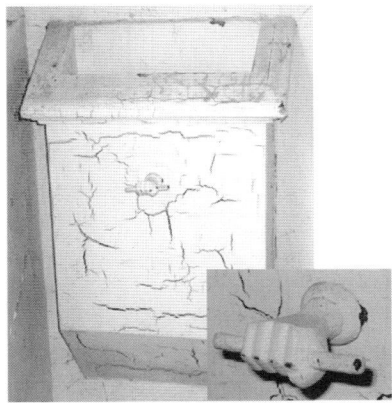

Photos: Jim Sanders, 2006
Top: "Tower" on the roof
Bottom: Vent on wall with small hand

None of the former pupils of the school remembers a bell being rung from the tower; most remember the teacher using either a whistle or a handbell. Whatever its purpose, the tower has now become a distinctive feature of the building and a separate section has been written on its later restoration.

On 4th April 1907 two of the Managers, Mr. Colthup (of Hatch House) and Mr. Arnold (of Nickle Farm) visited the school, presumably to see the new classroom.

Council School No. 73

The Local Education Authority was informed by the Board of Education on 24th July 1907 that "Chartham Hatch Council School No.73 is now recognised by the Board as providing accommodation for not more than 60 Mixed and 44 Infants – totalling 104 children".

Schooling continues

Unfortunately so did the illnesses. The summer of 1912 was a particularly bad year with cases of diphtheria and whooping cough in May and July, followed by measles in October. The school was ordered to close for a total of six weeks.

May 12th 1912: One child taken to hospital suffering from diphtheria and as there are five other children in the family this has caused low numbers.

The school was closed again in 1916, this time because of an outbreak of rubella.

Inspections and regular visits from the Managers and the Schools Attendance Officer also continued. Both Miss Mugford and Miss Letchford were praised for their teaching.

Medical inspections start

The Education (Administrative Provisions) Act of 1907 imposed on all local authorities the duty of providing for the medical inspection of children immediately before or at the time of, or as soon as possible after, admission and on such other occasions as the Board of Education directed. This Act marked the beginning of the state system of school medical inspections in this country and was reinforced by the 1918 Education Act. The Log Book now starts to record regular visits by the doctor and the nurse.

The First World War

Although we know that men from both Chartham and Chartham Hatch were either wounded or killed in battle, the following is the only entry in the Log Book which refers to the First World War:-

June 19th 1917: The children, at a given signal, now take places as for air-raid. Shortest time taken as yet for all to be in position, including youngest babies, 15 seconds.

Jam for the troops

There was also a comment in October 1918 on the closure of the school for two afternoons "for the purpose of picking blackberries as provided for by K.E.C. [Kent Education Committee]". This may have been part of the National Blackberry Scheme launched by the Board of Education in co-operation with the Food Production Department of the War Office in 1917 and 1918 where fruit collected went to make jam for the Army and Navy, but this cannot be confirmed.

The Village School – The Remaining Years

July 22nd 1966: It is with great regret that I make this last entry in this school log book.

T.W. Hime, Acting Headmaster.

Photo: Jim Sanders
The shield made by Mr. Holmes in 1944 still hangs on the wall in Village Hall

School life continued very much along the same lines until the school closed in 1966, when Mr. Hime wrote the last entry in the Log Book. The Head Teacher completed the Punishment Book, the Register and the Log Book, and the Managers continued with their regular meetings and visits. We have also been able to speak with several former and current residents of the village who have helped to 'flesh out' the facts contained in the Log Book and the Minute Books with their own school experiences and a special section with some of their memories has been included later in the book.

The inspections also continue

The first two inspection reports available to us after the appointment of Mrs. Wood were written following visits on 18th January 1922 and 27th January 1925 and were both very favourable.

The 1922 report tells us:-

> "There are three teachers for an average attendance of 55 children. The Head Teacher has high ideals and gives much thought and care to the instruction and training of the children under her charge. The older girls are quiet and well behaved; they show satisfactory interest and very fair ability in their work. In the 3rd Class – Infants and Standard I – the children seem very happy in their work and play. A recent change of teachers has proved a good one."

The 1925 report is equally complimentary:-

> "The Head Teacher has been successful in her efforts to train the girls to work independently. The individual programmes are thoughtfully planned and the periodical examinations provide reliable records of progress. Tests in Arithmetic set at the inspection gave good results and the oldest girls showed creditable knowledge of Geography and History". The Inspector does, however, comment that "speech training needs more attention. The children should be encouraged to cooperate more fully in oral lessons".

Photo: Courtesy of Ella Willmott – 1922/23
Back row left to right: Mrs. Wood, Eva Sims, Gladys Hearnden, Winnie Shilling, Dorothy Woodcock, Viney Bird, Mary Ross
Front row: Grace Wood, Edith Page(?), Nell Wood, Ella Hoare, Amy Moat

Schoolchildren from the 1920s

Photo: Courtesy of Ella Willmott – ca. 1920

Back row left to right: Edith Hoare, Winnie Shilling, Viney Bird, Dorothy Woodcock, Frances Roberts
Third row: Mary (or May) Maybourne, Grace Wood, Marjorie(?) West, Olive Butcher, Amy Moat, Maggie Smith, Eileen ?
Second row: Amy Featherstone, Gladys Woodcock, Lily Smith, Agnes Featherstone, Nellie Smith
Front row: Ella Hoare, Beatrice Wood, Dorothy Coombs, Lily Foster

Photo: Courtesy of Vi Barling – ca. 1921

Back row left to right: Vi Wood, Edie File, Gladys Pemble, ? , Sissy (Valetta) Moat, Rose Marshall, Rhoda Roberts
Third row: ?, Stan Moat, ? , Bill Bird, ? Hazelwood, Harry Brown, Alf Price, ?
Second row: Ada Page, Vi Hoare, Hilda Marshall, Rosa Woodcock, ? , Vera Evans
Front row: Perce Coombs, Cliff Shilling, ? , Stan Bird, Sid Wood, Kenny Hearnden

School - The Remaining Years

Photo: Courtesy of Rhoda Wills – ca. 1923/24
Back row left to right: Hilda Marshall, Edith File, Rose Marshall, Rhoda Roberts, Beattie Wood
Third row: Violet Reeves, Elsie File, Jess Marshall, George Roberts, ?
Second row: ?, Arbin Wood, Betty Ashbee, Joan Philpott, Ray Underdown, Florrie Page
Front row: Cyril Reeves, Wallace Croft, Ray Coombs, ?, George Page

Photo: Courtesy of Rhoda Wills – ca. 1924/25
Back row left to right: Rosa Woodcock, Rose Marshall, Ada Page, Edith File
Middle row: Violet Wood, Rhoda Roberts, Sis Moat, Vi Hoare, ?, Vera Evans, Hilda Marshall
Front row: Sister of Edith File, Ellen Woodcock, Florrie Page(?), ?, Violet Marshall

A surprise for the Board of Education

It was, however, the Inspector's report of 4th April 1928 that took the Board of Education by surprise. Again, it was a mainly favourable report:-

> "This is a cheerful school, the rooms are bright and well cared for, a friendly and quiet tone prevails; the classes are small – 19 and 21 respectively – and there is ample room for all activities …. In their written exercises as well as in their responsive answering to oral questions, there is indication of acquaintance with some good literature. A more systematic attack on elementary errors in spelling, punctuation and grammatical construction could well be made a little earlier."

The Inspector also commented that the Head Teacher, Mrs. Wallis (formerly Mrs. Wood) had changed the status of the school; this led to a flurry of correspondence. After the summer holidays in 1927, without informing the authorities, she had reopened the school as a Junior School, with both boys and girls going to Chartham at 11 and over.

The Board of Education consulted with the Inspector who wrote that:-

> "There was some opposition from the parents but this appears to have died down. The distance is just under two miles, I should say, and the road is pretty poor, although it crosses a main road. Chartham is a much larger school (8 teachers) and the LEA propose to eventually make it into a Central School. There are no particular arrangements at present for dinner, but I understand that a canteen is to be provided. There is plenty of room for the Hatch children at Chartham. The weak point is that Chartham does not as yet provide much in the way of Advanced Instruction, but I do not see that we can very well object to the new arrangement".

The Board decided it could raise no objection and informed the Local Education Authority of their decision, adding the following caustic comment at the end of their letter

> "It would be convenient if, in all future similar cases, the Board could be notified of reorganisations before they are made".

A happy Junior school

The report of 1933 talks about "a happy little Junior school in which the children who are well mannered and responsive are on good terms with their teachers". It does, however, find fault with oral training for the Infants – "great care should be taken with speech which is poor" – and "in the upper class points to which attention should be given are the improvement of the handwriting and neatness of written work in general, the development of oral work so as to obtain greater continuity in speech and the provision of more remedial and fewer routine language exercises in teaching composition".

Improvements

In 1937 we learn from the Inspector's report that the sanitary arrangements had been improved, a gas and water system had been installed and the offices modernized. The oil lamps would have been replaced by gas lights. The previous year the interior had been redecorated and the playground resurfaced.

School numbers

There were only 20 children on the roll at that time but the report mentioned that houses were being built in the area so that numbers would increase. These were the houses built by Mr. Baldwin in 1937 along Bigbury Road, Howfield Lane and Gravel Hill. School numbers did increase, reaching 46 in 1941. They dropped again to 20 in 1948, climbed up to 51 in 1957, only to be followed by a gradual decline. They were again on the increase when the decision was taken to close the school.

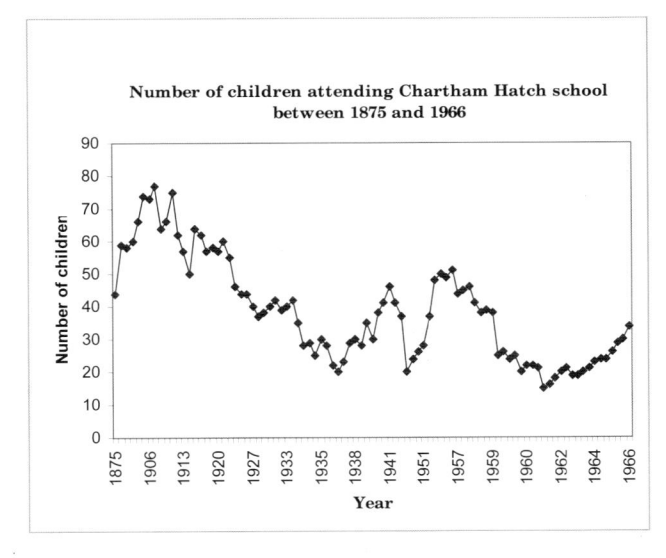

Attendance numbers from the Log Book

The Second World War

With a searchlight unit at the top of Howfield Lane, an anti-aircraft army encampment between Gravel Hill and Bigbury Road, and a camouflaged ambulance station in Bigbury Road - not to mention the occasional German prisoner of war - life in the village and the school during the Second World War was both exciting and frightening. The boys, in particular, recall the excitement of watching the dog fights in the sky and picking up the spent bullet cases and shrapnel, competing for the best collection. Many still remember the sirens and having to take cover as best they could. With its nickname of 'Hellfire Corner' or 'Doodlebug Alley', the whole of the county of Kent was both on the bombing run to London and a target in its own right.

Disaster at Apple Tree Corner

On 27th October 1940 the pilot of a Spitfire of the 603 Squadron, Pilot Officer R.B. Dewey, was killed when his plane hit a tree at Apple Tree Corner, Primrose Hill after it was shot down south of Maidstone in a surprise attack.

Air raids

Despite many air raids, school continued. In 1940, an air raid shelter was built on the Gravel Hill side of the cloakroom, creating an alleyway between the shelter and the school that led to the children's entrance. During practices or actual raids, the children sat in the gloom in the shelter, learning their times-tables, singing the alphabet (they even sang it backwards) or listening to stories. The schoolroom windows were crossed with sticky tape to minimise damage from broken glass.

The Log Book for October and November 1940 records some of the worst occasions:-

11th November: School opened four times on account of raids.

18th October: School opened nine times on account of raids.

1st November: Wednesday and Friday – no afternoon sessions owing to air raids.

15th November: Marked registers nine times owing to raids.

29th November: More air raids – two more children leaving for safer areas.

Earlier in the year children had come to Chartham Hatch as evacuees! The Log Book on 14th May 1940 mentions "two more evacuees admitted".

A doodlebug in Primrose Hill

Towards the end of the war, unmanned V1 rockets, commonly known as doodlebugs or flying bombs, passed overhead on their way to London. Many recall when, on Saturday, 22nd July 1944, one was brought down in Primrose Hill at the bottom of the garden belonging to 4 Baker's Row (now Broadview), destroying the end two of Laurel Cottages, Primrose Cottages (between Primrose Hill and Baker's Row) and the semi-derelict chapel at the end of Chapel Row, and badly damaging the houses in Chapel Row and Baker's Row. Four people were seriously injured, twelve people less so and fifteen houses damaged. The injured were taken to the hospital in Canterbury in army ambulances which came up through Chapel Field from the Hut Meadow Army Camp in Gravel Hill. The blast was felt as far as the village. The Managers' Minutes record that "the school premises were damaged by enemy action on the evening of 22nd July 1944 necessitating closure of the school for one week. The damage was superficial, the structure not adversely affected". The school was also closed for a week on 28th September 1944 because of air raids.

Photo: Sheila Barber

Taken in the late 1960s, this photo shows the remaining cottage of the row of three (Laurel Cottages) damaged by the doodlebug in Primrose Hill, with Highwood in the distance. Until it was extended in the 1970s and became one house called Fir Trees, it was often referred to as the 'Half House'.

Victory celebrations

The school celebrated the end of the war by holidays on 8th and 9th May 1945 (Victory in Europe) and 15th and 16th August 1945 (Victory in Japan).

The whole village also celebrated. Mrs. Holmes, the Headmistress, was asked by several of the children's mothers if she could help them to organize a party. This turned into a whole day of festivities on the meadow at the Royal Oak for both children and adults. The *Kentish Gazette* of

2nd June 1945 described the celebrations as follows:-

"The Victory celebrations at the Hatch on Saturday provided a day of keen enjoyment and pleasure for young and old alike. The children's sports were opened by Miss M. Arnold, of Nickle Farm, who hoped the children would have a very happy day. In the children's fancy dress parade, judged by Miss M. Arnold, Miss C. Arnold and Mrs. Blake Wacher, winners were: "Mrs. Mopp", (aged 2), Bevin Boy, "Sid Walker", a Soldier and a Gypsy. In the races for boys and girls there were many thrilling finishes. The children sat down to a real Victory tea. The tables were laden with good things and were decorated with red poppies, white pinks and blue iris. Ice-cream was served, and each child was given a threepenny bit by a lady helper. Three clowns were very much in evidence during the festivities. The children's sports prizes were presented by Mrs. Blake Wacher.

"In the evening the adults had their own sports and fete. The varied races caused a lot of fun; the crowd roared with delight as the ladies crawled under a tarpaulin in the obstacle race, and some 18 competitors wrestled with sticky buns. Sideshows, competitions, fortune telling, a fruit stall and a buffet all did a roaring business. The ladies' ankle competition was judged by two visiting W.A.A.F.'s, who were at first puzzled by an odd leg that was showing from under the screen, until a gentleman dressed as a lady was pulled out. In a tug-of-war competition between teams from Chartham and Nickle, the latter proved the stronger. After the tilt-the-bucket competition, the final event was the fancy dress parade; the Gypsy Bride and the "Gentlemanly" Lady were awarded prizes.

"The evening finished with dancing on the green to the music of Miss J. Arman and her friends. During the evening Major Cremer and the rector (Rev. A.R. Gore-Brown) visited the fete. The success of the day was due to the hard work and enthusiasm of the residents of the village who worked as a team. As a result of the effort, Chartham Hatch will send a donation of £40 to the Agricultural Red Cross Fund."

The Social Club is formed

This community event was also the starting point for a new venture in the village. Shortly afterwards, with money left over from the celebrations, the Chartham Hatch Social Club was formed. Until the club had its own premises, it hired the school regularly for bingo or whist evenings or for a social evening on Saturdays. A separate section has been written on the Social Club and its activities.

Teaching staff

Mrs. Wallis resigned in August 1944 and her position as Head Teacher was taken by Mrs. N.E. Holmes who taught until November 1947. When Mrs. Holmes left, there were 36 applications for the post, shortlisted to seven. Miss C.M. Mann from Herne Bay was appointed in January 1948 and she remained until 1965, apart from two short periods of absence. Mr. T.W. Hime (Deputy Headmaster at Whitstable C.P. Boys' School) had stood in for Miss Mann while she attended a course in Bristol for teaching handicapped children from September 1964 to September 1965 and he was appointed as Acting Head when Miss Mann left at the end of December 1965 to join the staff of the Amberley Ridge Special School in Stroud, Gloucestershire. It was already planned that the school would close in July 1966.

Photo: Courtesy of Lena Elvidge
Mrs. N.E. Holmes

There were several supplementary, assistant and trainee teachers. Apart from Mrs. Whitcombe who was at the school from 1906 until 1933 and Miss J. Brenchley who taught for a total of fifteen years between 1951 and 1966, the other teachers did not stay long. There was a time in the mid-1930s when Mrs. Wallis had no help at all and had to do all the teaching herself. She reported at the Managers' Meeting of 11th October 1934 how difficult it was to deal with Infants at the same time and in the same room as the older children - the Infants very frequently required music and the older children were disturbed by their lessons when in one room. She stated that the school was further handicapped by the fact that there were no children over eleven to give any kind of temporary help by taking charge of the younger ones. A Miss Garner from Dunkirk helped out on a voluntary basis for several months.

A request for an additional teacher was made in January 1938 in view of the steady influx of children from the new houses being built in the village: "14 of these houses were already occupied and the number on the roll had increased during the last 3 months by 25%". An assistant mistress (Miss M.L. Goldsmith) was appointed in May but only stayed for three months.

Other teachers mentioned in the records were Miss Wood, Miss Scott, Miss Addyman, Miss B. Blackman, Miss R.M. Williams, Miss M.W. Mount, Mr. Haynes, Mr. Broyad (from Chartham under the emergency scheme), Miss Levy, Mr. Bailey, Miss Waller, Miss Bowman, Miss Driver, Miss Brittlebank, Miss Vant, Miss Mawer, Miss Gore, Mrs. Holman and Mrs. Cook (temporary position).

Lessons and other activities

Lessons continued in very much the same way until the school finally closed, with the children split into two classes divided by the partition. Each class was split into small groups, according to the children's ability. The day started with an assembly where the register was taken, prayers were said and a Bible story read, followed by formal lessons in the morning with a break mid-morning.

School milk

Following the School Milk Act in 1946 after a campaign by Ellen Wilkinson, the first woman in British history to hold the post of Minister of Education, one-third of a pint of milk was issued free to all pupils under eighteen and this was drunk during morning break. Milk was already delivered to the school in accordance with the Government's Milk Marketing Board Scheme but the children had to pay the teacher for it. The Log Book in May 1946 says that the milkman had found it impossible to get the small bottles so he continued to deliver the milk in bulk. When the bottles became available, they had cardboard tops which were kept and used to make raffia mats in sewing lessons. The milk often froze in winter and had to be put next to the fire to thaw out.

School meals

School meals were provided in October 1944. They were prepared in Chartham School and delivered in large containers by van. Canteen supervisors were appointed - the records mention Mrs. Whitehead, Mrs. J. O'Meara, Mrs. H.E. Lowman and Mrs. E.A. Salvage. Before this date, the children either went home for lunch or brought sandwiches. In fact, local authorities had been permitted to provide school meals since 1906 following the Provision of School Meals Act, when Mr. Jowett, the Labour MP for Bradford, had managed to convince Parliament that hungry children had trouble learning, but many local authorities were very slow to respond.

Schools broadcasts

There was less formal teaching in the afternoon with physical exercises, stories, sewing and singing. A wireless set, bought with the proceeds of jumble sales, was installed in 1934 and the children listened to schools programmes broadcast by the BBC. On 22nd October 1937, the Visiting Manager, Mr. H.L. Cremer, was "very interested" in both the BBC lesson which was being broadcast during the time of his visit and the "excellent physical training arrangements in the playground". These schools broadcasts continued for many years, some more popular with the teachers than others if Miss Mann's comment of "interesting but not convincing" was anything to go by, following a talk and display on the new BBC programme 'Music and Movement and Mime' at Wincheap Junior School in 1962.

A shield is carved

When Mrs. Holmes became Head Teacher in 1944, she introduced the idea of school teams. Her husband, who was a carpentry teacher at the City Council School in Canterbury, carved the shield which is still in the hall today, and at the end of the week the team with the most points hung their team's coloured band over it. The shield hung on the wall between the two windows in the Junior classroom.

Photo: Courtesy of Lena Elvidge
Mr. C.L. Holmes

The oak motif on the shield probably refers to the oak trees which are now between the road and the car park. At the time of the school they were inside the school fence and it is even mentioned in the Log Book in June 1951 that "Mr. Baxter kindly fixed a climbing rope on to the oak tree".

Distant lands

In an attempt to "widen their outlook", the children regularly heard about the countries in the Commonwealth from visiting speakers of the Commonwealth Institute.

Many visits are recorded in the Log Book between 1958 and 1966, the first in July 1958 by Major Devereux-Colebourne who talked about his journey through Australia, New Zealand and Panama to England. Miss Mann wrote: "It was a delightful programme". Speakers talked about places as diverse as Central Africa, Antarctica and Cyprus and in 1962 there were three talks in as many months – on Burma, the Fiji Islands and Tanganyika.

Unlike today's children, most of these school-children would not have been further than the Kent coast. These lands must have seemed very distant indeed.

Hard working

The Inspector's report of 23rd November 1950 presents the picture of a hard-working, busy little school as shown in the following extracts:-

> "Since the appointment of the Head Mistress[Miss Mann] in 1948, four different teachers have been in charge of the Infants Class, but the work of the school has not suffered. The Head Mistress has worked with zeal and consistent energy to improve standards of work which, since the war, have not been high. The range of the pupils' abilities, limited partly by the low recruitment, presents peculiar problems which are being met by much individual instruction and by praiseworthy efforts to stimulate greater interest... Very good progress has been made in reading and oral expression is distinctly improved. Dramatisation has become a lively feature. Written English, although at present only moderate in quality, has acquired a vigorous and natural character through its association with the children's interests... The story of human activities has been enlivened by references to the locality and by the pupils' models and illustrations; the possibilities of narration by the children should be further explored. Interest in nature is particularly marked and the related practical work is considered most useful".

The Inspector was not, however, equally complimentary about the children's ability in arithmetic:-

> "The response in Arithmetic remains somewhat slow and, in spite of the thoroughness of the teaching, several pupils lack confidence in the handling of simple processes".

Such visits must have been quite stressful, both for the teachers and the children - Miss Mann records that the Inspector came soon after 9 am and stayed until nearly 5 pm. "He made a thorough examination of the children's work, in all subjects, both asking them questions and listening to answers given by the teachers."

Nevertheless, the School Managers were very pleased with the report and Miss Mann was congratulated by them at their meeting in January 1951.

Nature in the classroom

The "interest in Nature" commented on by the Inspectors is what is remembered most about Miss Connie Mann's time as Head Teacher. Previous teachers had taken the children on nature walks but Miss Mann also brought nature into the classroom and into School House. The children were very much encouraged to bring wildlife into school. This included the usual wildflowers, frog spawn and frogs, but more unusual creatures, such as stag beetles, a squirrel, a jackdaw and a dead badger also made their appearance (the children drew the badger before it was buried). Caterpillars have their own entry in the Log Book:-

12th September 1963: The children continue to bring caterpillars to school. These are being allowed to pupate as naturally as possible. Over 20 Tortoiseshells emerged and were liberated just before the holidays. Others are Satin Moth (eggs and chrysalids to date), Great Elephant Hawk and Privet Hawk Moths (caterpillars and pupae). Satin Moth chrysalids taken to London Zoo 27th July.

There were fish tanks and a resident ferret in a cage.

The sick and injured

Sick and injured animals were also brought in by adults for Miss Mann to look after. A fox cub was nursed back to health and strength before being taken to her house where it was described as "a lovely member of Miss Mann's 'menagerie' but is not allowed the freedom of the house. He may be in danger from her dog and the hens from the fox". After a month it was released back into the wild. Baby hedgehogs brought in after being disturbed by a dog were fed on warm milk from a doll's bottle.

She kept rabbits (at one stage there was a total of twenty-three) in hutches in the garden of School House which were often fed on the dandelions collected by the children on nature walks. She also kept a dormouse in her sitting room and a pet lamb. She had received special permission from the school authorities in Maidstone to feed the kitchen waste from the school to the animals.

Farm visits

There were also visits to nearby farms. At Nickle Farm they saw plantations of beech, poplar, Corsican pine and Douglas fir as part of their woodland study and, on another visit, they were shown over the oast house and told how the hops used to be dried. At Howfield Farm they were shown round the apple packing sheds and nearby greenhouses.

An anonymous complaint

Miss Mann owned a black and white collie dog which for ten years regularly came into the classroom with her. However, in December 1957, an anonymous complaint by a parent the previous month resulted in an unofficial visit from Miss Mount, one of the School Managers, and an official visit from Mr. Ball, the Medical Officer of Health. Even though Mr. Ball had no objections "on grounds of hygiene" to the dog being in the school, it was decided to put the dog in the other room at dinner time until, on 8th January, the Log Book records, without further comment, "the dog is left at home".

'Indirect methods'

There had been much more comment in the previous entries in December. Miss Mann was obviously very unhappy at the way the matter had been handled and made it quite clear in her Log Book entries:-

The visit caused some sadness to the staff because we try to be honest and direct in our approaches to things and are not used to indirect methods.

If a parent has a grievance, it is surely better to come and talk it over with the Head Teacher who hopes she is competent enough to discuss any matters. She is suspicious of anonymous persons.

Photo: Courtesy of Jean Brenchley
Miss Connie Mann (left) and Miss Jean Brenchley, with Miss Mann's dog, Rover, taken in the orchard off Town Lane

Plays and concerts

The 1950 report mentions that "dramatisation" had become a lively feature and there are many references in the Log Book and the Minutes of the Managers' Meetings to school plays and concerts which raised money for outings and Christmas parties. The partition was drawn back and wooden blocks used for the stage. The following is a selection from the records:-

14th December 1946: Children presented "The King's Pocket Knife" by Enid Blyton.

14th December 1950: The whole school took part in a Percussion Band Selection. The younger children acted "The Runaway Christmas Rabbit" and the older children performed "The Toys and the Magic Pot". The Youth Club acted Aladdin. Mrs. Barragon (tap dancer) and Mr. Wiseman (pianist) performed between the scenes. Old people over 70 were invited.

October 1952: Concert given and £25 collected for gym shoes and Christmas parties.

8th March 1962: Concert and sale of goods held on November 2nd raised £21 for funds.

Photo: Courtesy of Mrs. I. Port

Harvest Festival – 1953

Back row left to right: Roger Delo, Dave O'Meara, Michael Laker, Bobby Woodbridge, Michael Hoare, Keith Baker, Terry Simmons
Fourth row: Ann Kidd, Brenda Rumley, ?, Shirley Winter, Judy Mayes, Elizabeth Wiseman
Third row: Barbara Philpott, ?, ?, Jonathon Wiseman, Tommy Kidd, ?, Trevor Hinder(?), Ronnie Port
Second row: Jeanette Kidd, ?, Pam Delo, Terry Noble, Jean Philpott, ?
Front row: Sylvia Ruck, Bernard Moat, Patrick Beasley, Roy Delo, Ann Glover, June Baker, Jean Bradley

Fêtes and festivals

Other fund-raising events were the annual summer fêtes and harvest festivals:-

12th October 1945: Harvest Festival – Gifts to Kent Hospital.

13th October 1949: Harvest. Two large tables were decorated with various kinds of produce and it was a good display for such a dry year.

12th November 1953: Harvest Festival and concert in evening. Infants acted Nursery Rhymes and a short play "The Tale of a Turnip" and Juniors acted a play specially written for the occasion "Harvests of the World".

3rd November 1955: Harvest Festival. At the service the rector was bidden farewell – a phonogram was given him from staff and children. In the evening the Infants acted a topical play "Mary, Mary" and the Juniors one specially written for the occasion showing, sometimes humorously, the countries from which some of our food comes.

1st November 1956: Harvest Festival. In the morning a Service of Thanksgiving was graciously honoured by the presence of Mr. Woodhead, County Educational Officer and Mrs. Woodhead. Mr. F.J. King was the Guest Speaker. Mr. King's address was based on Amos. He brought a basket of fruit and gave each fruit a quality, such as apple – joy. Concert in evening. Mrs. Bradley thanked for making new curtains bought with money from the June fete and used for the first time that day. They will hang in the school afterwards. Material cost £15 1s. 0d.

27th June 1958: Summer Fair in school playground during evening.

10th June 1960: Fete to raise money for school fund. A very good evening resulted in £33 being raised, about £4 of this will be expenses. As usual many helpers did Trojan work at stalls and sideshows.

16th October 1964: School Fete on 26th June raised £48 for school funds. It was well supported.

School - The Remaining Years

Fête on No-Bus Friday

This is the heading for the *Kentish Gazette's* report on the school fête held on 27th June 1958. Miss Mann told the paper "We don't hold it on a Saturday because there is a bus then – and everybody goes shopping in Canterbury. There is no bus on Friday!" Apart from the PT display in the playground, "it was strictly an indoor affair, for the biting wind and dismal drizzle drove many of the visiting parents and friends to attractions inside the school building."

Source: Kentish Gazette
PT display at the school's third annual fête to raise money for the school's Outings Fund. The fête was opened by Mrs. Blake Wacher, a School Manager. The other guests – among them Rev. and Mrs. E.J. Field of Chartham and the Rev. Sir Reginald and Mrs. Champion of Chilham – sat wrapped in blankets.

Parties, pantomimes and puddings

There were parties and pantomimes at Christmas time. When Mrs. Holmes was the Head Mistress, her husband used to dress up as Father Christmas and, even though it was wartime, there were toys for the children. Later, Christmas puddings were made with the help of Miss Mann and Miss Brenchley, which, according to the Log Book on 18th December 1953, "were consumed and pronounced good". Sometimes there were sixpences in the puddings. The Log Book also records:-

16th December 1947: Xmas Party – Mrs. Wacher, Mrs. Mount, the rector and Miss Arnold visited. Children presented simple "Nativity Play".

17th December 1949: School used for children's Christmas Party. The Chartham Hatch Social Club and school combined to give all the village children a good time. Father Christmas and "Uncle" Colin (of Herne Bay) entertained after a good tea.

22nd December 1949: Concert – plays, carols and poems. Miss Boyne of Canterbury brought six little girls up to dance. £5 8s 10d to school fund.

16th December 1950: A Christmas Party was held in the schoolroom. Many kind friends helped to prepare the room and tea. Toys had been bought and parcelled up and "Father Christmas" in the form of Mr. Williamson of Boughton School came to make the evening complete. The rector joined in for part of the time.

12th December 1953: Party for all children below 11 and mothers of those under 5. Tea held in the school and the whole party was then conducted to the Village Hall for Father Christmas and a film show kindly given by the rector. Mr. F. King gave each child a packet of sweets.

29th January 1955: A concert pantomime was given by members of F Division Kent County Constabulary in aid of the school voluntary fund - £10.15s.

The 'Village Hall' mentioned above was the hall on the playing field belonging to the Social Club. For several years (unless the weather was too bad), the Christmas party followed the same pattern – tea in the school, followed by a film show in the hall, with sweets and apples provided by the Managers.

The Log Book also tells of the children singing carols – to parents and friends, to the Merry and Bright Club in the Social Club hall and in the Methodist Chapel opposite the school.

Village School to Village Hall

Holidays and celebrations

Empire Day continued to be celebrated and holidays to be given for Royal occasions and local events.

16th July 1928: A day's holiday for Sunday School treat.

30th July 1928: Holiday for Salvation Army treat.

15th August 1928: Holiday for Flower Show.

12th July 1934: Three children absent to visit Hospital for a ceremony connected with Duke of Kent's visit.

24th May 1935: Empire Day. Spent morning doing handiwork (flags), relating stories of the Empire and Empire songs, finishing with saluting flag.

28th January 1936: Holiday for the funeral of George V.

11th May 1936: School closed for Coronation of George VI.

20th November 1947: School closed for celebration of Princess Elizabeth's wedding.

24th April 1948: In the morning normal lessons were not taken, time being given to a rehearsal. In the afternoon at 2.00 pm parents and friends were entertained to a short display of PT by the Juniors, Percussion Band by the Infants and three Scandinavian and one English Country dances, again by the Juniors. In the morning a short talk on the Empire and a message to the children by the Earl of Gowrie was read by the Head Teacher.

26th April 1948: The afternoon was a holiday given by their Majesties on the occasion of their Silver Wedding.

29th May 1953: School closed for the Coronation holiday.

18th June 1957: Children walked to the main road to see the Queen Mother pass.

6th May 1969: School closed for Princess Margaret's wedding.

The Coronation

Celebrations for the Coronation of Queen Elizabeth II were held in the school on 26th April 1953. There were races in the afternoon on the playing field and a concert in the evening. The whole school took part – the Infants acted nursery rhymes, played singing games and performed in the percussion band, and the Juniors put on "The Cobbler and the Shoes" and sang songs. Children were presented with KEC [Kent Education Committee] beakers and saving stamps on a card. The Log Book records that the school had been given a flag pole the previous month by Mr. Hoare (presumably for the celebrations). Unfortunately, the flag pole itself is now missing but the fixing is still there on the wall above the tall window at the front of the building.

Photo: Courtesy of Bernard Moat
Coronation celebrations, 26th April 1953

Back row left to right: Tony Rumley, Bernard Moat, Tommy Kidd, Roy Delo, Simon Wiseman, Patrick Beasley
Kneeling: Pam Delo, Ann Glover, June Baker, Barbara Philpott, ?, Jean Bradley, Jeanette Kidd, Mary Hills
Sitting: Johnny Mayes, Jean Philpott, Robert Hulme, Richard Stone, Linda Hills, Lorraine Beasley, ?, Sylvia Ruck, ?
Audience: Margaret Hinder, looking back

School - The Remaining Years

Outings

As travelling became easier, outings were not just restricted to walks in the woods or walking down to Chartham, but the teachers were able to take the children further afield. The trip to London in July 1950 would have been a major event:-

22nd July 1950: The school had an outing to London to look at the zoo. Some of the children had never been on a train before and certainly not on an escalator.

There were annual outings to the seaside (Herne Bay, Broadstairs) in the summer, with parents helping the teachers.

27th July 1957: School trip to Herne Bay with Miss Brenchley, Miss Mann, Mrs. Lowman and Mr. Delo. Various friends kindly took parents who were unable to get there owing to the bus strike.

20th July 1961: Annual outing. A coach was hired to go to Broadstairs where a happy day was spent in glorious sunshine. About 20 parents and adult friends went.

Photo: Courtesy of Jean Brenchley
Miss Jean Brenchley and children at Broadstairs

Other outings mentioned include:-

16th May 1945: History visit to Canterbury

20th March 1951: The Juniors were taken to the Music Festival in Canterbury in the afternoon. They were conducted over the Cathedral and the Westgate Towers.

5th June 1952: All children present went to the Trooping of the Colour Ceremony by kind invitation of P.C. and Mrs. Wiseman.

10th June 1952: Children taken by East Kent Bus Company to a Music Festival at the Chapter House.

June 1958: Occasional closure of school so that both teachers could take the top Juniors to the County Agricultural Show.

8th April 1960: The school and two teachers visited the Friars to see a film on the Queen's Coronation.

22nd June 1965: The Juniors went on an educational outing to Sandwich, Deal and Dover.

Modernization

During 1935 and 1936 gas was installed, water laid on and the offices converted to WCs, though not without problems during the winter when the Log Book records many instances of frozen lavatories and burst pipes. The following Log Book entry in 1949 tells its own story:-

2nd February: A boy fell while sliding on the cesspool overflow and got very wet as it was not completely frozen.

There had been legislation covering housing, sewage, drainage, water supply and contagious diseases for many years - the 1875 Public Health Act had been the most comprehensive legislation of its kind. The pace of change, however, was very slow and it was not until the 1936 Public Health Act that legislation empowered local authorities to require that water closets replaced privy, pail and earth closets.

These 'outside' toilets were still in use when the school closed in 1966 and were not demolished until 1986 following the installation of 'indoor' toilets in the former air raid shelter in 1981. Mains drainage was put in during 1970. The shelter had been used as a store since October 1948 and was re-roofed in 1956.

Electricity was installed during the summer holidays in 1954 (electric lights were not, however, installed in the toilets until ten years later) and the school was repainted during the summer of 1958, though not, it appears, to Miss Mann's satisfaction.

15th September 1958: The school has been repainted during the holidays. All windows and wooden parts are of two colour greens (both pale) and the doors yellow. Outside office doors are grey as are those of the sheds. The painting has not been carefully done. Yellow paint bespatters the door posts, green and black paint are splashed all around the school on the playground – a very amateurish job.

New wooden floors were laid during the summer holiday in 1960 and a new kitchen unit and electric heater fitted. A stove in the Infants Room was also installed. While the work was carried out, "all the movable material and apparatus was stacked in the lodge" [Kentish dialect word for an outbuilding or shed]. It became apparent to Miss Mann that the room would not be ready for the start of term on 13th September. She recorded in the Log Book how she, Miss Brenchley and Mrs. Salvage arrived armed with dusters, etc., on 12th September to find no hot water, and desks piled on top of each other plastered with whitewash and paint. "The mess was indescribable". But "by dinner time there was some semblance of order". The Infants' chairs and tables had been stacked in the urinal with the result that every ten minutes water cascaded on six tables and over twenty chairs, making them unusable. However, she reported:-

School commenced on Tuesday, 13th September. Both classes were in one room, with workmen in the next room, electrical engineers in the cloakroom and a fair amount of noise and a large amount of dust. On Tuesday we were asked to go into the other room while work was finished in the big room.

The classrooms continued to be heated by coal fires until the 1950s when they were replaced by slow combustion stoves. The fire in the Junior classroom was the first to be replaced (by a Tortoise® stove with the well known 'Slow but Sure Combustion' motto) – at some cost, it appears, to the caretaker!

October 1952: The caretaker's hair and eyebrows were singed by new stove.

An Esse®-type stove was installed in the Infants room in February 1956 but, as this never proved satisfactory, it was replaced by a Cairn® slow combustion stove in June 1960.

Road safety

As cars became more commonplace and the volume of traffic increased through the village, road safety took on a greater importance, particularly in view of the position of the school. As far back as January 1946, a Safety Officer had brought a handbook to the school about safety on the roads. Road Safety films were specially made for school children and in December 1960 the whole school went to Chartham School by East Kent bus to see some of the films. Safety also became a frequent topic in the Minutes of the Managers' meetings, culminating in 1965 in a request for a 'kissing gate' to be installed in the fence next to School House. However, after consultation with the police, it was decided that this would increase rather than decrease the risk of an accident.

In the 1960s there were inter-school Road Safety Quizzes, and the Log Book records in June 1965 that "the children had beaten Waltham in the first round and were meeting Barham in the next round".

The new automatic barrier over the railway line in Hatch Lane was installed on 14th May, 1966 and the children walked down to see it in June.

Still from ciné footage: Courtesy of Mrs. W. Dissington
The new automatic barrier in Hatch Lane from a ciné film taken in the summer of 1966. When the new barriers were fitted, the crossing which had been previously called 'Chartham Siding' was renamed 'Chartham Hatch Level Crossing'. The gatekeeper's cottage or 'lodge' was demolished shortly afterwards.

Doctors and dentists

Medical inspections also continued, with regular visits to the school by the doctor, the nurse and the dentist, as shown by a selection of Log Book entries:-

21st November 1927: Dr. Day visited for Medical Inspection.

21st December 1927: Dental examination.

2nd April 1936: Dr. Watts visited school.

21st January 1943: Nurse Robinson visited and found all the children very clean.

26th June 1946: Medical examination for children leaving to attend Chartham School and for new entries.

September 1953: The nurse came to look at the bad legs of a brother and sister owing to constantly wearing wellington boots.

From the following entry, it would appear that the dentist's visit was not always welcomed:-

School - The Remaining Years

7th November 1930: Attendance poor owing to misunderstanding about Dentist.

The nurse examined the children's heads, eyes and ears and prepared them for the medical inspection by the doctor. The doctor also immunised the children against diphtheria (in the 1940s) and against polio (in the 1950s).

Mobile units also visited the school.

14th June 1937: Visit of cinema van showing Health and Cleanliness Pictures

19th July 1960: The dental van was brought into the school playground

The mobile dental clinic became a regular visitor, with the dentist often "working all day".

Source: Independent Television News Limited
The dental van at Chartham level crossing on its way to Chartham School in 1954 taken from a British Pathé News film

Adults were also catered for:-

28th October 1960: The Mobile X-Ray Unit (Chest) was in the playground for several hours to enable adults to take advantage of the service.

Exercises and team games

There was still physical exercise in the playground, or inside if it was really cold, with regular inspections and visits by the Physical Training Advisor. The teachers also had to be taught:-

11th November 1948: Last lecture of a series of six being given in Canterbury by Miss Hampton on Physical Training for Infants. Miss Brittlebank and Miss Mann have both attended.

Miss Mann attended a course of Physical Training Classes in Canterbury in October 1950 taken by Mr. Baxter, the Assistant Physical Training Advisor for the area, and she and Miss Brenchley also attended lectures on Physical Education given by Mr. Baxter at St. Stephen's School in Canterbury in October 1955 as well as a PE course for Infants at Reed Avenue Infants School in 1961. Mr. Baxter was a regular visitor to the school and was "able to give helpful criticism and suggestions for use of apparatus". In 1955 the Log Book records that he "brought 14 pairs of plimsolls for the school".

Rounders and other sports

There were also team games, with the children wearing coloured bands in the 1950s to gain points for the shield introduced by Mrs. Holmes. We learn from the Log Book that the children played rounders from around 1950, taking part in inter-schools matches. It was also in 1950 that the playing field of the Chartham Hatch Social Club (the current recreation ground) was levelled and seeded and the Kent Education Committee agreed to help in the upkeep of the field in return for its use during school hours for organised games. Until it was ready, the school used the playground, the meadow at the Royal Oak or the gravel pit along Bigbury Road. The Log Book records some of the events:-

18th May 1950: Ten children went with Miss Brenchley to Hoath to play a rounders match. Result 2-1 to Hoath.

31st May 1950: Lower Hardres School came to play a rounders match. Mr. Groombridge of the Royal Oak kindly mowed and lent his field. Lower Hardres won 1½ rounders to nil.

7th June 1950: Hatch played Chislet. Chislet had to leave before the end because of catching a bus.

20th July 1950: Junior children went with two teachers to Blean School for the interschool Sports Rally.

26th July 1950: The school had a sports evening in the meadow at the Royal Oak (by kind permission of Mr. Groombridge). A programme of Physical Training and races had been arranged and Mrs. Blake-Wacher was present to present the ribbons. Mrs. Mount and the Reverend Gore-Browne were also there to represent the Managers. Councillors Smith and Clough of the Bridge/Blean Road Safety Committee came to present prizes won in a Road Safety Competition in the area.

Photo: Courtesy of Bernard Moat

School Rounders Team – 1959

Back row left to right: Jean Philpott, Mary Lowman, Bernard Moat, Peter Beasley, Robert Hulme
Front row: John Mayes, Jeanette Kidd, Mary Hills, Roland Beasley, Frederick Philpott

There were regular rounders matches against Hoath, Lower Hardres, Waltham and Chislet. The Log Book records some heavy defeats but, in October 1959, the school shared the Rounders Shield with Chislet.

As numbers decreased in the early 1960s, there were not enough children to make up a team; members from the visiting team had to be "borrowed" so that a match could be played.

Scholarship examination

Most of the children went to Chartham County School at the age of eleven. Selected children were entered for the Scholarship Examination Test (also referred to in the Log Book as the Kent Intelligence Test and the Kent Junior Tests) and, if they were successful, they went to school in Canterbury. Following a visit to the school in July 1942 the Reverend M.L. Man wrote:-

It is good to note that Mrs. Wallis' coaching has enabled yet another child to get a scholarship (the fourth from this school).

It has to be said, however, that some years there were no passes at all and a year with two passes was a rare occurrence.

Other interesting snippets

Of all the entries in the Log Book, those written by Miss Mann give us the most insight into what was else was happening in the school, in the immediate neighbourhood and, indeed, in the world! Here are a few examples:-

12th July 1948: Two Dutch ladies youth hostelling in Britain called in to ask for directions. One was a school teacher until the German occupation. They came into school and listened to some singing and "taught" us two Dutch singing games and joined in one of ours.

[Miss Mann also recorded their names and addresses; we have written to them and an article has been posted in a popular Dutch magazine, but so far with no luck!]

17th March 1949: Two children brought to school from the tents (on the sandpit). Parents hope for a house soon.

3rd February 1953: Clothing was collected and sent to the Relief Centres for the Flood victims.

The above entry in February 1953 was a result of both national and local appeals after storms on January 31st flooded much of the east coast of England. Whitstable and Herne Bay were badly affected.

27th January 1955: Eight children were taken to the Regal Cinema to see Climbing of Mount Everest.

7th November 1956: Mr. Eisenhower was again elected President of the United States. The unrest in Egypt seems a little less strained. A cease-fire is in being.

30th April 1958: Children watched the cars (including the bride) going and returning to and from Church at Chartham on the occasion of the wedding of the eldest daughter of Mr. and Mrs. R. Mount.

15th September 1958: Chartham Secondary School – new school opening today.

19th March 1959: Head Teacher absent to attend official opening of Chartham Secondary School.

6th July 1959: PC Fairhall instructed a group of children for the Cycling Proficiency Test.

13th February 1960: We had the National Savings Shield for East Kent for one week.

21st February 1961: Juniors went with Miss Mann to see the television pictures of Col. Glenn to Mrs. P. Hubbard's. We would like to record the fact that at 2.45 pm yesterday we heard Col. Glenn shot into orbit and we are thankful that he made a safe return.

9th June 1964: We sent 49 lb wool via the "Wirral Wool Co." van.

14th December 1964: Kent County Library van visited to make the termly exchange of books.

Although the school photographer probably visited the school each year, his visit is not recorded until 1949 when we learn that the photograph was taken by Messrs. Recordafoto Ltd. Messrs. Sunbeam Photos Ltd. took the photographs in subsequent years.

Closure threatens

School numbers started to decline after 1957, reaching a record low of 16 in October 1961, caused in part by parents sending their children to schools outside the village. The numbers had been regularly monitored by the Divisional Education Office and, at a meeting in October 1965, the Managers were asked for their reaction if a proposal were submitted that Chartham Hatch School be closed and the children transferred to the school at Chartham. At that time there were 30 children on the roll.

The Managers (the Reverend E.J. Field (Chair), Lady Boucher, Mrs. E.E. Mount, Major R. Plowman, Mr. C.J. Riddell and Mr. P.B. Wacher) replied that no objection would be raised provided the Committee undertook to convey all children who would normally attend Chartham Hatch School across the main Canterbury/Maidstone Road to Chartham Primary School. A meeting of parents was held on 31st December when the Divisional Educational Officer explained the reasons for the proposed closure.

Strong opposition from some

There was strong opposition to the closure; letters of objection were sent to the Secretary of State for Education and Science and the support of Canterbury's Member of Parliament, Mr. David Crouch, was sought. The *Kentish Gazette* of 1st July 1966 reported the case as presented by Mr. Anthony Payne of Woodside, Bigberry Hill. He stated that the objections fell under two headings – educational and social – and he outlined them as follows:-

(i) The classes at Chartham Primary School were already much larger and the influx of an additional 50 pupils would worsen the position.

(ii) The personal attention and tuition given to individual pupils in the small classes of the village school would never be achieved in a large school.

(iii) The personal contact made between the child, teacher and parent in a small school was educationally of immeasurable value.

(iv) The present village school was well equipped and in good repair and was able to offer adequate facilities for efficient education.

(v) The roll for next term stood at 50. This was an ideal number, being sufficiently large to more than justify the existence of the school, at the same time allowing for small classes.

(vi) It was educationally undesirable to extend the time away from home for young children. In many cases, this would be from 8 a.m. to 4.30 p.m., a day of 8½ hours, 40 percent of which would not be used for education.

The main points under the social heading were:-

(i) Young children should not be deprived of the security which stems from the knowledge that they are not far from home.

(ii) There was no public transport available between Chartham Hatch and Chartham and, having once arrived at school, they could not return home neither could their parents reach them. For those children who would

Village School to Village Hall

have to walk to school the route was formidable. There was the negotiation of two level crossings, one unguarded, crossing a trunk road – the A28 – on a bend and the whole route was steeply downhill to school – and very steeply uphill home at the end of the day.

(iii) Chartham Hatch was a distinct community, geographically separate and impossible to integrate into Chartham. Closure of the village school would undoubtedly result in the destruction of a neighbourhood unit. The school was the centre around which the village revolved. If it were not there, who the devil would want to come and live here?

Mr. Nicholas Polmear, Canterbury's Chief Education Officer, replied that the decision rested with the Secretary of State for Education and Science. On the question of transport, he stated that the Committee guaranteed that all pupils transferring would be provided with transport as a special circumstance because of the danger of crossing the A28, adding that this was a promise they had given.

Mrs. Ewan Mount, one of the School Governors, had been a staunch campaigner for the provision of transport for the Hatch children and was instrumental in arranging for the children at Denstead to be collected instead of having to walk along the dangerous road to the village.

... but not from others

Not all parents, however, were against the closure. Some felt that their children would benefit from the extra facilities at the larger Chartham school and were keen for their children to be transferred.

The school finally closes

The Department of Education and Science finally confirmed that the school would close at the end of Summer Term 1966 and that arrangements had been made for the Castle Motor Company to convey the Chartham Hatch children to and from the Chartham school from the beginning of the Autumn Term 1966.

Miss Mann left at the end of December to take up a position in Gloucester. She was presented with "a beautiful case from 'the village' and a travelling clock from the children". Her last entry in the Log Book reads:-

20th December 1965: Miss Mann and Miss Brenchley were dismayed to find that the reason given in the paper for the closure of the school is that numbers are declining. They have doubled in a year and 35 at least are expected next term.

Mr. T.W. Hime took over for the remaining two terms and school continued as usual. Miss Brenchley left on 21st July 1966. Mr. Hime recorded the event:-

Managers and friends were invited to a presentation of gifts to Miss Brenchley for her devoted and faithful work to the children of the school and village over the past 13 years. She is leaving to take up an appointment at Petham School.

The last entry in the Chartham Hatch Log Book reads:-

22nd July 1966: The school closed for the summer holiday. Notice was received that the school will be closed and the children transferred to Chartham C.P. school. It is with great regret that I make this last entry in this school log book. T.W. Hime, Acting Headmaster.

A positive start

However, the first report to the Managers by the Head Teacher of Chartham School, Mr. Richard Nisbet, on 14th October 1966 was very positive:-

The Department of Education and Science ruled in favour of the closure of Chartham Hatch school and the children were transferred here from the beginning of this term. They have adapted to the change of environment remarkably well and now seem quite happy in their new classes. The operation of the school bus between the school and Chartham Hatch is proceeding smoothly.

To this day, there is a school bus taking children from Chartham Hatch to the Primary School in Chartham. Regent Coaches now provide this service but for many years these transport arrangements were provided successively by Roy Tours and Smiths' Coaches.

Memories of the School

1915-1930

Hilda Fagg, née Stokes – Born 1910. Lived in one of the two cottages at Puddledock. Started school in 1916 during the First World War. Had polio as a child and went to school on a scooter with wooden wheels which she says ended up being square with so much use.

Ella Willmott, née Hoare (1912-2004) – Born 1912 in 2 School Cottages. Started school in 1915 at the age of 3 and left at the age of 14 in 1926.

Dorothy Tong, née Coombs (1914-2005) – Born 1914 in 1 School Cottages. Started school in 1919.

Rhoda Wills, née Roberts (1914-2006) – Lived at 3 Hatch Lane Cottages. Started school in 1919.

Sid Wood (1914-2006) – Born 1914 in 4 Baker's Row, Primrose Hill. Started school in 1919.

Vi Barling, née Wood, and Bernard Wood – Born 1915 and 1922 respectively. Lived at 8 New Town Street.

Harry Brown – A friend of Sid Wood. Lived at Steed Cottages, Howfield Lane.

Ellen (Betty) Smith, née Ashbee (1917-2006) – Lived initially in Primrose Hill and then in New Town Street. Started school in 1922.

Violet Winter, née Marshall (1918-2006) – Lived next door to Rhoda Wills in Hatch Lane. Started school in 1923.

Hazel Lewis, née Newton – Came to Chartham Hatch in 1924. Lived at 2 The Mount at the top of Primrose Hill, moving to 13 New Town Street when she was 10 years old. Attended Chartham Hatch school from 1927 to 1933, after which she went to Chartham school.

Kathleen Edwards, née Fuller – Born in Mill Row, Chartham. Moved to Primrose Hill when she was very young and then to Puddledock. Went to Chartham school at the age of eleven.

Greville Raines (1924-2006) – Born July 1924 in 1 School Cottages and moved to 2 Primrose Cottages, Primrose Hill when only a few weeks old. Moved to Shalmsford Street, Chartham when he was 7.

Mabel Sparks, née Featherstone, nickname Robin, (1925-2006) – Born in 1925 in No. 2, New Town Street.

Photo: Courtesy of Ella Willmott - ca. 1919
Lily Smith, Albert Evans, Olive Butcher, Ethel Butcher, Gladys Hearnden, Grace Wood
Ella Hoare, - ? -, Gladys Pemble, Edith Pemble, Freddie Hearnden, Fred Wood

Photo: Courtesy of Rhoda Wills – ca. 1920

Left to right – Back row: Nell Wood, Ethel Butcher, Eva Sims, Win Shilling, Daisy Thomas, Lucy Price, Edie Underdown, Viney Bird, Edie Price, Gladys Hearnden, Dolly Woodcock, Rose Holiday

Middle row: Lily Bishop, Amy Moat, Olive Butcher, Norman Jeanes, Margaret Pemble, Alf Price, Vi Wood, Grace Wood, Ella Hoare, Vi Hoare, Gladys Woodcock, Ellen Woodcock, Ken Hearnden, Gladys Pemble

Front row: Sydney Wood, Stan Bird, Clifford Shilling

Happy days

Several of those we spoke to commented how happy they were at school. All the children got on with each other – it was a friendly school. Harry Brown remembers the happy atmosphere – he says there were no quarrels and the children were well behaved. Punishments were few and usually resulted in having to stand in the corner or to stay in at playtime, with the occasional caning on the hand.

Mrs. Hoare

Ella's mother, Mrs. Hoare, was the school cleaner; they lived next door to Dorothy Coombs and her family. Mrs. Hoare would get up early to light the fires, which had guards round them, and after school had finished she would sweep up and clean ready for the following day. In addition, helped by Ella, Ella's sister and brother, she would blacklead the huge "donkey stove" in the big room once a week, prepare enough coal and firewood for a whole week over the weekend and scrub the floor once a month. Ella says that, after her mother left, the floor was only scattered with sand and swept. Betty Smith and Mabel Sparks remember her making up a bed for any sick child as the mother usually had to go to work on the farm. When Ella Mary Letchford, the Head Mistress, died of typhoid fever, her sister, Isabella Letchford, asked Mrs. Hoare if she would name her baby after her if it was a girl. It was – hence Ella Mary Hoare.

Mrs. Wood, Wallis and Whitcombe

The Head Mistress after Miss Letchford was Mrs. Helena Wood, who reverted to her maiden name of Wallis after her husband died. She is very well remembered. Rhoda Wills describes her as "wonderful", "brilliant at everything". Mrs. Wallis taught the Juniors and Mrs. Whitcombe the Infants.

Dorothy remembers Mr. Whitcombe dressing up as Father Christmas. The two classes were divided by the partition that is still in the hall today. Hazel Lewis recalls Mrs. Wallis giving them dancing lessons to try to make them into "ladies and gentlemen", although she says that, being farm labourers' children brought up happily but roughly, they didn't really know what a "lady" or a "gentleman" was. They had to knit a kind of slipper with a drawstring at the top that they would wear for the lessons instead of their usual lace-up boots so that they could slide easily on the floor. At that time the floor was bare scrubbed wood.

School Memories

Playtime

The entrance to the school playground was by large double gates on the corner of Bigbury Road and Gravel Hill, opened and closed each morning and evening by Mrs. Hoare. The playground was surrounded by railings made of steel bars and posts. Ella remembers hooking her pinafore over the bar and swinging upside down. At playtime the boys kicked a football around or played 'tag', while the girls played hopscotch, and had whips and tops, hoops and skipping ropes. They hung their coats up on hooks in what they called the porch. Opposite the school were open fields called "The Green" where Hazel remembers playing at playtime and Dorothy remembers playing games with old tennis racquets and balls, rounders and cricket. There was no problem then crossing the road! The pump in the playground was the only source of water and was used both in the school and School House – Dorothy remembers the boys throwing the water over the girls!

Dipping Tank

The children walked to school and back each day. Vi Marshall and Rhoda walked from Hatch Lane, turning into Dipping Tank by the oast houses, up Chapters Hill and along New Town Street. Rhoda remembers the road being repaired, before it was tarred. The holes would be filled with stones and the steam roller would flatten them. Dipping Tank probably got its name from a tank in the field which was filled with creosote and used to dip the hop poles to preserve them. In Rhoda's time there was a water tank at the bottom which stored the water used when the orchards were sprayed. The name Dipping Tank is still used by many people.

The 'Atchites

When they went down to Chartham School the children would walk down Hatch Lane, though in good weather Harry Brown and Sid Wood went through the fields, crossing the Canterbury to Maidstone/Ashford road at the Corn Mill. Hazel remembers the Chartham children calling the children from the Hatch the 'Hatchites'. The majority of the Hatchites (or 'Atchites as they were called) were the children of farm workers and Hazel felt that sometimes they were looked upon as being 'different'. Quite often they would arrive at Chartham dirty from walking through the fields. Kathleen Fuller had to walk along a rough track from Puddledock and used to clean her shoes before she got to the school with rags hidden in the hedge at the other end. Hazel remembers Chartham Hatch always being called a hamlet (the 'amlet) rather than a village. Before the Hatch school became a Junior School in 1927, the girls stayed at the Hatch until they reached the school leaving age of fourteen; the boys transferred to Chartham at the age of eight. After 1927, all the children remained at the Hatch until they were 11 or 12 when they transferred to Chartham. The first girls to go to Chartham were Rose Marshall, Ada Page, Ida Ford, Rhoda Roberts, Sissy Moat, Vi Wood and Rosa Woodcock. They went when they were 12 but children from subsequent years went at 11. Greville Raines remembers the teacher at Chartham (Miss McKay) calling him out in front of the class on his second day there to go through his tables – he was "absolutely jittered" and could get no further than seven sevens.

Postcard: Courtesy of Norton Harries
Hop picking in 1905 looking from the bottom of Dipping Tank towards the oast houses and Hatch Farm House in Hatch Lane. Apples have now replaced the hops. The water tank was at the bottom of the field on the left.

Village School to Village Hall

Photo: Courtesy of Rhoda Wills – ca. 1925

Left to right – Back row: Olive Featherstone, Eileen (Leny) Collinson, Dorrie Coombs, Sis Moat, Rhoda Roberts, Beattie Wood, Ada Page, Ella Hoare, Amy Faulkner

Fourth row: Vera Evans, Elise Irvine, Elise (Rosa) Woodcock, Vi Wood, Vi Hoare, Hilda (Dolly) Marshall

Third row: Leslie Maybourne, Tom File, Edith File, Elsie File, Helen Woodcock, Amy Wood, Betty Ashbee, Vi Marshall, Vic Datlen, Violet Reeves, Ron Irvine

Second row: Florrie Page, Mary Hubbard, Cyril Reeves, Arbin Wood, Tommy Link, Joan Philpott, Doreen Gilbert

Front row: George Page, Wilfred Hills, Cyril Hills

The daily routine

Both Mabel Featherstone and Hilda Stokes had a tin tray containing sand and a stick to write in the sand, while Dorothy and Rhoda remember writing with pencils. Slates, chalk and pens dipped in inkwells were also used. The desks were in rows and the Head Mistress would walk up two steps to a platform and sit at a high desk. She had a blackboard and easel next to her desk. After the register had been called, there were prayers and a Bible lesson. Other lessons included reading, writing and arithmetic, and sewing, knitting, dancing and singing. Rhoda describes making cushion covers and chair backs, even cutting out pinafores which the girls wore to school. If the sewing was good enough, it used to be bought by the children's mothers. They wore what they liked to school but Dorothy says it was usually white pinafores with lace. Vi Wood wore a big floppy ribbon and a white apron, like most of the girls, and the boys had flat caps with peaks. They also learnt about history and different places in the world and had drill in the playground. Nature walks were taken through Bigbury Woods. Dorothy remembers three oil lamps hanging down on thick wire – one for the Infants and two for the Juniors. The outside 'bucket' toilets were emptied by horse and cart very late at night. There were long summer holidays, and Rhoda and Sid went hop-picking to earn money to have new clothes to go back to school. Greville also remembers hop-picking, with families coming down from London to live in the hoppers' huts at Denstead and Nickle, working during the week and celebrating each weekend.

Lunch time

Most children would go home for lunch but those from the outskirts of the village, e.g. White Wall and Denstead, would bring a packed lunch as it was too far to walk home and back again. Hazel and Kathleen also brought a packed lunch as their mothers were out at work, but nothing to drink as they would get water from the pump. They sat at their desks to eat it and afterwards they would fold their arms on the desk, put down their heads and go to sleep as most of them had been out in the fields with their mothers before 7 am.

Hazel remembers the Horlicks® drink made by the teacher - one Horlicks® tablet was dropped into their enamel mugs. According to Hazel, the resultant drink was pretty weak and tasted "like dishwater", as they were only allowed one tablet. The children took it in turns to be given the empty tin by the teacher.

The 'Bug Nurse'

Hazel describes a visit by the 'Bug Nurse' where the children had to line up and the nurse would part their hair with two spatulas to see if they had head lice; 'clean' children were told to stand in one line and 'dirty' children in another. 'Dirty' children were given a note to take home to their mothers.

Empire Day

Hazel also describes Empire Day at the school - they made a little flag which they took home for it to be fastened to a stick and on Empire Day itself they would all wave them. Dorothy, Rhoda, Violet, Betty and Mabel all remember dancing round the maypole in the back playground on May Day.

Sunday School

They all remember the Primitive Methodist Chapel in Town Lane where Mrs. Whitcombe used to play the organ. Both she and her husband were Sunday School teachers and lived in New Town Street. Rhoda, Violet and Hazel attended Sunday School regularly, going on the annual outing. Hazel's father, Sid Newton, was very involved with the Chapel – Hazel recalls the Wednesday evening Joy Nights he used to run where everyone gathered for choruses, stories and sometimes lantern slides, with the youngsters sitting at the back roasting chestnuts on the old 'tortoise' stove. She recalls harvest festivals, sales of work and prize-giving days. Mrs. Whitcombe taught her drawn-thread work once a week in the Sunday School room and how to make tablecloths and duchess sets for the dressing table. Adults made clothes, all by hand.

Photos: Courtesy of Hazel Lewis and Kathleen Edwards
Hazel Newton (left) and Kathleen Fuller (right)

Photo: Courtesy of Hazel Lewis
Sid Newton picking apples in the orchard along Town Lane in 1938

Photo: Jim Sanders
A vase rescued from the chapel by Mr. Albert Bradley. It had been thrown onto a pile of rubbish and was in need of repair.

Mr. Whitcombe also used to help Mr. Newton - weeding the small flower borders, emptying the bucket from the wooden privy at the back and taking visitors from Canterbury to see the rhododendrons and azaleas in the woods at the back of the Mount. Dorothy recalls Mrs. Polly Hubbard taking on the running of the chapel until it was pulled down in late 1960s.

A tiny clasped hand

Sid was intrigued by the ventilators on the walls of the Hatch school, each with their tiny clasped hand, forming a knob to enable the ventilators to be opened.

Into service

Betty was offered a place at the Simon Langton school in Canterbury but family circumstances were such that she was unable to go and, after leaving school, she went into service as a children's maid at Mystole.

Photo: Courtesy of Sid Wood
Sid Wood tending the carnations in the glasshouses belonging to Mr. Leslie Mount at the bottom of Howfield Lane

Photo: Courtesy of Vi Barling

A Methodist Chapel outing to Whitstable, some time in the 1920s

Back row left to right: Mrs. Ashbee, ?, Mrs. Woodcock, Mrs. Ashbee senior (?), Mr. Alf Woodcock, two mothers with babies, Mrs. Wood, ?
Middle row: Rosa Woodcock, Betty Ashbee, Eileen Collinson, Olive Butcher, Grace Wood
Front row: Stan Bird, Bernard Wood, Bill Bird

1930-1950

Arthur Faulkner (1928-2006) – Born 1928 in 5 New Town Street. Started school when he was five and left in 1939 to go to the Simon Langton School for Boys

Alan Joyce lived at The Bungalow in Howfield Lane. Started school in 1934 and left in 1940 to go to Chartham school.

John Piper – Born 1935 and moved to Rozel, Bigbury Road from Primrose Hill when he was three. Went to Chartham School when he was 11.

Pat Amos (née Butcher) – Lived at Yew Tree Cottage, Howfield Lane. Started school in January 1941 and left in July 1947 to go to the Simon Langton School for Girls.

Brenda Delsignore (née Coombs) – Lived at Puddledock. Started school in 1941 and left in 1947 to go to Chartham School.

Shirley Woodward (née Lemar) – Lived at Dove Cot, Bigbury Road. Started school in January 1943 and left in July 1947 to go to the Simon Langton School for Girls.

Sylvia Rose (née Delo) – Lived at Avis, Bigbury Road. Started school in 1944 and left in 1950 to go to Chartham School.

Margaret Talbot (née Hinder) – Lived at Alicia, Howfield Lane. Started school in 1944 and left in 1950 to go to Chartham School.

Lena Elvidge (née Butcher) – Lived at Yew Tree Cottage, Howfield Lane. Started school in 1946 and left in 1952 to go to Chartham School.

Jessie Bradley – Has lived in Bigbury Road since 1939. Helped to set up the Social Club.

Peter Rumley – Was at home at 4 Baker's Row, Primrose Hill when the doodlebug landed in 1944.

Photo: Courtesy of Sylvia Rose – late 1940s

Back row left to right: Michael Hoare, Kenny West, Michael Osborne, Brian Moat, Patrick O'Meara, David Coombs, Ronnie Piper

Front row left to tight: Valerie Hinder, Sylvia Delo, Brenda Rumley, Valerie Matthews, Margaret Hinder, Susan Murray

Sometimes on a Friday afternoon the children were allowed to bring in their toys

Mrs. Wallis and Mrs. Holmes

The Head Teacher was still Mrs. Wallis when they all started school. Arthur Faulkner describes her as "a particularly good teacher … very conscious of the welfare of the children", remembering especially the Horlicks® warmed on the stove that they could have with a biscuit for a penny during winter and was very grateful for her coaching in the evenings which helped him to pass the grammar school examination.

Mrs. Wallis left in August 1944 and was followed by Mrs. Holmes, who with her husband also lived in School House. Shirley Woodward describes Mrs. Holmes as being "young and vibrant". Pat Amos remembers earning points for the shield – "She [Mrs. Holmes] would ask things like 'Who cleaned their teeth today?' or 'Who polished their shoes?' and 'How about your finger nails?' and if you put your hand up you got a point for that."

Photo: Courtesy of Shirley Woodward

Left to right: Alec Osborne, Richard Miles, Michael Jury, Peter Rumley, Maurice Port, John Piper, Derek Rumley, Pat Butcher, Brenda Coombs, Shirley Lemar

Both photos taken by Mrs. Holmes in Bigbury Wood, ca. 1947

Photo: Courtesy of Shirley Woodward

Back row left to right: Brian Phillips, Alex Salvage, Colin Wood, Diane Hills, Joan Piper

Front row: Rosie Osborne, Jacqueline Chenneour, Evelyn Delo, Violet West (Tootsie), ?, Shirley Jury, John Miles

Children with dirty fingernails had to go into the cloakroom and scrub their nails in the little sinks. Pat also recalls Mrs. Holmes reading the Enid Blyton magazine, 'Sunny Stories', to them on a Friday afternoon and particularly remembers the anticipation of listening to the next instalment of the serial. Mrs. Holmes played the piano for morning assembly and also taught Pat how to play. Both Pat and Shirley remember using the telephone in School House to tell Chartham school how many school dinners to deliver. A different child each day was asked to ring down the numbers – this was Mrs. Holmes' way of getting the children accustomed to using the telephone. The children were tested on their mental arithmetic and times-tables by having to go out of the classroom and answering the questions put by the class when they came back in. Shirley remembers listening to the schools programmes on the wireless – history, geography and nature studies – and the Christmas parties when Mr. Holmes dressed up as Father Christmas – "we all knew or thought we knew it was him but it was never let on".

Both Brenda Coombs and Pat learned "Land of Hope and Glory" for Empire Day and also danced round the maypole on May Day. The girls and boys had separate playgrounds, with the boys round the corner at the back. The entrance to the building was at the end of the alleyway between the newly built air raid shelter. The children had to stand to attention, the girls lining up against the school wall, the boys against the wall of the air raid shelter, until the teacher said they could go in.

Both Pat and Brenda also recall going on a nature walk down the track by the present Warren Cottage to the woods between Bigbury Road and Howfield Lane and having their photo taken by Mrs. Holmes. Shirley also remembers looking for fox footprints in the snow. They had a Sports Day in the nearby gravel pit.

Hop picking

Pat and Shirley also remember hop picking, Shirley going to the hop gardens along Sandy Way opposite Denstead Oast and Pat working in the hop fields at White Wall and Denstead at the end of the summer holiday. Pickers from London lived in the hoppers' huts at the bottom of Gravel Hill.

Behind you!

After they had both left the school, Shirley and Pat took part in the two pantomimes, 'Aladdin' and 'Cinderella', performed in the school by the Youth Club with help from many villagers.

'Aladdin' was part of the concert held on 14th December 1950 which also included items from the percussion band and three playlets by the school children, with P.C. Wiseman at the piano and a tap dancer giving "welcome entertainment between the scenes". Pat played the title role in 'Aladdin' and Shirley the Princess. The *Kentish Gazette* also comments on the "lighting effects and ingenious footlights provided by Messrs. J. Hubbard and S. Delo, there being no electricity in the village".

A big day out

Several children remember the trip to Westgate Towers as a "big day", when they met up with some of the pupils at the City Council School in Canterbury, had lunch in their dining hall and were taken to the Westgate Towers.

Photo: Courtesy of Pat Amos and Peter Tong
Trip to Westgate Towers, Canterbury – mid 1940s

Odd job man

Alan's father, Frank Joyce, used to do repair jobs in the school – the Minute books record him repairing the pump, the fireplace and fixing leaking pipes in the toilets, and Alan tells of him whitewashing the toilets during the summer months and putting tape on the school windows at the start of World War II.

Photo: Courtesy of Alan Joyce
Alan Joyce and his father

Sunday School and First Aid

Arthur went to the Sunday School in the chapel in Town Lane from 1934 to 1943. Margaret Talbot recalls a Sunday School outing on a steam train from Chartham to Broadstairs. Pat, Brenda and Shirley all went to a Girls' Club where they had First Aid classes in the little room at the back of the chapel.

Scholarship examination

Arthur, Pat and Shirley recall taking the Grammar School selection examination. Pat and Shirley did theirs at the same time and both passed – it was considered "fantastic" that Chartham Hatch had two passes in the one year as there were often no passes at all. They had to go into Canterbury to take the examination which included an oral examination. When Pat and Shirley took their examination, the Simon Langton School for Girls was temporarily located at St. Martin's Hill as the main building in Canterbury (in Whitefriars) had been bombed. Arthur successfully sat his examination in the Simon Langton School for Boys, which was also in Whitefriars, just before the start of the war. After both Langton schools had been bombed, he attended school in the mornings only – there were not enough buildings habitable so the authorities decided that the boys would go in the mornings and the girls in the afternoons. As there was only a Wednesday and Saturday bus service to and from Chartham Hatch, on the remaining days everyone had to walk about a mile to the Ashford Road (A28) to catch the bus to Canterbury – downhill all the way there but uphill all the way back!

World War II

Pat and Brenda hadn't started school when the Second World War broke out and only gradually realised its implications as they got older; they remember the blackouts during the air raids and having to take shelter, both at home and in the school air raid shelter. Both remember the air raid in 1942 on Canterbury; Brenda was in Canterbury at the time and sheltered under the seats at the station, and Pat watched it from Shalmsford Street. Pat also recalls a German prisoner-of-war being marched past her house one Sunday to the army camp at the top of Howfield Lane. His plane had come down in the White Wall/Fishponds area and he was badly burned. Sid Wood tells how his brother, Ern, captured a German airman who landed in what is now Nightingale Close after baling out from his burning aircraft. He took his gun away from him and handed him over to the troops in Gravel Hill.

The doodlebug

Many remember the doodlebug landing in Primrose Hill.

Arthur was pedalling home up Howfield Lane when he saw the doodlebug being attacked by a Spitfire to divert it from its target and heard the spent shells landing on the road beside him. The doodlebug had landed by the time he got home so he rode down to Primrose Hill. He still recalls being shaken up by seeing one of the nearby residents in Chapel Row coming out of her house crying. There was nothing left of the doodlebug but Arthur remembers seeing the damaged cottages. Alan also remembers the spent shells in Howfield Lane "all the way up the hill" and also went to see what damage had occurred.

Pat's mother looked after evacuee children from London. Their father used to visit them on a Saturday and it was on one of his visits that the doodlebug landed. He was used to air raids and made them all shelter under the kitchen table.

Peter Rumley was at home in Baker's Row in Primrose Hill when the doodlebug landed at the bottom of the garden – it was 8.20 pm on Saturday, 22nd July 1944. Their house was very badly damaged and they had to move out while it was repaired. The Spitfire pilot who had forced the doodlebug to land visited them the day afterwards. He was very upset that the houses had been hit – he had followed the doodlebug across Canterbury and, thinking that it was all woodland over the brow of the hill, he brought it down after it had passed over the village.

Brenda was also down Primrose Hill at the time and was knocked to the ground. She ran all the way home crying, came to her grandma's house first (Hatch Green Cottage) and hid under the table.

Shirley was in Chartham at the Salvation Army Hall. They heard the doodlebug go over and rushed outside when they heard the engine stop as they knew this meant that it was going to land. The comment was made that "it was all right, it was going Chartham Hatch way", so Shirley and her family had to walk back home not knowing whether they would have a house left when they got there.

Rationing continued after the war and Pat's sister, Lena, remembers food parcels from Australia being delivered to the school and being distributed to the children to take home.

Victory party

Jessie Bradley recalls the Victory party at the Royal Oak Meadow at the end of the war where all the villagers joined in, and she was an active member of the Social Club that was formed shortly afterwards. Jessie was the Social Club Secretary for thirteen years and her husband, Albert, was the Show Secretary for the Gardeners' annual Produce Show.

Miss Mann takes over

In November 1947 Mrs. Holmes resigned, to be replaced by Miss Mann in January 1948. Miss Mann is remembered by all her former pupils for her love of nature and animals. Sylvia Delo and Margaret Hinder, who were friends at school and still are, went on nature walks with her and her dog. The school children also walked in rows to the playing field to pick up stones to prepare the field for sowing.

Miss Mann had a pet lamb and Margaret's sister, Valerie, appeared with the lamb when dressed as Bo-Peep at a fête in Chartham in 1951.

Photo: Courtesy of Valerie Gosbee

Valerie Hinder with Miss Mann's pet lamb

School Memories

When the school put on a play, the partition between the two classrooms was drawn back and blocks set up at the end of the Infant classroom. Margaret was Sneezy in 'Snow White'. The children were taken into School House to choose their outfits for the play. At harvest festival times Sylvia's father, Bert Delo, used to auction the fruit and vegetables afterwards to the parents. Sylvia and Margaret remember the Friday afternoons when they were allowed to play with their own toys.

Bert also dressed up as Father Christmas for the school Christmas parties. Bert and his brother, Sid, did odd jobs in the school. There were still coal fires with a square guard around them when Sylvia and Margaret were at school. They also remember the two pictures that hung on the roadside wall of the Junior room – one of the Queen and one of Winston Churchill with a cigar. They describe how they made mats by winding raffia round cardboard cut into circles and ovals or round milk bottle tops with the centres pressed out. Sylvia still has the bag she made. Sylvia and Margaret also recall taking part in egg and spoon, sack and three-legged races at a Sports Day on the playing field.

Photo: Courtesy of Sylvia Rose – late 1940s
Back row left to right: Valerie Hinder, Sylvia Delo, Margaret Hinder, Susan Murray
Front row: Brenda Rumley, Valerie Mathews

Photo: Courtesy of Syliva Rose – 1950

Back row left to right: Valerie Hinder, ? Osborne(?), Terry Simmons, Roger Delo, Bobby Woodbridge, David O'Meara, Ronnie Piper, Lena Butcher

Middle row: Jean Beale, Reg Baker, Sylvia Delo, David Coombs, Margaret Hinder, Pat O'Meara, Valerie Jury, Joyce Beale

Front row: Ann Kidd, Brenda Rumley, Rachel Chenneour, Keith Baker, Maureen Hoare, Michael Hoare, ?, Shirley Winter

Sitting: Trevor Hinder, ? Stillwell(?)

1950-1966

Dave O'Meara – Born in 5 Hatch Lane in 1942 and moved to Woodlands, Gravel Hill when he was two years old. Attended school from 1947-1953, when he went to Chartham School.

John Bradley lived at Avon, Bigbury Road and was born in 1940.

Jean Cutting (née Bradley) and Ann Payne (née Bradley), John's sisters, were born in 1947 and 1950 respectively. Jean was Head Girl in her last year at Chartham Hatch.

Maureen Dunn (née Allerton) – Born at 1 Seed Mill Cottages in 1944. Lived at White Platt Cottage, Fishponds. Initially went to school in Faversham. Attended school at Chartham Hatch for short while until 1952 when she moved to Canterbury.

Bernard Moat – Born at No. 3 New Town Street and moved to No. 20 New Town Street when a few months old. Attended school from 1953 to 1959, when he went to Chartham Secondary School.

Jane White (née Woodbridge) and Sandie Burns (née Woodbridge) – Jane was born in 1958, her sister Sandie is seven years older. They lived in various tied cottages in Chartham Hatch. Sandie later worked for Mr. Downs in his New Town Street shop.

Jean Brenchley – Taught the Infants class from 1950 until it closed in 1966, with a break for two years in 1951-52 to go to Training College.

Pauline Dearing (née Sparks). Lived at 2 New Town Street and attended school from 1959. Went to Chartham Secondary School.

Geoffrey and Brian Fitch – Born in 1959 and 1960 respectively. They lived in Nightingale Close and were at the school when it closed.

Katherine Ahmad (née Thomson) and Kitty Bowler (née Thomson) – Lived at Hatch Farm House and were also among the last to attend the school.

Billy Skeet – Born in 1960 and lived in Howfield Lane. Went to the school for one year only before it closed.

Photo: Courtesy of Jean Brenchley – ca. 1950

Top row left to right: Joyce Beale, David Butcher, Margaret Hinder, (Big) Brenda Rumley, Jean Beale, Sylvia Delo

Fourth row: Bobby Woodbridge, Roger Delo, Lena Butcher, Valerie Hinder, Michael Hoare, Reg Baker

Third row: Valerie Jury, David Coombs, David O'Meara, Ron Piper, Pat O'Meara, Derek Smith

Second row: Shirley Winter, Maureen Hoare, Michael Laker, Terry Simmons, Keith Baker, Ann Kidd

Front row: Maureen Allerton(?), (Little) Brenda Rumley

Miss Mann continues

Miss Connie Mann, the Head Mistress until December 1965, was a strict teacher but also is well remembered for her love of nature and animals. Sandie Burns describes her as having "a deep love of the countryside and [she] seemed to epitomize country living to the eyes of an eleven year old girl". Pauline Dearing says Miss Mann's vast knowledge of country life and wild flowers was "incredible" and says that her own knowledge of wild flowers comes from Miss Mann. Miss Mann encouraged them to look at everything. The Juniors completed a diary every morning and, if they didn't know what to write, she would say that they "must have seen something of interest". There are many recollections of nature walks and nature in the classroom. Often she would take broken biscuits and mealworms with her on the walks for the birds and the children would bring back dandelions for the rabbits she kept at School House. Katherine Ahmad remembers Miss Mann keeping a fox in the space surrounding the stove and the railing around it. She now says "it didn't seem odd at the time, but then little children are not very discriminating!" As Bernard Moat says "it was always sort of nature orientated at the school". Pauline remembers going to Miss Mann's bungalow, Appledene, in Primrose Hill at lunch time to collect eggs and let out her dog. This was a regular duty for the two oldest in the class.

All creatures great and small

Bernard had a pet jackdaw at home and it often used to fly to school with him, land on his shoulder and sit on the fence round the playground. If the windows were open the jackdaw would fly in, pick up pencils and fly back home with them. Bernard also took great interest in the stag beetles that flew in through the window from the oak tree during the summer months – "we used to count them, we used to race them along the desks and then we would try and catch them and see which one had got the biggest antlers". The pickled snakes in jars on top of the cupboard in the Junior room made a big impression on both Bernard and Lena. Bernard says "I can see them as though it was yesterday .... I always wonder what happened to them".

Photo: Courtesy of Bernard Moat
When Bernard was at school, there were no longer group photographs. Each child was photographed with a card showing his/her age.

Dave O'Meara remembers Miss Mann's lamb which she kept in her garden, though it often came into the playground! He also remembers one particular visit by the "School Board Man" who wanted some frog spawn to take to another school; he and Terry Simmons who lived at White Wall cottages went with him in his car to the pond at White Wall and filled up the jars he had brought with him.

Sandie had a pet badger which she and her father had saved after its family had been gassed. Miss Mann took Sandie to show her badger to the children at the Vernon Holme Junior school in Harbledown which she says "was quite something to the eyes of a farmworker's daughter, as they came from wealthier backgrounds than she did". She has very fond memories of Miss Mann.

A long way to walk

Maureen Dunn and her brother, Michael, lived at Fishponds and walked to school past the cottages at White Wall, past Apple Tree Corner and up Primrose Hill. Maureen was born at her aunt's house in Seed Mill Cottages, Primrose Hill. Her aunt was Mrs. Eva Ruck and was married to Sid Ruck. It was November and her mother was worried that the midwife would not be able to get to their own house at Fishponds.

Photo: Courtesy of Maureen Dunn
Maureen and Michael Allerton outside Seed Mill Cottages which were demolished in the 1950s

Miss Brenchley

Miss Jean Brenchley taught the Infants until the school closed in 1966. For the first two years she used to cycle from Selling but then came by car which she used to park under the oak tree in the playground. The Infants remained in her class until they were seven, when they transferred to Miss Mann's Junior class. The classes were divided by the partition, with the Infants on the Gravel Hill side and the Juniors on the other. When the children were eleven, they sat the grammar school selection examination, the Eleven Plus. A teacher from another school would come to invigilate, while Miss Brenchley would go to another school to do likewise.

A typical day

Miss Brenchley describes a typical day where all the children got together in the Junior classroom "to have a hymn, a prayer and a good morning". She would then go with the children into her classroom where they learnt "a little bit of everything", concentrating on the 3Rs. All ages were taught together – each child had their own work according to how far advanced they were. The desks were arranged in groups of four and the children had cardboard boxes for their books. Miss Brenchley's desk was "quite large", with a step and a lid, though she says she didn't use it much. There were also PT (Physical Training) lessons, either in the classroom or outside (sometimes on the playing field) depending on the weather, with balls, hoops and ropes, and in the latter years a vaulting horse and other equipment. There was also needlework, raffia work and "French knitting", a cotton reel with four nails that the wool would be wound around to make a knitted string that was pulled through the hole in the centre of the reel. Bernard remembers making teapot covers or teapot stands with it. Lena remembers the children sitting with Miss Brenchley round the small fire in the Infants' room learning how to knit; Lena knitted a bag and remembers one of the boys, Ronnie Piper, knitting a royal blue tie. Miss Mann had a blackboard and easel in the Junior classroom. Jean Bradley remembers listening to music lessons on the radio – Time and Tune, Music and Movement. There was an accompanying booklet – Jean remembers one telling the story of Peter and the Wolf and another the story of Coppelia. Kitty Bowler remembers lots of paintings hanging up to dry on the fender that surrounded the stove.

In the centre of the cloakroom were metal frames with pegs for the children's clothes; a cupboard stood against the wall overlooking the back playground with little sinks to the left for the children to wash their hands, paint pots and brushes and ink wells and, to the right of the door nearest School House, there was a sink with cupboards underneath for crockery. The toilets were outside and had paraffin lamps placed in them in winter to try to stop them from icing up. Library books for both children and adults were kept under the window in the Junior room. The adults used to change their books on a Monday evening. The library van visited once a term to change the books.

School meals and milk

School dinners were delivered from Chartham Primary school in large containers and, in Miss Brenchley's time, served out in the Junior classroom by the teachers and the dinner lady – plastic covers were put on the tables. The dinner lady, who was also the caretaker, would wash up afterwards. Dave remembers the dinners being served out in the kitchen on a trestle table and being nearly always stew; Bernard remembers that the puddings always had custard! Billy Skeet's memory of the dinners is slightly more colourful – he remembers how important it was to get the right colour plastic plate because "pink makes you stink, yellow makes you a strong fellow, blue makes you …!" Milk, in one-third of a pint bottles, was delivered for drinking in the morning break. Bernard remembers the milk crate being left outside in winter – something would be put over the top to stop the bluetits pecking at the tops. The milk would freeze, pushing the frozen cream to the top which they would then eat.

Dave's mother, Jessie O'Meara, was the school caretaker in the late 1940s and used to help serve the school dinners. Mrs. Whitehead also used to help with the school meals and would supervise the children in the playground. Dave remembers the dinners being delivered by Mr. George Mercer who ran a taxi service in Chartham. Bernard, who was at school six years later, remembers them being delivered by Mr. Sara in his van.

Keeping warm

Dave used to help his mother, going with her to the school at 6 o'clock in the morning. He would break up the kindling wood and bring in the buckets of coal for her to light the fires (they were still open fires during Dave's time at the school). The coal and faggots (kindling wood) were delivered by Mr. Gibson, the coal merchant in Chartham, and were stored next to the toilets. Bernard remembers the coke stoves; he often had the job of filling the tall scuttle with coke. John Bradley describes how Mrs. Holmes and Miss Gore used to make cocoa on the stove from the bottles of milk and then pour it back into the bottles. He also remembers them giving the children a teaspoon of the cod liver oil and malt provided by the Government.

Playtime and games

Dave recalls playing marbles and conkers in the playground. When he was at school the fence was low so they couldn't play very many ball games. By the time Bernard was at the school, there was a high fence which meant that they could play football. There was a sand pit under the oak tree when Lena was at the school and the children would climb the tree and jump into it. Kitty remembers the old water pump "umbrellered by evergreens" being a focal point for gatherings and games. Even though the war had finished, Dave remembers watching from the playground soldiers marching by. Bernard also remembers the farm workers at harvest time on their way from Denstead Farm to the storage units in Howfield Lane throwing apples and plums over the fence to the children during playtime.

Lena played in the school rounders team and remembers playing against Chislet and Lower Hardres on the playing field.

Fun times

Miss Brenchley remembers the annual summer outing, which was usually to the seaside and very often to Botany Bay, Broadstairs. They would hire a coach and some of the parents would go along to help. She recalls one particular year when "the Dads all burned their feet" on the hot sand. The costs of the trip were met out of the school fund – no-one had to pay.

Fund-raising was by the annual concerts and plays, summer fairs where parents would look at the children's work and there would be a PE display outside, and harvest festivals where the children would bring in produce and the rector from Chartham (the Reverend Gore-Brown and later the Reverend Field) would conduct a service.

Bernard describes one particular play when he was "all covered in drinking chocolate" because he was an African hunter. He can't remember what the play was about but certainly remembers licking his fingers to wipe the chocolate off afterwards! He also remembers trips to the County Show at Maidstone and Miss Brenchley tells of one trip when there were huge puddles which the children were more interested in jumping in than in looking at the animals.

John tells of one trip to the seaside when he had been given 2/6d to buy drinks and ice cream but he changed it all into pennies and lost it in the slot machines – one of the teachers bought him an ice cream as he had no money left! Jean remembers regular trips to Herne Bay and Uncle Collins' Magic Show. They would have tea in the King's Hall and go boating on the lake. The boys often got into trouble for jumping off the pier at Broadstairs. Jean also remembers the Coronation celebrations when the children were given a Coronation mug and Union Jack button badges.

A stir and a wish

Bernard, Jean and Katherine remember the Christmas puddings that the children made with Miss Mann and Miss Brenchley. The ingredients were put into a big bowl and all the children had a stir and made a wish. Katherine describes how the whole school circulated around a great long table and everyone would get a turn at stirring the enormous vat of Christmas pudding mix with a wooden spoon. The pudding was then divided into two or three smaller bowls and Miss Mann cooked them in School House. They were eaten in the school at a special Christmas lunch. The presents for the Christmas party also came out of school funds. Miss Brenchley remembers Dr. Lipscombe from Chilham dressing up as Father Christmas.

Village School to Village Hall

Photo: Courtesy of Mrs. I. Port

Christmas concert, ca. 1955

Performers back row left to right: David O'Meara, Roger Delo, Ron Port, Rachel Chenneour, Ann Kidd, Brenda Rumley, Shirley Winter, Elizabeth Wiseman, Judy Mayes, Bobby Woodbridge, ?, Michael Laker, Terry Simmons

Performers front row left to right: ?, Keith Baker, Maureen Hoare

Audience: Left hand group - Ann Glover, June Baker, ?, Jean Bradley; right hand group: Tommy Kidd (centre), Bernard Moat (right)

The final term

Geoffrey and Brian Fitch were among the last children to attend before the school closed. Geoffrey remembers the Head Teacher, Mr. Hime, reading a story from the Bible every morning. He also remembers taking part in the school play when he played Humpty Dumpty and his brother Wee Willy Winkie. If one of the pupils had a birthday, everyone was given one dolly mixture – "it was fun to make it last and imagine that it was your most favourite food". His sadness at leaving the school was soon forgotten in the excitement of going on the school bus to Chartham.

A sad day

Miss Brenchley was there when the school closed on 22nd July, 1966 and also came in for several days afterwards to help sort things out. The Headmaster, Mr. Richard Nisbet, and the Deputy Headmaster, Mr. Robert Masters, from Chartham came to select items for their school. She describes it as being very sad, "like a bereavement".

Still from ciné footage courtesy of Mrs. W. Dissington

The Village School in the summer of 1966

Note the front double gate with the post box, the notice board and the oak trees inside the boundary fence

School House

Drawing by Jon Wilmot, June 2005

When the school was built in 1873, it was surrounded by fields and woodland, and when the teacher's residence followed in 1874, these two buildings must have stood in isolation for several years. The nearest houses would have been the small cluster at the bend in Howfield Lane. It wasn't until the 1890s that the village as we know it started to evolve. Most of the first school children would have come from the Hatch Green, Primrose Hill, Denstead, White Wall and possibly the Fishponds areas.

Some background history

It was common practice in the 19th century for the Master's or Mistress's residence to be provided rent-free as part of their contract of employment, with free fuel often included, as there was usually a shortage of suitable accommodation in the area for rent. After 1843, Government grants were available for the building of school houses for the Head Teacher "not too large so as to exalt him too much in society, but to take him out of a cottage and into a decent residence so that persons lower than himself will feel respect for the person who teaches their children". Many school houses were comfortable but many were unsatisfactory, as if anything were good enough to be lived in rent-free. There were numerous complaints about sub-standard houses to the National Teachers Union - even if the house was satisfactory, it was often poorly equipped. School teachers in a village were very isolated, as their status was not high enough to mix with better-off members of the local community. Marriage, unless to a teacher, was also difficult socially. School Managers were advised to make sure a young unmarried woman did not live alone, to avoid scandals.[i]

The house is built

We are very lucky in having some first-hand information of life in School House. For the most part, however, we have had to rely on what we have been able to find out from the records. We know that, when the Managers approached the National Society in October 1872 about a school at Chartham Hatch, they intended to build a teacher's residence at the same time. It was to be a house with five rooms – a sitting room and a living room each measuring 11 ft x 11 ft 7 ins x 8 ft, and three bedrooms, measuring 10 ft x 10 ft x 8 ft 3 ins, 10 ft x 9 ft x 8 ft 3 ins and 7 ft 7 ins x 6 ft 10 ins x 8 ft 3 ins. There would be a grant of £15 from the National Society. However, as the Managers only had £280 available to build both the school and the teacher's residence and the lowest quote they had received was for £272 excluding the teacher's house, "the residence was abandoned through want of funds" and only the school was built. There is no record of where the very first Mistress, Miss Dyason, lived.

Building a teacher's residence became top priority when the school became a Board school in 1874 - the provision of a partly furnished house was part of the Mistress' contract - and a Mr. Ellsmore was asked to draw up plans. He estimated that the cost would be £300 and this was accepted by the Managers in July 1874 "subject to any alterations which can be made in them with a view to saving any expenditure which is not strictly necessary". The plans were approved by the Education Department subject to a yard and privy being provided attached to the house.

Village School to Village Hall

Four tenders were received:-

Featherstone and Lucas, Littlebourne	£340 0s 0d
I.H. Knight, Whitstable	£328 10s.0d
I.E. Wiltshier, Canterbury	£300 0s 0d
Wallace Gentry, Canterbury	£285 15s 0d

Mr. Gentry's tender was accepted and a contract drawn up at the School Board meeting of 13th August 1874. A loan from the Public Works Loan Commissioners of £443 over 21 years was agreed in October 1874. This amount also included £98 to pay the National Society for the fixtures and fittings of both Chartham Hatch and Chartham schools. The loan was duly received and in January 1875 bills could be paid - £9 9s 0d to Messrs. Barnes and Bernard, the solicitors used in obtaining the loan, £337 18s 2d to Mr. Gentry for the teacher's residence and £21 7s 3d to Mr. Ellsmore, the architect. Mr. Ellsmore had also valued the schools' fixtures and fittings and his payment included £3 3s 0d for this valuation. Mr. Gentry had had to pay for water to be delivered but, in spite of several requests, the Managers refused to reimburse him. The house was insured in December 1874 for £250.

The house and its first inhabitants

Standing alone next to the school, the house would have assumed a certain importance. Its shape, gables and roof tiles matched those of the school building - it was certainly much grander and larger than any of the village's farm cottages. Even with a companion, the Head Mistress's life must have been a lonely one and also very dependent upon the decisions of the Managers. When Miss Jeffries started in 1876, the Minute Book records that Mr. Foreman, one of the Managers, "undertook to find a suitable person to reside in the house with her", and in 1896 Miss Haslam herself requested a companion. Unfortunately, in both cases, there are no further details. The house was partially furnished and the teachers had to apply to the Managers for any additions, changes or repairs. These were not always dealt with immediately and quite often deferred from one Managers' meeting to another. It appears that "partially furnished" did not even include provision for curtains as the first request, from Miss Colman in March 1875, was for "wooden frames to be placed across each window for curtains". Ordinary items as a "mat, coal scuttle and poker", as requested by Miss Letchford, had to be agreed by the Managers.

Although many references are made in the Minute Books to the supply of water and its associated problems, it is not clear exactly what

Photo: Courtesy of Ella Willmott
The Misses Letchford in the garden at School House, where they lived from 1897 to 1912.

system was used. We can only assume, because of their proximity, that the house would have had the same water supply and sanitary arrangements as the school and would have experienced the same problems. We do know that the pump in the school playground and an inside pump over the kitchen sink were used for supplying the house in the late 1920s.

Repairs and resignation

It appears that most major repairs and purchases were made either before a new teacher moved in or at the request of the new teacher. One of the first things Caroline Mills did when she arrived in December 1878 was to write to the Board, bringing to their attention all the repairs that were necessary – these included preventing the chimney from smoking, fastening the windows, putting chains to the doors, painting, whitewashing, colour and graining in the house, and cementing portions of the house. When Mary Haslam came in 1894, she was authorized to obtain a new blind for the front room, 13 yards of stair carpet and 14 stair rods. However, many of her requests were deferred and, in January 1897, complaining that the recently bought furniture which she had stated "was absolutely necessary if she was to remain" was unsatisfactory, she tendered her resignation. When Ella Mary Letchford started as Head Teacher in 1897, she too wrote to the Managers on the subject of repairs, which were subsequently agreed in 1898. These included repairing the brick scullery floor, repairing the copper and stopping the smoke going into the kitchen. Also included was the supply of a new half-gallon iron tea kettle and a new hearth rug for the kitchen.

Between 1897 and 1917 the Head Teacher became responsible for paying rent and for coal – these were no longer deducted from the salary (although we have not been able to find out what adjustment, if any, was made to the salary) and from December 1917 the Head Teacher paid a quarterly rent to the Committee and provided her own coal.

Duties of a Cook General

Photo: Courtesy of Rhoda Wills
Rhoda in her afternoon uniform holding a kitten. Taken by Mrs. Wallis' son in the garden of School House.

After leaving Chartham school in 1928, Rhoda Roberts worked for six years as Cook General for the Head Teacher, Mrs. Wallis, and her widowed sister-in-law, Mrs. Bright. Mrs. Wallis had been widowed some years previously. Rhoda, who had attended the Hatch school until the age of twelve, lived in Hatch Lane and would either walk or cycle to work along New Town (as New Town Street was then called), using the footpath that cut through the field in Howfield Lane to come out on to Bigbury Road. She worked every day, with Saturday and Sunday afternoons off and with two weeks holiday when Mrs. Wallis had her annual summer holiday.

Hard work

Rhoda describes her daily routine – "it was hard work, it really was". The day started at 6.30 am when she would draw two bucketsful of water from the pump and heat it on a paraffin stove. It had four burners with the oven over two of them. She had to fill the stove up daily with paraffin which was delivered weekly and stored in a tank in the shed. There was a large glass container on the side of the stove with a spring which had to be removed so that it could be refilled with paraffin. The little pump over the kitchen sink supplied rainwater. Rhoda would first cook the breakfast and then take up a cup of tea and a big can of hot water for Mrs. Wallis and Mrs. Bright to wash.

Rhoda did the cooking and cleaning but not the washing – that always "went out" – and looked after the fires and got in the coal. Rhoda cooked and ate the same mid-day meal (dinner) as her employers, but she ate hers in the kitchen after she had waited on them at table. After she had washed up after dinner, she would wash and change in one of the bedrooms from the overall she wore in the morning to do the housework into her afternoon uniform of an apron and cap starched by her mother. Her last job of the day was to get tea ready at four o'clock and then she was free to go home at half past four.

Most provisions - milk, bread and groceries – were ordered in advance and delivered to the house.

Modernization

The hard work remembered by Rhoda would have gradually become easier. Mains water was laid on in 1935, followed a year later by gas. Consent was given by the Managers in 1938 for the construction of a "motor garage", though we are not sure whether this was ever built – the people we have spoken with have no recollection

Village School to Village Hall

of one. We have no record of when a telephone was installed, but former pupils remember Mrs. Holmes teaching them how to use the telephone in School House in the mid-1940s to order the school dinners from Chartham school. At that time, there were only two or three telephones in the whole of Chartham Hatch. The bathroom first suggested in December 1945 became reality in late 1948/early 1949 with the conversion of one of the small bedrooms. There was also an increase in rent to 6% of the expenditure involved. Electricity was installed in September 1954.

The end of an era

Miss Connie Mann was the last Head Teacher at the school who lived in School House, living there for just over eight years following her appointment in January 1948. In 1956 she bought a plot of land in Primrose Hill including the by then dilapidated Yew Tree Cottage and lived in the bungalow she had built, Appledene. Yew Tree Cottage was demolished. She lived at Appledene until she left the school in 1965 and moved to Gloucestershire.

School House was rented out to Jeff and Christine Bean in July 1963 who bought it when the Diocesan Board put it on the market in 1967. It has had several owners since then. It still boasts the same tiled roof, echoing that of the old school.

---

[i] "Education in Rural England 1800-1914, P. Horn, published by Gill and Macmillan 1978.

Photo: Jim Sanders

School House in 2006

The Social Club

Source: Kentish Gazette

"Family Spirit Predominates" – the fund-raising fête held on the Royal Oak Meadow, August 1946

Left to right: John Miles, John Bradley(?), Barbara Miles(?), ?, Violet West, ?, Valerie Jury, Lena Butcher, ?, Joan Piper, Colin Wood, Michael Hoare, ?, Diane Hill, Shirley Winter, Brenda Coombs, ?, Shirley Lemar, ?

Fund-raising

The Social Club was established with the money left over from Victory celebrations at the end of World War II and, with Maurice Jenkins as its first Chairman, Jessie Bradley as Secretary and Col. Robert S. Mount as President, soon started to raise funds. Permission was received from the Education Authority to hold events in the evenings in the school. These included social evenings, fêtes, bingo and whist drives.

One of the first events, a fête held on the Royal Oak Meadow on 10th August 1946, was reported as follows by the Kentish Gazette:-

"Family spirit predominates"

"The most attractive feature of the highly successful fete held at Chartham Hatch on Saturday was the happy family atmosphere which characterised the whole of the proceedings. It was a real community effort, effectively led by Mr. and Mrs. C.L. Holmes.

"The fete was graciously opened by Mrs. Gracie of Bigbury House, who wished the effort every success. The children's fancy dresss competition gave Mr. and Mrs. R.E. Mount, the judges, a difficult task. Some twenty boys and girls in clever and pretty costumes paraded and after much consideration Brenda Coombs (Painted Doll), Shirley Winter (Family Allowances), Diane Hill (Make Do and Mend) and Michael Hoare (Grow More Food) were the winners. During the afternoon the children had their races, a Punch and Judy Show and a ventriloquist, Mr. Stokes, of Canterbury, worked hard with his portable roundabout.

"The highspot of entertainment was a splendid display by the gymnastic team led by Q.M.S. Roberts. These fine athletic young soldiers were applauded throughout their show.

"The evening events included adult races, fancy dress, tilt-the-bucket and community singing. The fancy dress parade was again a first class event, the costumes being varied and original. Mrs. Goodhew and Mrs. Kendall acted as judges and Miss Moore and Miss Winter (Family Allowances), Miss D. Hammond (Baker's Nightmare), Mrs. Faulkner and Mrs. Woodbridge (Old Mother Riley and Kitty), and Miss V. Hubbard (a Japanese lady) were the winners.

"Throughout the day the stalls, sideshows and buffet were doing good business. The success of the fete was once again due to the wonderful team work of the ladies and gentlemen of the Social Club Committee".

Village School to Village Hall

Photo: Courtesy of Sylvia Rose

Another fund raising event – Fancy Dress "Twenty Questions", 1949

Back row left to right: Jean Beale, Lena Butcher, Pat Butcher, Brian Moat, ?, Valerie Hinder, ?, Joyce Beale(?), ?, John Piper(?), ?, Alex Salvage, David Butcher

Front row: Sid Butcher with Peggy, his dog, Sylvia Nightingale, Valerie Jury, Sylvia Delo, Roy Delo, others unknown

A hut is delivered

By the early 1950s enough money had been raised for the Club to start looking for a building, and a wooden, ex-army hut was found in Belvedere, Kent. Chartham Parish Council allocated a section of the recreation ground for it to go on and several villagers set to work to make a concrete base. The hut was delivered and erected by Bert and Sid Delo, helped "by the men of the village"; water was laid on and it was ready to go.

We haven't been able to find out the exact date the hut started to be used as the Club's official records have unfortunately been thrown away. We know that it was being used in December 1953 as the school Log Book mentions that the children went there for a film show after their Christmas party.

Source: Kentish Gazette

The Social Club hut on the recreation ground, 1961

Free subscription for all

Initially, there was no subscription – everyone living in the village was entitled to free membership. Funds continued to be raised by regular events, such as the Monday evening whist drive when a tote was drawn based on the first letter of the leader in *The News of the World* newspaper, and fêtes and horticultural shows. Betty and Sid Smith held the weekly whist drives and all the prizes, such as fruit or a leg of lamb, were donated. The *Kentish Gazette* reported regularly on these events – including a whist drive in October 1956 to raise money for the Nurses' Recreation Fund where refreshments were "ably served by Miss Mann", and a Christmas Social in December of the same year where there was an ankle competition won by Miss Shirley Winter and judged by Col. R. Mount. An article on the fête and show held three years after the hut was erected to raise funds for a kitchen mentions the entertainment provided by an American Barber Shop Quartet from the air base at Manston. Jessie Bradley remembers that, until rationing after the war finished, they had to get a permit to get rationed goods to make refreshments.

Both Jessie Bradley and Sylvia Delo remember the Old Time Dancing classes, and going as a group to dances in the area, even going to London to take part in one of the Saturday evening dances broadcast on the radio. Sylvia often partnered Jessie's son, John. The hut was also hired regularly for weddings and by other clubs, such as the Youth Club, and the Derby and Joan Club. It is the produce shows, however, that Jessie remembers most as her husband, Albert, was the Produce Show Secretary for many years.

Photo: Courtesy of Jessie Bradley

A Produce Show in the Social Club

Back row left to right: Bob Philpott, Connie Mann, Arthur Ballard, Howard Glover, Ada Faulkner, Win Moat, Albert Bradley

Front row left to right: Bernard Moat, Barbara Philpott, Liz Mayes, Jean Bradley, Ann Bradley, Jessie Bradley, Roderick Glover, Mary Glover, David Glover

Village School to Village Hall

Photo: Courtesy of Jessie Bradley

A fund-raising fête on the playing field to raise money for the hut
Taking part in the adults' race, left to right: Lil Downs(?), Mary Hubbard, Jessie Bradley, Gwen Parker (Mystole), Ewan Mount (President of the Gardeners' Society) and Joan Glover

Lack of support

Unfortunately, the support needed from the village to keep the club going did not continue and, even though a small subscription had been introduced, funds dwindled. A meeting of hall subscribers was held and a decision made to close it. This resulted in several non-subscribing villagers complaining to the *Kentish Gazette* that they should have been consulted; a flurry of correspondence followed from villagers and committee members alike, but the decision was unchanged. Remaining funds were distributed amongst several charities and the building was demolished in 1961.

A concrete suggestion

There was also disagreement on the future of the hall's concrete base until Chartham Parish Council decided it could stay. The base still exists and was converted in 1995 by the Parish Council into a picnic area.

Photo: Jim Sanders

The playing field in 2006 with picnic tables on the concrete base of the Social Club

The Village Hall – A Factual History

For Sale

The Freehold Property being Chartham Hatch Primary School near Canterbury, Kent.

It is in a somewhat isolated position being over a mile from the Canterbury to Maidstone and the Canterbury to London roads. The only bus service is one bus on a Saturday.

(Extract from Agent's particulars)

The Village Hall by Jon Wilmot, 1995

A campaign and a film

Several villagers were concerned that the building would be demolished when the school closed and saw an opportunity for the village to buy it and use it as a social centre. Mary (Virginia) Thomson of Hatch Farm House led a campaign, going round the village asking for support. Initially, many villagers were sceptical and there was a great deal of opposition. She also asked one of the residents, Mr. Bobby Dissington, to make a ciné film of the village. The film was shown to a capacity audience in the school building in November 1966, with Elgar's Enigma Variations as accompaniment. A representative from Kent Council for Social Services said that a grant would be available. However, during the course of the meeting the audience realized that, if they did not grasp the opportunity to create a social centre for themselves, there would be a serious risk of the village losing its identity and becoming merely an outlying part of Chartham. A vote was taken and 100% were in favour of going ahead.

Decision-making time

The school premises were put on the market through agents Messrs. Collier and Gardner of Mercery Lane, Canterbury. The price was £3,150 excluding the teacher's residence. It was time for quick thinking, decision-making and planning. The agents were already pressing for a decision, giving 28th February 1967 as a deadline date, and needed a deposit of £315.

The Committee is formed

A meeting of interested residents was arranged at the Chapter Arms on Friday, 9th December 1966. It was decided to grasp the opportunity to purchase the building and to set up the Chartham Hatch Village Hall Society. Plans for fund-raising were discussed and Mr. Leslie Mount of Howfield Manor offered to take legal advice regarding the use of the school building for such fund-raising events prior to the sale being completed. It was agreed that the main source of fund-raising would be the issue of One Pound Shares, operating in a similar way to that governing the issue of Premium Bonds, with regular draws. Prize money was initially set at £10, £5 and £2 10s 0d.

A certificate was issued to everyone who bought shares in the Village Hall

The Chartham Hatch Village Hall Society was now well and truly launched and the first meeting took place on Friday, 6th January 1967 at the Royal Oak. Those present were Messrs. Auty, Bennett, Dissington, Faiers and Smith, with Mr. Leslie Mount in the Chair. An apology for absence was received from Mr. K. Thomson of Hatch Farm House. At this meeting Mr. Mount announced that it would be possible to use "The Hall" for fund-raising purposes prior to purchase completion and it was agreed that a letter would be written to all villagers to let them know what was happening.

The newly formed Chartham Hatch Village Hall Committee certainly did not let the grass grow under its feet. The sale of the One Pound Shares was approved, many fund-raising events were discussed and sources of grants were explored. Officers and Trustees were appointed at a meeting on 20th January 1967 as follows:-

Officers: Chairman: Mr. L.A. Mount
            Secretary: Mr. J.H. Bennett
            Treasurer: Mr. J. Auty

Trustees: Mr. J. Auty
            Mr. J.H. Bennett
            Mr. L.A. Mount
            Mr. K. Thomson

Early fund-raising

By February 1967, just two months on, over £300 had been raised, which included a donation of £50 from the F.H. Hooker Group, profits from a bring-and-buy sale and £50 from a sponsored all-night walk. The 30 mile walk along the Pilgrims Way from Detling to Chartham had been sponsored at a penny a mile and doubled for those who completed the course. It was organized by villager Hazel Bennett, a student at Canterbury Technical College. Both village residents and students from the college took part, with Wendy and Brian Allen providing rolls, soup and coffee at the top of Charing Hill. Hazel's father, Joseph (Ben) Bennett, was first home with a time of 7 hours and 15 minutes. According to the newspaper article reporting the event, fifteen of the walkers took a wrong turning and ended up in Faversham!

Source: Kentish Gazette
Walkers checking the route at the start with Hazel Bennett centre, facing the camera

A deposit of £315 was paid but the vendors were pressing for a completion date and it was anticipated that interest would have to be paid on the balance of the purchase price.

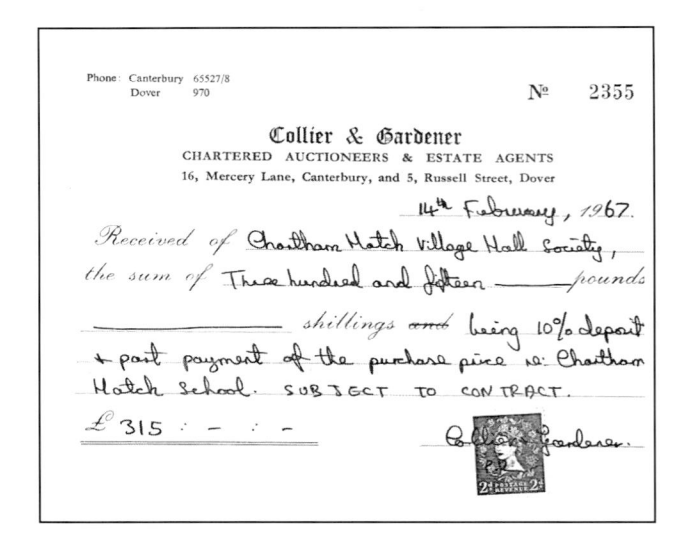

Official and domestic arrangements

Before the Hall could be let, several official and domestic arrangements had to be made, including seeking planning permission for change of use of the building.

Permission to purchase had been obtained from Kent Education Committee. The Department of Education and Science advised that a grant might be available. The sum of £1,625 was suggested, held open for 12 months. The Kent Education Committee was approached regarding the purchase of certain items remaining in the building, resulting in £12 being paid for fire extinguishers, curtains and an amount of coke. Mr. Faiers had given and installed an electric cooker which was in good working order and Mr. Dissington obtained some old cinema seats at a cost of £6 10s 0d, including delivery.

Donations had also been received from Messrs. Robert Brett & Sons Ltd. for £50 and from the Parish Council for £400, which greatly boosted the funds.

Fund-raising and lettings

Serious thought had now to be given to formal lettings as a means of regular income. The first organization to rent the Hall was the nursery school run by Mrs. Heather Fitch (a State Registered Nurse) and Mrs. Philippa Bennett. When the Nursery School opened there were just six children, not all from Chartham Hatch. Very often Mrs. Fitch would collect and return the children to their homes in her own car.

The premises were inspected by the appropriate authorities who demanded that a fire exit should be created and part of the playground fenced off for the safety of the children. Also, adequate insurance cover had to be obtained. All this was wise advice, but it is ironical to recall that the old village school had operated without all these restrictions and with many more children!

It was hoped that a Youth Club would be established, as well as a Gardeners' Society, an Old Age Pensioners' Club and a sewing class (a sewing class organized by Julie Sheckleton had met soon after the school closed as a fund-raising activity). It was agreed that the Assembly of God could rent the hall for a Sunday School every Sunday afternoon. The Chartham Hatch branch of the County Library started operating from the building during the spring of 1967 at a rent of £13 per annum with the assistance of Wendy Allen, Philippa Bennett and Mrs. Bailey and it was hoped that this would continue. The Minutes record that this was because Mr. Hammond was leaving the district. (In fact, the hall library opened once a fortnight until November 1976, with the library van coming every three months. The helpers chose a supply of books to last until the next visit. In November 1976 it was replaced by a mobile van which still visits the village every Friday afternoon.)

The services of a caretaker were sought and a notice board and target thermometer were made.

Fund-raising started in earnest during 1967 with such varied events as dances, film shows, whist drives, bingo sessions, beetle drives, a jumble sale and barn dances with music provided by The Rigadoons. Still remembered by many is the Jamaican evening on 18th March organized by Heather and Peter Fitch. A dance group and a steel band, Peter Hovery and his group, came down from London (organized by Heather's sister-in-law, Christine, who was in the dance group). A number of villagers attempted to limbo dance, with varying degrees of success! The hall was decorated in Jamaican style, and home-made Jamaican delicacies were prepared by Heather and her family and friends. Also not to be forgotten were the tables decorated with dressed pigs' heads which had come from an event that had been held the evening before at St. Augustine's Hospital in Chartham. Over 100 people attended the Jamaican evening. It raised £50, a record at the time for a fund-raising activity.

The very first Whitsun fête was on 29th May followed by a Tramps' Supper and dancing in the hall in the evening.

Photo: Wendy Allen
Philippa and Ben Bennett centre, with Arthur and Joan Hull, Philippa's sister and brother-in-law, at the Tramps' Supper in 1967

The fête was a financial success, raising £110. It is interesting, however, to read the comment in the Minute Book – "the need for more active help was again stressed" – a comment that is still repeated today!

Serious doubts and more ideas

Outwardly all seemed to be going well, but there were serious doubts within the committee. The grant had not yet been received from the Department of Education and Science. The vendor's solicitors were pressing for the sale to be finalised, stating that another party had made an offer. Consequently, an Extra-ordinary Meeting was held on 29th June 1967 to decide whether or not to proceed with the purchase. The question was put to the vote.

Village School to Village Hall

All the committee members voted in favour of proceeding. However, at the next meeting held on 20th November 1967 it was revealed that the grant expected from the Department of Education and Science (£1,625) would not be forthcoming until 1st April 1968 at the earliest.

The Chairman also reported that he had had a meeting with Her Majesty's Inspector of Village Halls, the Solicitor, the Architect and a representative from Nasons. The proposed changes to the building would cost a further £4,000 and the cost of furnishings and fittings another £400.

The situation was grave but still the committee was undaunted and decided to continue with their efforts until forced to do otherwise. (In the event, these changes were achieved at considerably less cost by using volunteers and donations of labour from local contractors.)

This indefatigable team carried on with their task to raise funds with more exciting and original ideas – in July 1967 a performance of 'The Enchanted Circus' by Group 64, a Putney-based theatre group directed by Maurice Copus OBE, entertained an audience of 150 in the grounds of Hatch House, the home of Mary (Plum) and Maurice Copus; there were car treasure hunts in July and August, organized by Wendy Allen, and a trip to Sheffield Park.

However, the most lasting of these ideas was the Pram Race held on Easter Monday. This was the first of what was to become a regular event, although the initial rules were amended in 1973 to exclude the pub stops, much to the disappointment of some competitors!

Photo: Courtesy of Audrey Copus
A scene from 'The Enchanted Circus', July 1967

Photo: Courtesy of Wendy Allen
Wendy and Brian Allen in the first pram race

Source: Kentish Gazette
The first Easter Monday pram race in March 1967 organised by "the go-ahead Village Hall Association"

Many of the activities that have taken place over the years are described in more detail in a separate section.

A few changes

One year had slipped by since the formation of the Chartham Hatch Village Hall Society and a few changes on the committee had taken place. Mr. T. Lyons had been co-opted in April but resigned in June 1967, together with Mr. Faiers. Mr. R. Williams and Mr. B. Allen joined the Committee in November 1967 and Mr. W. Andrews in January 1968. Mr. K. Thomson had given notice of his intention to resign as he would be leaving the area.

As with other societies, committee members and officers changed frequently. The names of those elected at subsequent Annual General Meetings, as recorded in the Minute Books, are given in the Appendix.

Fund-raising continued apace and was reported weekly in the local newspaper. Events included a Hobbies Exhibition, regular dances, a Sweepstake on the Grand National and a Halloween Night.

Source: Kentish Gazette
Joe Auty talking to visitors at the Hobbies Exhibition

Good news

Good news was on the way! In March 1968 planning permission was granted subject to the lowering of the boundary fence and the provision of a new access to replace the entrance in Gravel Hill that had been used by the school. A bridging loan had been obtained through Barclays Bank. At last the purchase could go ahead!

26th August 1968 was a momentous day when a cheque was paid for the purchase of the hall.

Having carried the proceedings to the point of purchase, it was decided that the present committee should be dissolved and that a Public Meeting be called for 30th September when a new Management Committee would be elected.

First Management Committee meeting

The first meeting of the Management Committee, which included representatives from the various organizations hiring the hall, was held at the village hall on Wednesday, 16th October 1968. Present were:-

Chairman	*Mr. L. Mount*
Treasurer	*Mr. J. Auty*
Mrs. W. Allen	*Woodcraft Folk and Library*
Mr. D. Andrews	
Mr. B. Allen	
Mrs. J. Bailey	*Whist Drives*
Mrs. K. Barker	*Chartham Parish Church*
Mrs. P. Bennett	*Keep Fit Class and Morning Nursery*
Mrs. H. Fitch	*Morning Nursery*
Mrs. N. Harrison	*Welcome Club*
Mr. A. Moat	*Chartham Parish Council*
Mr. R. Nash	

Apologies were received from Mr. J.H. Bennett.

It was reported that the grant from the Department of Education and Science had still not been received and a supplementary grant had been applied for to cover the cost of the new access, the alterations to the boundary fence and the installation of gas.

It was decided that groups should pay what they could for the hire of the hall until they had more members. It was also agreed that people living outside the village should pay 30 shillings a night.

Arrangements for an annual fête were discussed with the most ambitious ideas put forward. The Chairman was tasked with finding someone suitable to open the fête – "a TV personality, a film star or a foreign princess"! Attempts would be made to hire Morris Dancers and a train or fire engine. What type of train was not specified!

Although funds were still low, the committee still maintained their community spirit by sharing their carol singing proceeds between a charity and a fund for the village children.

Village School to Village Hall

A Declaration of Trust was drawn up on 7th December 1968 detailing the duties of the Trustees and the Management Committee, the constitution of the Committee, and the Rules and Regulations for the conduct of business.

Moving on

The first Annual General Meeting took place on Monday, 16th April 1969 with representation from the following organizations:-

>   Welcome Club   Woodcraft Folk
>   Senior Citizens   Church of England
>   Gardening Club   Nursery School
>   Keep Fit   Sewing Class
>   Library   Whist Drives

The number and variety of these organizations show how well and widely used the hall was becoming, obviously proving to be a great benefit to the community.

During 1969 and 1970 there had been many problems that needed urgent attention.

Plans had been submitted to Bridge-Blean Rural District Council for the creation of the new entrance to the hall from Bigbury Road following the purchase of land from the owners of School House and the blocking-up of the old entrance in Gravel Hill.

The Fire Brigade had advised regular inspection of fire extinguishers and replacement of faulty electric plugs. They had also recommended the installation of a fire door.

Dry rot had been discovered in one room and the toilets were in need of repair.

The scale of charges for hiring the hall had been reviewed and it had been decided that:-

> A payment of 1s 0d per head be made for the meetings of each organization.
>
> A charge of 2s 0d per session would be made for activities for children under the age of 15 years.
>
> There would be no charge for the Services held by the rector.
>
> A charge would be made for parking in the area surrounding the hall of 5s 0d per week for lorries and 2s 0d per week for cars, with the proviso that, if necessary, other arrangements would be made when there were activities in the hall.

On the domestic side, an inventory was to be made of all the crockery. A lockable notice board would be erected outside the hall in the same position as the old school notice board.

A donation of £25 was received from an organization calling itself "The Ancient Order of Purchasers" and this was used to buy an immersion heater for the kitchen.

Fund-raising activities continued with:-

> 'Know the Hatch' Walk
> Jumble and Harvest Produce Sale
> Guy Fawkes Night Celebrations
> An Old-Time Music-Hall Evening
> Carol Singing
> Christmas Bazaar
> Summer Fair
> Chicken Supper and Dance
> Michaelmas Supper
> Barbecue organized by the Senior Citizens

Source: Kentish Gazette
Entertainment at the old-time music hall evening in March 1967

The competitions on Easter Mondays included pram races, Easter bonnets and decorated eggs.

It was reported that the Country Fair held in May 1969 had not made a reasonable profit. The coconuts had proved expensive and many were bad! £90 had been raised which was generally felt not to be "fair income for all the effort".

The second Annual General Meeting, held on 16th April 1970, opened with a presentation by Mr. A. Moat to Mr. L. Mount on his resignation as Chairman of the Society and in gratitude for all the effort he had put into the running of the hall. At the meeting it was proposed and carried unanimously that Mr. Mount should take the office of President of the Society.

Village Hall – A Factual History

Source: Kentish Gazette
A fund-raising supper in the hall in November 1970

Major issues

There were two major issues to be faced - toilets and heating.

The toilets, still the outside ones used when the building was a school, were in need of repair and conversion to adult use. It was suggested that, instead of spending money on these toilets, it would be better to convert the old air raid shelter into ladies' and gents' toilets, particularly as mains drainage was soon to be laid. In February 1971 the committee felt confident that, with a concerted effort and a 50% grant from the Council, they would manage to raise the capital and agreed that plans should be drawn up. The Minutes of 6th May 1971 record that an estimate of £645 had been provided and that plans had been prepared and submitted for planning permission. The accounts, however, showed a surplus of only £77.98 and the committee learned that they could not be considered for a grant before April 1973 or even April 1974.

Paraffin heaters had been installed in the autumn of 1970 as a more economic alternative to the coke stoves. However, as many of those who used the hall were elderly or very young, the stoves sometimes had to be lit as well as the paraffin heaters, increasing the running costs even more.

In spite of these difficulties, fund-raising and hirings continued. A Youth Club was formed. The Gardeners' Society, however, was disbanded. The hall was cleaned and painted by volunteers.

At a committee meeting in June 1972, it was suggested that, in view of the amount of money required to maintain the present building, the following proposal should be considered:-

THAT THE BUILDING AND SITE OF THE PRESENT VILLAGE HALL BE SOLD AND THAT ALL THE MONEY RECEIVED FROM THIS SALE BE SPENT ON BUILDING A NEW HALL ON PART OF THE PLAYING FIELD.

The proposal was given a cautious welcome and it was decided to investigate the possibility. The hall was valued at £6,500 by Messrs. Collier and Gardner.

Democratic decisions

In view of the seriousness of the matter and future implications, a Public Meeting was held in the hall on 19th February, 1973. The *pros* and *cons* of the scheme were put to the meeting:-

FOR THE PROPOSED SCHEME

The present building was not built as a village hall and was difficult to heat and expensive to maintain.

A purpose-built hall would be designed to be labour saving with the minimum of maintenance.

Toilet facilities for the present hall were seriously inadequate and the kitchen was barely satisfactory. A new hall would have better amenities.

A new hall on the recreation ground would stimulate the use of the field and it could be used as a changing room for sports teams.

AGAINST THE PROPOSED SCHEME

A building on the proposed site would be leasehold, whereas the present hall was owned by the Society and would increase in value.

A building on the recreation ground would be of much less value should the need arise to sell in the future.

There was limited access to the proposed site.

The site would be vulnerable to vandalism.

The proposal was put to the vote, resulting in:-

FOR THE PROPOSED NEW BUILDING - 15

AGAINST - 19

Councillor Roy Cooper congratulated Chartham Hatch on having put forward an imaginative idea and considering it intelligently.

It is left to the imagination to envisage what sort of development might have taken place on the site of the former Victorian school, now much loved for its place in the village scene and its historic interest.

Renovations, alterations and determination

The decision not to re-build must have been a disappointment to some and a relief to others. Whatever their views, the committee pressed on with determination.

At the Annual General Meeting on 4th April, 1973, the Secretary reported that, during the past year, the work of the committee had been dominated by the proposal to build a new hall. The Society now had to make the best of the present building. The elaborate plans for building new toilets in the old air raid shelter would have to be dropped in favour of a simpler scheme to renovate the existing toilets. Some of the money saved would be used to make the hall more comfortable and, in particular, to provide a source of quick heating.

Consequently, by April 1975, more heaters had been purchased, and the end wall of the Hall had been rendered, damp-proofed and re-painted inside. Volunteers had painted the outside front of the building. New curtains had been provided, fifteen wooden chairs purchased from Chartham Primary School and work was nearly completed on improvements to the kitchen, including the removal of the old iron frame for hanging coats.

Hiring charges had again been increased in May 1974 but only for occasional users from outside Chartham Hatch. They now had to pay double the rate as follows: £2.00 for a weekday morning or afternoon and £2.50 for a weekday evening; £3.00 for a Saturday morning or afternoon and £4.00 for a Saturday evening.

By the end of 1975 an electric urn had been purchased and a better piano donated. (In fact, in response to an advertisement in the local paper three pianos had been offered!) Tablecloths had been made by Mrs. Judy Knight and eighteen new plastic stacking chairs purchased. Repairs and improvements had been made to the outside toilets.

The accounts showed that finally the Society was in a healthy state. To achieve this, the committee had kept to the premise that the receipts from lettings should cover the day-to-day running costs of the hall and money raised from special events would be used for fixtures and fittings and general improvements. There had been an increase in private hirings.

Special events had been numerous. The Easter Monday activities and Michaelmas Fairs had become established as regular events and each year brought more imaginative fund-raising ideas - Summer Fair, Barn Dance, Christmas Fair, Halloween Party, Fish and Chip Supper, Country and Western Evening, Tramps' Supper, New Year's Eve Party with Disco, St. Valentine's Party.

Photo: Ann Sanders
Heather Fitch enjoying being a tramp with a heavily disguised Philippa Bennett in the background at the Tramps' Supper in 1976

It's cold outside!

January 1976 brought with it frozen pipes and cracked toilets and a renewed call for better facilities. Committee members volunteered to help. At the committee meeting in May 1976 Anthony Jankowski presented a detailed Energy Conservation Report which included lagging the ceiling, installing two gas heaters with fan blowers and converting the air raid shelter into toilets. A toilet sub-committee was formed! It was, however, to be several years before work on the toilets could start. The ceiling was lagged the following month by Mr. David Downs of Folkestone at a cost of £80 and the two heaters installed in 1977. There had been some discussion in the minutes about also lowering the ceiling to conserve heat. There is no record that the ceiling was actually lowered at this time, but it seems highly probable.

There were also other changes. Following a string of accidents to the boundary fence, in 1976 the committee and Kent County Council agreed that an improved road junction was needed. It was agreed that, if the Society would consent to sacrifice a strip of land from the corner of its property, the Council would move the fence back and also relocate the Society's notice board.

In the meantime, fund-raising continued with the usual Easter Monday activities, Michaelmas Fairs, and New Year's Eve parties.

A timely memorial

Many visitors to the hall have admired the clock on the wall above the fireplace and wondered about its inscription. The clock was bought by the committee in December 1975. It was suggested that Mrs. Opie be asked if it could be dedicated to her late husband, Mr. Ernest Opie, in recognition of his services to the hall. Mrs. Opie volunteered to pay for the clock but the committee agreed that she should be asked to pay for a plaque only. In the event, a substantial donation was made. The plaque was finally attached to the clock in January 1977. The clock is still going strong, thanks to regular maintenance and winding by Mr. Paul Wadhams.

Newsletters and AGMs

From the very beginning villagers have been kept informed about what is happening in the hall and given the opportunity to join the committee, to organise events and clubs or simply to come along to any of the activities. This has been done by means of newsletters, delivered by committee members or volunteers to every house in the village, and at the Annual General Meeting when official reports are given by the Chairman, the

Source: Kentish Gazette

Children in their Easter Bonnets in 1976. First prize went to Fay Groombridge (third from left front row), second prize to Catherine Cooper (to the right of Fay) and third prize to Julie Dyer's daffodil (centre)

Secretary and the Treasurer. In the early days, the newsletter deliverers were given the official title of "Street Warden". When there was a forthcoming event, they also had the duty of going to each house to sell tickets!

Money worries continue

The financial situation continued to be worrying. After the heaters had been installed, there was a deficit of £173 which was met by an offer from a committee member to buy more shares. Hiring charges were again revised in 1977. In 1980 there was only one regular hirer and this was at the time when work had started on the new toilets.

Celebrations

1977 and 1978 brought with them occasions for celebration – the Silver Jubilee of Her Majesty Queen Elizabeth II in 1977 and, in the following year, the tenth anniversary of the formation of the Village Hall Society.

Chartham Hatch as a whole community joined in the Silver Jubilee celebrations organised in the Parish of Chartham, manning a stall at the fête in Chartham on 9th July and providing a decorated float for the Carnival Parade. The float depicted characters from Walt Disney® and took first prize in the Community Class. Joe Auty, Chairman of the Village Hall Society, was presented with a framed photograph of the float at a ceremony in the Royal British Legion Club in Chartham on 3rd April 1978.

Source: Kentish Gazette

Left to right: Tony Clark, Chairman of the Jubilee Committee, with Joe Auty, David Glover and Joan Salmon receiving their awards from the Deputy Mayor, Cllr. George Hodges and Mrs. June Hodges

In Chartham Hatch itself, on 12th June there was a party in the hall, which had been decorated in red, white and blue and, with some money left over, a splendid children's Christmas party was organized by local villagers with party games and a conjuror in the afternoon and a disco in the evening.

At the tenth Annual General Meeting held on 17th April 1978 the Secretary said in his report:-

> "The outstanding event of the year had been the Silver Jubilee celebrations. The party for the children had probably been the high-point of the hall's history and something which those present would remember for the rest of their lives.
>
> "It was worth noting that this had been the work of a committee separate from the Village Hall Management Committee, although, of course, they were represented. It was heartening that a major event like this could be initiated and brought to a very successful conclusion by people in the village, other than those who ran the village hall."

Also, to the mark the occasion, repairs were carried out to the pump which stood on the forecourt of the village hall, formerly the source of water for the village school and house, and a suitable inscription was engraved on the wooden support.

Photo: Jim Sanders, 2006

The loan for the hall was finally paid off on 26th August 1968 and a buffet lunch was held on Saturday, 9th September to celebrate its tenth anniversary.

Self-help

With the improvement of the financial position in 1978, it was decided to go ahead with the drawing up of plans for the new toilets and requests for tenders. It was not until 1980 that the work actually started, made possible by the efforts of committee members and volunteers who were busy with pick and shovel, those who generously gave materials and their professional advice free of charge, and grants from Canterbury City Council and the Department of Education and Science. There was, however, still much work to be carried out by builders,

92

plumbers, electricians, etc., which would drain the Society's funds.

An anonymous loan

Help was at hand when the committee accepted an anonymous offer of an interest-free loan of £500. This was just another example of support for the Village Hall Society.

....At last

On 23rd June 1981 it was reported that the new indoor toilets were now in use, although there was still a certain amount of work yet to be completed.

Two tempting offers

Meanwhile, in May 1981, an offer had been made from the owner of School House to buy the old toilet buildings. The offer was for the lavatories, the shed and the rough strip of the old playground between the building and Denstead Lane, approximately 1300 square feet. The purchaser would provide an alternative shed for use as a store, but the Society would have to provide a fence on one side of the site.

A Public Meeting was held on 22nd April 1982 to put forward the following proposition:-

> "That the Management Committee of the Chartham Hatch Village Hall Society be empowered to sell, to a prospective purchaser, at the full market value as agreed by an independent valuer, and subject to approval by the Charity Commission, part of the village hall property for which it has no further use viz:-
>
> A range of outbuildings at the rear of the hall, currently being used as WCs and stores;
>
> The land on which they stand;
>
> A strip of land extending from the rear of School House to Gravel Hill;
>
> The whole having a total area of some 100 feet by 13 feet (1300 square feet)."

The proposal was carried unanimously but the offer was held in abeyance owing to a disagreement over the responsibility of erecting and maintaining fencing.

In May 1982 it was recorded that another offer had been made to buy, lease or rent the buildings etc., for storage of building materials.

Having considered all the advantages and disadvantages of both proposals, it was finally decided not to sell the land but keep it for the Society's own use. The buildings would be pulled down, the bricks and tiles to be retained for sale and for future repairs to the hall.

Therefore, it was proposed and carried that:-

> "The committee is no longer interested in the disposal of the surplus land and buildings"

The prospective purchasers were advised.

Fund-raising and social activities

It might be assumed that the committee's activities over the past few years had been confined to the installation of the new toilets and removal of the old. This was not the case, even though much time and effort had been put into these most important improvements.

Fund-raising and social activities had continued with cheese and wine parties, coffee mornings, a book sale, and a bonfire party (to name a few), with the Easter and Michaelmas events still holding their own. The attractions at the 1981 Michaelmas Fair give an idea of the variety of entertainment for all:-

> Pony and Trap - Fancy Goods - Plants and Garden Produce - Cakes - Tombola - Teddy Bears - Children's Stall - Coconut Shy - White Elephant Stall - Kick-a-Football - String Game - Lawn Mower Race - Raffle and, of course, refreshments.

By now, because of the difficulty of obtaining pram wheels, the Easter pram race also included whatever form of wheeled transport was available.

In 1980, the first of several village hall New Year's Eve Parties took place, with 61 villagers sitting down to a meal and entertainment provided by the 'Movin' Sound' disco run by Adrian Williams.

Photo: Courtesy of Kenneth Dawes

A useful contribution to the funds was the 100 Club which had started in April 1982. By August, Grace Davies had successfully built up a subscription list of 100 members and the first draw was able to take place.

Even committee meetings had their lighter moments - minutes from meetings in December 1982 and 1983 held by the Chairman, Dr. Kenneth Dawes, at his house, Sayes Court, each Christmas record:-

> "The control of the committee gradually slipped from the Chairman's grasp, shouts of "order" were misinterpreted, appeals for "Any other business" ignored, and it was impossible to distinguish when the meeting ended and Christmas conviviality took over" and "The committee held itself together just long enough to set the date for the next meeting for 25th January 1984 and then promptly collapsed under more glasses of sherry. A call for thanks to Dr. and Mrs. Dawes came from somewhere under the piano and was seconded from another body somewhere under the chairs. At this point the Secretary's notes came to a bleary halt and it is assumed that the meeting came to an end, with cries of Happy Christmas and New Year".

Charity No. 302709

An order was made on 17th December 1982 vesting the hall and its land in the Official Custodian for Charities and the village hall became a Registered Charity, No. 302709.

Fencing problems and solutions

The fencing was still causing many problems - not only to do with making the area safe, but also with establishing correct boundaries. Happily, we can now report that, even though it has taken over twenty years, all fencing issues have been resolved. The boundary fence between School House and the hall was renewed in January 2003. Joint ownership, with some realignment, was agreed with the owners of School House at the time. However, final legal agreement with the Land Registry Office was not achieved until 2006, with the hall paying over £2,000 in legal and surveyors' fees for their part of the proceedings. The upkeep of this fence is now the joint responsibility of the village hall and School House. The fence to the front of the hall was also renewed in 2006.

The 100 Club comes to the rescue

There were still not enough hirers in the early 1980s to ensure that all the bills could be paid from the income account and the committee relied heavily on the income from special events. There were only two regular hirers of the hall, bringing in £8.40 per week, and only a few private hirers. Luckily, a grant of £350 was received from the Canterbury Lottery Fund which meant that the materials could be bought to finish off the work in the toilets. In August 1982 a decision had to be made whether to pay the rates bill of £36.08 or an electricity bill of £13.41 from a total of £18.05 in the bank. The Treasurer was advised to pay the electricity bill which led to his receiving a summons in September to attend the Magistrates Court for non-payment of rates! However, borrowing sufficient money from the 100 Club account to add to the £4.64 hall account meant that half the rates and the £5 costs could be paid. The proceeds from a coffee morning repaid the 100 Club and proceeds from the Michaelmas Fair brought the bank balance back into the black.

Joe Auty

So many people have been involved with the hall that it is not possible to mention them all. However, many villagers fondly remember Joe Auty and speak of his unassuming dedication and unstinting commitment to the hall. The Minutes of March 1992 record that, without Joe, "there would never have been a hall". The hall has even been described by some as "Joe Auty's hall". Joe, who lived in Yew Tree Cottage, Howfield Lane, served on the committee from the first meeting in the Chapter Arms in 1967 to April 1983, initially as Treasurer then as both Treasurer and Secretary.

One of his early initiatives was to design a 'cut-out' model of the hall on card complete with instructions on how to assemble it using the flaps and slots provided. There was even a tiny tower to go on the top. He had several copies made and they were sold to raise funds. The original card measured 25 ins x 20 ins flat; the model on the next page was made recently from a copy of the original card reduced to A4 size.

Joe resigned at the 15th Annual General Meeting on 20th April 1983 after presenting his fifteenth annual report as Treasurer and his twelfth annual report as Secretary. His last report as Secretary records his resignation as follows:-

> "The Chairman paid a generous tribute to Mr. Auty on his retirement, mentioning

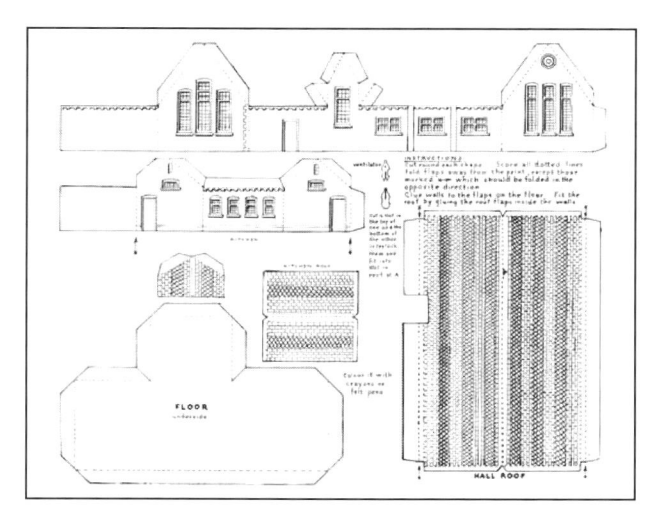

Photos: Jim Sanders
Model of the village hall made from an A4 copy of Joe Auty's original flat card

his work both seen and unseen, and then presented him with a fine gift of a pair of binoculars. That gentleman, finding the apt phrase eluding him for once, muttered a few halting, embarrassed, inadequate words of thanks."

Photo: Margaret Pomfret
Jessie Bradley with Joe Auty at his retirement party

To mark his retirement, the committee held a Cheese and Wine party on 23rd June 1983.

Joe died suddenly on 16th March 1992. After the funeral, mourners returned to the hall for tea. He very kindly left £500 in his will to the hall.

The committee commemorated his name by having a shield engraved which became known as the Joe Auty Shield and was presented each year to the winners of the tug-of-war competition at the Michaelmas Fair.

A year for action

The 1984 Annual General Meeting saw the resignation of the Chairman, Kenneth Dawes, before (in his own words) "he became an embarrassment to be got rid of!".

The newly appointed Chairman, Dennis Millis, declared that 1984 would be a year for action. The hall must be made into an attractive commodity by repair and decoration, in which all must be involved.

The local Manpower Services, who had already expressed an interest in assisting with the re-decoration of the hall, confirmed that they would start in March. However, it was only after much urging by Stan Walton, who was co-ordinating the scheme, did work eventually start in September.

It was reported on 8th October 1984 that, just by looking around the hall, it was clear that much improvement had been made and the transformation in the kitchen was obvious. At the same time committee members and other volunteers were still doing much work themselves, such as repairs necessary to the toilets and enclosing the children's wash basins.

The heating and lighting had been improved, new linoleum laid in the kitchen and new tables and chairs purchased.

The decision was taken to demolish the outbuildings, to sell off the bricks and tiles and to go ahead with the construction of a stage with storage facilities underneath. Mr. Ken Shilling was employed to build the stage, which was completed at the end of 1985 when a final coat of varnish was applied by members of the committee.

Indeed, it certainly was a year of action, though not the first nor the last!

Sadly, one who had faithfully served the village hall for many years was diagnosed as suffering from a corroded bottom and succumbed in July 1984. How many cups of tea and coffee had been made by an old and dear friend, the kettle, is impossible to calculate!

Ladies' Group

1984 also saw the formation of a Ladies' Group, meeting on the first Thursday of every month. The group still meets regularly and is one of the longest-running hirers. A more detailed account of the Ladies' Group is given in the next section.

Taking stock

Over the next few years serious thought was given to obtaining more bookings for the hall and to increasing the letting fees to a financially viable level.

The prizes for the regular draw of the Share Certificates were becoming a drain on funds. It was therefore decided to end the scheme, offering shareholders the opportunity to redeem their share money. Very few did. After a period of four months it was declared that any claims on the Society were invalid.

On the practical side, repairs were carried out to the fencing and guttering and a wrought iron gate was installed (which, unfortunately, was stolen shortly afterwards). The old toilet block was at last demolished in October 1986, the bricks and tiles sold and the area resurfaced. In December 1986, a concrete block wall was erected to replace the old boundary wall at the back of the toilet block which was found to be unstable.

Photo: Ann Sanders
Demolition of the toilets at the back of the hall next to School House

Photo: Courtesy of the Ladies' Group
First Ladies' Group Christmas meal at Lily's Diner, Canterbury on 6th December 1984
Left to right: Linda Crawley, Doris Arnold, Grace Walton, Helene Jones, Pam Williams, Alma Hill, Grace Davies, Lilla Dawes, Lorraine Bishop, ?, Hilary Lingham, ?

The stage was proving to be a welcome asset to boost lettings. In April 1987, The Channel Theatre Company made its first booking for a production of Chaucer's "The Canterbury Tales", particularly apt in view of the village's proximity to Harbledown, Chaucer's "Bob up and doun". The Village Hall Society received 25% of the proceeds, as agreed. This was to be the first of several very enjoyable evenings.

The Easter and Michaelmas festivities continued to bring in revenue, supplemented by events organised by members of the committee or villagers, including coffee mornings, car treasure hunts, beetle drives, dances, a Caribbean evening and a Hoppers' Harvest Supper.

A new addition to the forecourt

When David Kemp announced in February 1986 that he would resign as Postmaster on 6th May, a meeting was held to discuss the possibility of having a post office in the village hall. However, this came to nothing. The post box was re-sited a year later to its current position at the entrance to the car park. The Society tried to claim rent from the Postal Authority, but this was not forthcoming. However, with the post box now outside the village hall, more people would pass the notice board and, it was hoped, read of and attend forthcoming events.

With the closure of the shop and Post Office, the red telephone box was replaced with the modern style kiosk opposite the hall.

Trouble ahead …

…and overhead. In the great storm of 16th/17th October 1987, the village hall did not escape damage. The ornate 'tower' on the roof was brought down in the ravages of the night. It was sadly missed. Perhaps a replica could be made? Not so easy as the damaged structure had disappeared leaving no prototype from which to work. The story of its reconstruction, replacement and further repair is recounted in a separate chapter.

Of course, there was much other damage to the hall caused by the storm, all of which was repaired by local tradesmen who offered their services free of charge. It is in times of emergency like this that the community spirit comes to the fore, yet again.

A crisis is averted

It became clear at the AGM of March 1989 that, unless more people were prepared to serve on the hall committee, either as a full committee member or as a representative from an organization hiring the hall, there was a serious risk of not meeting the requirements of the constitution. An Extra-ordinary Meeting was called. Luckily, several villagers stepped forward and the committee was able to continue.

Into the nineties

The new decade started off well with a lunch for Senior Citizens, held in the hall in March 1990.

The event was organised by Leslie Larrigan, Secretary of the Village Hall Society. The costs were mainly covered by the society, with donations from local businesses and residents.

The lunch, prepared and cooked by volunteers, was followed by entertainment which included a magician and a sing-along.

Photo: Courtesy of Kenneth Dawes

The Senior Citizens of Chartham Hatch enjoying their lunch in March 1990

Village School to Village Hall

An enterprising venture

In 1990, Leslie Larrigan, the hall Secretary and Booking Clerk, hired the hall to run a 'Village Shoppe'. This initiative was subsequently adopted by the committee and run as a hall activity.

With no shop in Chartham Hatch, this enterprise, selling groceries, cakes and greengrocery, was much appreciated by the villagers.

'The Shoppe', which also served teas, opened on Monday and Thursday afternoons, providing a welcome amenity and rendezvous for residents and visitors alike. The autumn 1990 village hall newsletter gave a summary of what was on offer:-

VILLAGE SHOPPE

OPEN MONDAY AND THURSDAY AFTERNOONS 2 - 5 pm

LOTS TO BUY, INCLUDING HOPPERS' GOODS AT REDUCED PRICES.

PLUS XMAS FARE:- DUNDEE CAKE, CHUTNEY, MINCE PIES

COME AND HAVE A CUPPA AND BROWSE.

THE LAST DAY TO SHOP BEFORE XMAS WILL BE MONDAY 17TH DECEMBER

Another new addition

This time to the side, not the front, of the hall. Still in use for the storage of chairs, etc., the shed was erected in June 1990, helped by a grant of £350 from Shell Research Ltd. under their Community Grant scheme and £80 from the Lotteries Commission.

Looking good

With the new curtains made by Barbara Miles in August 1989 (and still looking good today!), the hall was beginning to look much smarter and more attractive to hirers, and improvements continued over the next few years. In October 1990, Mel Martin from the Royal Oak and a team of helpers volunteered to sand and seal the hall floor. There was a new cooker in the kitchen, outside sensor lights were installed and the ceilings in the toilets plastered. In the summer of 1993, a work party supplied by the Kent Probation Service decorated the hall, both inside and out. The three shades of green chosen for the inside by the Chairman, Jon Wilmot, have remained ever since.

An opportunity to advertise

In 1994 Chartham Parish Council celebrated its 100th Year by organizing an exhibition in Chartham Primary School. All local groups, businesses and other activities were invited to have a stall to promote themselves.

Photo: Courtesy of the Ladies' Group
Jill Simmons with the Ladies' Group scrapbooks at the Parish Council Exhibition in 1994

The Parish Council also asked the hall committee to take part in their Parish Picnic on The Green in Chartham on 25th June 2000, when members of the committee ran a very successful tombola stall. The committee provided another tombola stall for the Parish Council's Festival on The Green the following year, on 16th June.

Local crafts in the hall

In 1995, an Arts and Crafts Festival was introduced, with local people invited to hire a stall and sell their crafts. This has now become an annual event, though with the simpler title of Craft Fair.

What a show of talent! Paintings, etchings, pottery, candlemaking, needlecraft, woodwork and calligraphy, to name but a few of the displays, not forgetting the craft of cookery with home-made cakes, quiches, jams and preserves for sale.

Held at the end of November, the event heralds the Festive Season, lightening the dark days at the end of the year with a friendly atmosphere, and a chance to ease the burden of the inevitable Christmas shopping.

At the Craft Fair held in 1997 £230 was raised for the village hall fund.

The event usually coincides with National Tree Week and for the first few years visitors were invited to celebrate the tradition of tree dressing by hanging a decoration on the oak trees outside the hall. These decorations were a reminder that trees are precious and vital to our existence and therefore should be loved and respected.

Source: Kentish Gazette

Dressing the oak trees are, from left to right, Jenny Harries, Sheila Webb, Veronica Litten, Camilla Tuite and Margaret Pomfret

Under its own logo

It was also in 1995 that Jon Wilmot, former Chairman of the Society and a talented artist, made a delightful drawing of the hall. This was reproduced as notelets which have become a very useful fund-raiser. Later the picture was adopted as the society's logo and now appears on all letters, posters, newsletters and publications, including the title page of this book and the first page of this chapter.

Some fund-raising changes

The nineties saw some changes to the regular fund-raising events. Attendances had been gradually dropping at both the Michaelmas Fair and on Easter Monday, and the committee felt it was time to make some changes.

In 1993 the Michaelmas Fair became a May Fayre. It was still held on the playing field but it was felt that there was less risk of bad weather in May. The Michaelmas Fair became a Michaelmas Bazaar in the hall and was held in 1992 and 1993. The May Fayre was renamed the Summer Fête in 1995 but was to be held for two more years only.

The last Easter Monday Funday, as it had become known, was in 1995. It was decided to make this the last one as entries for all the indoor competitions seemed to be mainly from committee members. Only the egg and spoon race attracted other competitors, probably because this involved much less work and ingenuity and a guaranteed prize of a chocolate egg!

The committee felt that the loss of these two events had left a gap in the calendar and decided in 1997 to hold a Plant Sale where villagers could hire a table to sell their own plants and produce, giving 10% of their profit to the hall. There was also a village hall table where donated plants were sold. The first plant sale was at the height of 'garden makeover' programmes on television and the queue waiting for the doors to open stretched to the road! The plant sale still continues, not quite as well attended as when it started, but the addition of a White Elephant stall in 2006 has helped to attract more visitors.

Photo: Courtesy of the Village Hall Committee
John Lewis with his plants outside the hall

Still going strong, the Wine and Wisdom Quiz was first introduced in 1992 and is held twice a year. The City of Canterbury Brass Band started hiring the hall in December 1995 and their summer concert, either in the hall or on the playing field, has also become a regular event, as has their carol concert in December. These and the other regular events held over the years are described more fully in a separate chapter.

Regular and one-off events (musical evening, barbecue, treasure hunt, poetry evening with Group 81, beetle drive, boot fair) continued to bring in revenue as did the lettings. One regular letting, to a meeting of local driving instructors, could not help but draw attention to itself – the sight of so many 'learner driver' cars parked at all angles in the car park was one not to be missed!

The hall celebrates thirty years!

Members of the committee and hall supporters celebrated the hall's thirtieth anniversary on 8th August 1997 by a 'bat and trap evening' at the Royal Oak in Hatch Lane. Mel and John Martin, the landlords, had always supported the hall and were only too happy to host the evening, introducing the uninitiated to the delights of floodlit bat and trap, a typically Kentish pub game.

Repairs and renovations

By 1996 funds were in a much healthier state with income from hirings rising steadily each year. However, every penny was needed as a new heater had to be installed to replace the old one which had been condemned by the Gas Board and the kitchen needed refurbishment and redecoration. Luckily a grant of £350 from the City of Canterbury Lottery went towards new flooring in the kitchen and the proceeds of a jumble sale organized in the hall by St. Mary's Church, Chartham, were donated to buy new crockery. New kitchen units, worktops, tiles, etc. were paid for out of hall funds.

Keeping a hall going has always required more than a regular income – it has also required regular maintenance and cleaning, and over the years many people have stepped in to help. In February 1996 Mike Armstrong offered his services, to unanimous approval of the committee, as a 'general services and utilities man' and in March 1998 Phyllis Cage offered her services as a cleaner. Both Mike and Phyllis are still carrying out these duties and it is to their credit that the hall continues to be well looked after.

A new century

And so, entering its fourth decade, the Chartham Hatch Village Hall Society forged ahead. The kitchen had been refurbished and was well equipped. Chris White was employed to redecorate the outside of the hall in 2002 (in its present pale yellow colour) and to renew the guttering. At the same time, several cracked windows were replaced and minor damage to the woodwork was repaired. The toilets, however, were old, cold and damp and did not comply with legislation governing disabled access. There was a healthy balance in the bank but not enough to fund both the new toilets and the other renovations necessary to combat the damp. It was decided to look for an additional source of funding.

Applications and rejections

There had already been one disappointing rejection from the National Lottery Awards for All scheme in September 2000 for a grant to continue research into the history of the hall. Veronica Litten had written a brief account of the history of the hall some years previously and it had been hoped to mark the Millennium by carrying out further research to produce a small booklet. The project had to be put on hold. Another application to the National Lottery in 2002 for a complete refurbishment of the toilets was also turned down. However, the committee decided it should learn from the experience, and two sub-committees were formed – one to look for funding for the toilets and for other improvements to the building and the other for funding for the booklet.

The renovations project

Renovations have played a prominent part in this history of the hall and the next few years were no exception. A sub-committee of John Lewis, Mike Armstrong, Jenny Harries and Richard Langley lost no time in commissioning a survey of the hall from Lee Evans de Moubray in Canterbury and in drawing up a business plan. An application to the Brett Environmental Trust under the Landfill Tax Credit Scheme in April 2003 was successful. Their grant of £14,000 was conditional on the committee raising 11% (£1,540) from other benefactors. An appeal letter was therefore sent to villagers and several local organizations.

The target is reached

There was a very generous response of just over £2,600 which included significant donations from Chartham Parish Council and Coombs (Canterbury) Ltd. In addition, there were donations from the Ladies Group and a sponsored walk (the Flora Light Walk) by Ann Baggeley, a local member of the Keep Fit class in the hall. Together with just under £400 returned by the Inland Revenue under Gift Aid and £500 donated by Railtrack under a charity nomination scheme to the winners (who just happened to be members and friends of the committee) of a Wine and Wisdom Quiz organized by Chartham Primary School, the total money raised locally amounted to £3,520, almost twice that requested. The renovations could start.

A cheque and a plaque

Sir John Gugeon, representing the Brett Environment Trust, presented the cheque for £14,000 to the Society's Chairman, John Lewis, on 17th July 2003 in front of an invited audience of donors to the project. Sir John also presented a plaque to commemorate the event.

Photo: Norton Harries *Photo: Jim Sanders*
Sir John Gugeon presenting the cheque and the plaque to John Lewis. The plaque now hangs on the wall in the hall.

Work gets underway

Nearly forty years after the hall was bought and just under twenty years after the toilets were 'brought inside', the hall's funds had grown sufficiently to be able fund the additional £15,000 required to pay for the project. The contract was awarded in 2004 to builder, Chris Mayne, and he, together with sub-contractors, started to attack the problems both inside and outside the hall, with Mike Armstrong acting as agent for the committee and general unpaid assistant.

The survey had identified damp problems at both the front and south-east end of the hall. These were caused by the rising ground level from successive playground resurfacing over the years covering the existing damp proof course – by up to two bricks at the south-east end! Trenches were cut to expose the damp proof course and filled with shingle. New soakaways were created to replace the old, blocked ones.

Meanwhile, inside the hall, much of the wooden panelling had rotted because of the damp and it was decided to replace the entire panelling along the front of the hall. The panelling was spaced off the wall and ventilators added to ensure a flow of air from both inside and outside the hall.

There was much to be done to refurbish the toilets. This was essentially a complete stripping out and rebuilding, with the added restriction that one toilet had to be functional at all times as the committee had decided to keep the hall open for hirers throughout the building work – quite a challenge for the builder!

As it had been originally a World War II air raid shelter for the school, the toilet block had an eight-inch thick reinforced concrete roof – very good for keeping out various missiles and the odd meteorite but useless for preventing the ingress of cold and damp! So the first job was to line all the outside walls and ceiling with Celotex® insulating board which, although only an inch thick, has the thermal properties of six inches of fibreglass.

The rest of the refurbishment of the toilets was conventional, with the exception of the entrance door which had to match the existing doors in the hall. This was cleverly achieved by the carpenter, who fashioned a matching door from a solid wood door.

The new toilets required alteration to the main drain connections which offered the opportunity to modernize the kitchen drains and replace all the manhole covers which were not substantial enough for cars to drive over.

Even with the extra work that was found to be necessary during the refurbishment, the project was completed within budget, thanks in large part to the builder.

A complete report, with photographs, has been produced by Mike to act as a record for future trustees of the hall. It was all a far cry from the early days when most of the work had to be done by volunteers!

Keep Fit class raises cash and heartbeats

Thus reads the headline of the Adscene article of 13th February 2004 when, on the previous Saturday, a fund-raising aerobathon was organized by Mel Lea, who ran a Keep Fit class in the hall on Monday evenings. The gruelling three hours of exercise raised more than £150 for the renovations project.

Source: Kent Regional Newspapers
Mel Lea, centre, setting the pace at the aerobathon

Thank you and farewell

A 'thank you and farewell' evening was held on 16th June 2004 to thank all those who had helped to make the renovations project a success and to thank the 100 Club members for their continued support. It was also to say farewell to Pat and John Lewis who were leaving the village for northern climes. Presentations were made to Mike Armstrong for his work alongside the builders and to Pat and John for their support to the hall. Pat and John made a presentation in return – a very generous gift of five new hall tables.

The history project

It was also decided to have another attempt at obtaining funding for the booklet. The Local Heritage Initiative was identified as a potential source, and a sub-committee of Valerie Elvidge, Ruth Harling, Jenny Harries and Ann Sanders completed the application form, requesting funding for a book, a DVD, web-site training and software, a plaque and a project with the local primary school. In September 2004, Jenny was able to announce that just over £16,000 had been awarded to the group and that the history project, as it had become known, would start in November with the purchase of a CD recorder to record memories of the school and hall and with visits to various archives.

Many villagers have donated their time – both in talking with members of the sub-committee and in typing up transcripts from recordings – and also their photographs and postcards for us to copy to use in this book and to deposit in the archives for future researchers.

The project has created much interest and, at the request of several villagers, a reunion and fact-finding exhibition was held on 5th June 2005. The hall was packed and buzzing with the sound of visitors from all over the UK recalling their memories of school and renewing old friendships.

Photo: Norton Harries

The History Project Group waits for the Kentish Gazette to arrive to publicise the Reunion and Exhibition in June 2005

Left to right: Valerie Elvidge, Jenny Harries, Ann Sanders and Ruth Harling

Photo: Jim Sanders
Visitors at the reunion and exhibition in June 2005

Photos: Courtesy of Chartham Primary School
Some of the children from Chartham Primary School experiencing the reality of World War II with gas masks made in the classroom while others find out what schoolboys would have worn

The school children at Chartham Primary School had also been busy, dressing up and reliving both Victorian school days and life during World War II, in preparation for a pageant. They had also prepared questions on school days for the Over 50s group on 5th October 2005 when questions such as "did you ride a penny farthing?" and "did you get the cane?" caused much amusement.

Four new events

The regular events of Plant Sale, Wine and Wisdom Quizzes, Craft Fair, Summer and Carol Concerts continued. The decision was taken not to hold any more New Year's Eve parties after a very low turnout in December 2003.

There were also four new one-off events.

The first was a Family Musical Evening on 7th April 2001 which Heather Fitch volunteered to organize to pay for the new piano which had been installed in the hall the previous September at a cost of £100, with muscle power provided by John Lewis, John Martin, Joby Martin and Sean Casey. The evening, which was compèred by Steve Wassell who also arranged the programme, was a great success and £331.20 was donated to pay for the piano and its tuning, with the balance going into hall funds.

Another very successful event, again purely a voluntary effort with refreshments provided by members of the family, was a Croquet Day organized by Margaret and Tim Pomfret on 20th August 2004 where the quality of the croquet decreased as the evening wore on!

In 2005, several villagers agreed to open their gardens to visitors to raise money for the hall. A sub-committee of Liz Anderson, Jill Simmons, Jenny Harries and Jon Wilmot decided that a different approach would be to organize a 'treasure trail' with visitors to be asked to solve clues either in the gardens or along the way. Liz and Jon volunteered to provide en-route refreshments. However, maybe it was the thought of having to solve the clues or the overcast weather, but only a disappointing thirty-five people took the opportunity on 12th June to visit some surprising gardens and the village hall, where the Painting Club had an exhibition and the Chartham Gardeners' Society had produce on display and for sale.

The latest new event, a Slide Quiz, was organized on behalf of the hall by villager Tim Flisher in November 2005, where participants had to work out the location of his slides by means of cryptic clues – surprisingly difficult but also very interesting, particularly the slides showing old Canterbury and the surrounding area. Soup and rolls were provided by Valerie Elvidge and Ruth Harling.

Into 2007

The year 2007 sees a hall that is used regularly by many individuals and organizations. The hall now has a new wire fence, a new heater has just been installed at the Gravel Hill end of the hall and, to ensure a presence in this age of the internet, the hall's web-site was launched in 2006 (www.charthamhatch.org).

A new venture, suggested by Margaret Pomfret for the Grumpy Old Men of the village, is a short course in croquet, with the fee going to hall funds. Whether this makes them more or less grumpy, only time will tell!

The hall has also been used regularly as a polling station, going back to the time when the building was the school. The most recent polling day was on 3rd May 2007 for the local council elections.

Fund-raising will continue to help pay for the repairs and renovations that are always necessary and to try to ensure that the community spirit essential to a small village is not lost.

Stop press!

We have been amazed at the amount of information we have collected over the past two years but nothing quite as amazing as our recent acquisition which came to light only one week before going to press.

Margaret Pomfret was repainting the kitchen and decided to replace the old hall notice board by the kitchen door. Imagine her surprise when she discovered underneath, hidden probably since 1966/67, the school notice board below!

Photo: Jim Sanders

Painted in a pale green/blue colour with white writing, this is the notice board that can be seen in the photograph of the school on page 74. The board itself is made of plywood measuring 36" x 30" and is on a softwood timber frame. There are holes on the back showing how the board was attached to two vertical poles.

The St. Augustine's Division of the Kent County Council Education Committee was administered from Canterbury and was responsible for the surrounding village schools as well as schools in Herne Bay and Whitstable.

Village Hall Activities

Clubs and Hirers

The Nursery

The impetus behind the purchase of the school to form a hall was fuelled by the desire to serve the needs of the community. Obviously children formed a large part of the community, and the first use of the hall was as a nursery for pre-school children. Heather Fitch and Philippa Bennett were keen to get started. Fortunately, they did not have to wait for the purchase of the school building to be completed – they started the nursery as a business in September 1966 with part funding from Kent County Council, contributing the rest themselves. Formal approval from the newly-formed Village Hall Committee was given at a meeting on 10th February 1967 when a hire charge of ten shillings per morning was agreed. A Ministry of Health official visited and ordered some necessary changes - a fire door and fire hydrants had to be installed.

Fixtures and fittings

Half a dozen tables, some chairs and a Wendy House were bought from London County Council which was selling educational equipment surplus to their requirements. All the equipment had to be carried to the outside store every Friday and brought in again on Monday morning apart from what could be stored in a wooden cupboard beside the fireplace.

The nursery only used the Gravel Hill end of the hall and Philippa had to fill the stove with coke and light it at 6.45 am in the colder months. The partition was kept across the middle of the hall. The two, oval-shaped, black pot-bellied stoves were blackleaded by the caretaker, Mrs. Salvage, who in the early days agreed to carry on working for the hall when the school closed. There were fireguards with brass knobs which also had to be cleaned. The stoves were later replaced with Calor Gas heaters. On Monday mornings there was often much clearing up to be done after the weekend lettings, especially when the committee could no longer afford to employ a caretaker.

Dog days

As some of the children came from Chartham and even further afield, in the early months of the nursery, Mrs Fitch used to collect them in her car, accompanied by the family dog, Paws. As the nursery became established, parents organized car-sharing as there was concern about the question of car insurance. Paws, however, a Labrador/spaniel cross, continued to attend the nursery and became a firm favourite with the children, even with those who were nervous of dogs.

Source: Kentish Gazette

Children at the nursery donned overalls and busied themselves with paint brushes while their parents had tea and buns at the nursery's first fund-raising event nearly ten years after it was formed. Around £40 was raised for new equipment.

The coffee morning included exhibits by the children, with the self-portrait gallery attracting particular interest, and a sing-song.

Activities

The nursery opened with only six children, aged between three and five, who soon settled into a routine. On arrival, the children hung their coats on the pegs in the kitchen, each hook having a tag with a coloured picture so that the children could recognise their peg. Wellington boots were lined up under the peg for outdoor activities. Indoors there were all the usual activities – painting, pastry making, puzzles, games. Heather and Philippa wanted to introduce an element of learning through play rather than just free play, so they made all sorts of things from egg boxes, the insides of toilet rolls and cardboard. They did "music and movement" and acted out nursery rhymes. In the summer, a large paddling pool was filled and used in the car park, where they also played on a seesaw or on ride-on toys. There was a patch of garden which the children were encouraged to help with. In good weather, there were many nature walks to the woods and, with a pram loaded up with milk bottles and lunch boxes, picnics in the orchard. Flowers were picked and brought back to press or copy. Whenever they walked (in twos in a crocodile) up Primrose Hill or Gravel Hill, they always sang "The Grand Old Duke of York". At Christmas, there was always a Nativity Play for the parents to watch. There were also trips to the Marlowe Theatre's puppet shows and to the seaside.

Bitten by a pig

Both Heather and Philippa clearly recall an unusual incident on one of the walks - a little girl was bitten by a pig when they went down Denstead Lane. She had to be taken to Casualty where the nurse couldn't believe her story.

Milk memories

Milk was delivered every day in one-third of a pint bottles - not at all popular with Nicola Whyte and Diane Janman ("it was not very nice as it was always warm"). When it was time for the milk break, the children took it in turns to carry in the tray with the bottles on as there was a policy of shared tasks. Philippa gave the milk out and Heather would say Grace and so became known by Dean Elvidge as Grace Flitch (never Fitch) and Milk Bennett.

When two or three ....

The rector, the Rev. Lloyd, came from Chartham on Friday mornings to take Communion in the other half of the hall, so the children had to be given quiet things to do. Philippa says "you could have heard a pin drop while the service was going on". Heather remembers hearing the rector through the partition saying "When two or three are gathered together..." which was often changed to "When one or two are gathered together .." The two or three were usually Mrs. Barker from Primrose Hill and Heather and Philippa who took it in turns to attend the service.

Spidery toilets

The toilets were unpopular with staff and children alike. They were still outside in the playground and were liable to freeze in cold weather. Because of the numerous spiders, many a child learned to 'hang on' until they got home!

Labour of love

Heather and Philippa managed on the whole without helpers, and describe their time at the nursery as a labour of love. The children were usually very well behaved, and discipline, apart from a quiet word, was unnecessary. They reluctantly had to give up the nursery in the summer of 1978 when Heather returned to nursing, and still have many happy memories of the hard work and fun they shared.

Source: Kentish Gazette

Children from the nursery with Heather (fifth from right), Philippa (sixth from right) and mothers on an outing to Wealden Woodlands in 1978.

Before leaving, flowers and book tokens were presented to Heather and Philippa in appreciation of 11 years work.

Village Hall Activities

Photo: Courtesy of Diana Kentish – 1982/83
Back row: Wendy Dyer, Christopher Kentish
Middle row: Ricky Bromley, Judith Harling, Lucy Kentish, Steven Pomfret, Nigel Dron, Adrian Rymill, Damien Watkins, William Rogers
Front left to right: ?, Emma Mellor, Cassie Hill, Joanne Brooker, Angela Baker,?, Colette Scott, Marie Scott, Charmaine Bromley

A new leader

Wendy Dyer, who had previously stepped in to help Philippa when Heather returned to nursing, took over in September 1978 and followed more or less the same routine. By this time there were between ten and fifteen children each morning. Wendy describes her time there as an enjoyable challenge. She was able to buy more small tables and chairs which the council was selling off from an Infant school in Canterbury and these were spruced up and painted in bright colours. As in Heather and Philippa's time, the hall was divided on Friday mornings so that the rector could conduct a communion service and afterwards pop in to say hello to the children.

To whom it may concern ...

Milk continued to be delivered each morning. Wendy remembers that, on several occasions when she arrived at the hall, the small milk bottles which she had rinsed and left out for the milkman looked as if they had been filled with urine. A note saying "To Whom it may Concern: We've had your sample analysed and suggest that you see a doctor immediately" soon solved this problem.

Volunteer help

Wendy was assisted by a rota of volunteer mums who stayed to help while their own children were attending. These helpers were Margaret Rymill, Yvonne Hill, Ruth Harling and later on Angela

Photos: Jim Sanders

The nursery float in the Stones Carnival in Chartham, July 1982 with Wendy Dyer (top left) and Margaret Rymill (top right) and Margaret with some of the children (bottom)

Bradfield, and Wendy pays tribute to the help they gave her and the fun they had. In May 1981 the nursery held a coffee morning which raised £27 towards the proposed new indoor toilets for the hall. The hall was redecorated in the summer of 1984 and cupboard seats installed by local villager, Stan Walton, for the playschool to use. Wendy has happy memories of her time in charge of the nursery and was sad to leave when the business which her husband Ken and she had started in Upper Harbledown in 1983 expanded so much that her time was needed there.

The business is sold

After Wendy moved from the village in late 1982, she continued to run the nursery until Easter 1985, when she sold the business to Mrs. Angela Bradfield from Chartham, who was one of her helpers. Unfortunately, we have been unable to contact Angela but we know that she continued to run the playgroup to the great satisfaction of the parents until her resignation at the end of the summer term in 1992. The money she paid for hiring the hall contributed significantly to the hall's annual income – 30% of total income in the financial year 1991/92. Rose Mills, who helped from time to time, had a grandson at the playgroup and remembers that, in fine weather, the children would come to play in her garden. There was also a 'Sports Day' on the playing field. She recalls that, despite Angela being very strict, the children all adored her.

A Playgroup Committee is formed

An emergency hall committee meeting then agreed that the playgroup could be run by a Playgroup Committee. The playgroup still had to pay for the hire of the hall. Initially, two people put up the money to buy the business and equipment from Mrs. Bradfield. They were later reimbursed when donations and money from fund-raising came in. The new playgroup started in September 1992 with Jenny Elvey as playgroup leader, run by a committee of Nick Tooth (Chairman), Donna Davis (Secretary) and Kate Linkins (Treasurer). The Parish magazine advertised it as being open from 9 am to 12 noon on Tuesday, Wednesday and Thursday mornings at a cost of £2.50 per session. In the following month new legislation for playgroups came into force which resulted in the Village Hall Committee having to pay nearly £500 to make the hall safe for children.

Source: Kentish Gazette

End-of-term playgroup Christmas party in December 1992 with games, a buffet and a visit from Father Christmas who had a present for each of the twenty-one children

Special doors were made at the foot of the steps to the stage, new fireguards were bought and a half door was fitted to prevent the children from going into the kitchen.

By December 1992 the playgroup was running well and had held an Open Day where people reported that the atmosphere was caring and the children were well disciplined. A Christmas party had been held in December paid for by the proceeds of the Open Day and a sponsored matchbox fill. By April 1993, however, it was beginning to struggle financially because of falling numbers. The position grew worse over the following months with the result that the playgroup decided in November not to continue after the end of December.

The hall has since been hired from time to time by several private mother and toddler groups, including Hey Diddle Diddle, a group for toddlers to learn music and singing using percussion instruments.

Youth Groups

The *Kentish Gazette* of 17th March 1967 records the opening of a Youth Club for eight to eleven year olds under the leadership of Wendy Allen and Sue Barrow, and for twelve to twenty year olds under the leadership of Ron Barrow and John Faiers. There is nothing on record about the activities of the older group but the younger group became part of the Woodcraft Folk movement and ran until 1969.

Woodcraft Folk

This national organization, considered the youth arm of the Cooperative movement, had been established as an educational movement and charity in 1925 as a non-militarist, pro-socialist alternative to the Scouting and Guiding movements. Its aim was to give both boys and girls an understanding of important moral issues such as the environment and to take an active part in the world around them. The children took part in games, drama, discussion, projects, crafts, singing and dancing and wore a uniform of green shirts onto which they sewed Woodcraft Folk badges and achievement badges in the same way as in the Scouts and Guides. However, when attending a rally at Ashford, the leaders of the Chartham Hatch group agreed that they did not want the children to be involved with a politically biased movement and reluctantly decided to cease running the group.

Youth Club

No further mention is made of a Youth Club until April 1972, when the minutes record that "several young people" had asked if a Youth Club could be formed. This was agreed, providing there was adult supervision. Up until then, several children had been playing darts, table tennis, etc., in the playroom that David and Joan Kemp had converted from their New Town Street shop for their own children and friends when the shop moved into new premises in Howfield Lane. David Kemp, along with David Leach, volunteered to be the leaders of the new club.

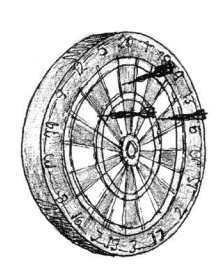

Drawing: Stephen Croucher

The club started well, with fifteen members who met every Friday evening for three hours at a hiring cost of £1 per evening. Various grants were obtained to buy equipment and the (by then defunct) Gardeners' Club donated the £6.55 remaining in their funds. As well as activities such as games, table tennis and music in the hall, there were visits to the swimming pool, to the speedway and also to Dreamland in Margate. One of the original members, Nigel Dawes, remembers a camping trip to Seasalter.

David Kemp recalls constantly turning the volume of the record player down in the hall and member Steve Levine turning it up as soon as David walked away. When asked why he did this, Steve replied "so that I can hear the quiet bits". Steve Levine is now the producer of Culture Club and the Beach Boys, amongst others.

The club regularly held rounders matches on the playing field with the boys versus the girls. The playing field had benefited in October 1970 from new goal posts which the Parish Council had authorized Mr. Evan Wills to buy. New swings and slides had been erected by the Parish Council just before this time, so there was plenty to occupy the Youth Club in fine weather.

In the summer of 1972 the club also carried out a door-to-door collection (raising £11.72) towards the New Toilet Fund.

Unfortunately, this good relationship with the committee was spoiled following a Youth Club disco in June 1973 attended by over 80 children, most of whom were not residents of Chartham Hatch, when the hall was left in a bad state and the fence of School House was damaged. Formal letters of complaint were written to both leaders and David Leach resigned as Youth Club representative on the committee, but continued as one of the leaders.

David Kemp appealed for more help with running the club, particularly from the ladies. Georgie Talbot helped for a while, mainly making 'Blue Peter' type things with the girls – she remembers showing them how to turn a margarine tub into a photo frame! When David Leach left the village in July 1974, no other leader could be found to replace him and, as the other David could not manage on his own, the Youth Club closed.

Chartham Hatch Lyons Table Tennis Club

In July 1977, after the Prince of Wales Youth Club in Canterbury burned down, the hall was for a brief while the venue for the Canterbury Table Tennis Club, run by Chris Laming from Hatch Farm House. Chris was in the process of bringing his barn up to the standard required for county matches but, as improvements were not complete at the time of the fire, the hall was hired by Chris for two seasons for the club, renamed the Chartham Hatch Lyons Table Tennis Club, for both coaching and matches. When the barn was ready, the club and equipment moved there.

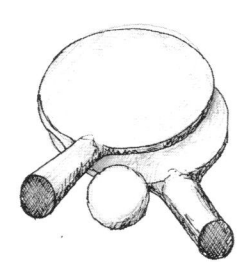

Drawing: Stephen Croucher

Sports Club

The next initiative for young people was the formation of a Sports Club, started by Bob and Barbara Miles in April 1980. Meetings took place on Monday evenings. When they left the village in 1981, the club was taken over by Bob Elvidge who was one of the helpers. Again, both the hall and the playing field were used. Helpers were Lorraine Bishop, Gina Flynn, Jim Wayre, Georgie Talbot, Doreen and Trevor Pilbeam. By 1982, the club was held on alternate Monday evenings.

The Minutes mention several donations to the club from hall funds to help with equipment and parties. The Sports Club, like the Youth Club before it, also helped the committee. It organized a children's party for the village in December 1987 and also contributed £25 to the fund for the toilets (now indoors, but by no means finished).

Photo: Barbara Miles
Elaine Popplewell with some of the children of the Sports Club on the Recreation Ground, 1980/81

It also held an event in the hall in March 1983 with stalls, side-shows, handicrafts, etc., to raise money for netball and rounders posts. Doreen and Trevor Pilbeam remember a trip for the older children when they took four carloads to Dover swimming pool and then on to Langdon Cliffs to eat sausage and chips.

By the early 1990s, the club was run by Lorraine Bishop, helped by Janice Tuite. In 1991, local members of the Winkle Club, a national charitable organization, gave the Sports Club £160, the proceeds of a disco at the Chapter Arms, where Vic Redpath was Chairman of the local group. Lorraine also organized a Halloween Fancy Dress party when twelve children from the Sports Club were tied together by the wrist with string and then went into the woods with torches. On the way back along Bigbury Road, they called at the homes of Grace Walton, Sue Wellard and Hilary Lingham for 'trick or treat'. When Lorraine left, Janice persuaded Vince McCormack to join the band of helpers, as his two daughters were already members. Vince had many new ideas for the club and became its leader in July 1992. At the Michaelmas Fair the children, with the help of Pat Torralba, organized several games and competitions.

The Monday Club

When Vince left at the end of the year, Pat and Janice, with helpers, saved the day by continuing the club as the Monday Club. Pat was the last leader of the club, which closed in 1995 when she and her son Ramón moved to London.

Ladies' Groups

Welcome Club

In 1967, in the early days of the village hall, a Welcome Club for ladies of the Hatch was formed and run by Nancy Robinson. This group enjoyed outings and speakers, and continued to run until 1975 when a lack of numbers brought about its demise. Outings included a visit to the Police Headquarters in Maidstone and the Paper Mill in Chartham. One outing which many villagers still remember is the trip to Bettshanger Colliery, when ladies and their husbands went down into the mine. All emerged with blackened faces except for Jessie Bradley who had had the foresight to cover her face with a headscarf!

When it closed in 1975, a small group of friends from the Welcome Club continued for a while to meet in one another's homes and were known as 'The Coffee Set'.

Ladies' Group

In the Village Hall Society's Summer 1983 newsletter there was a suggestion that a new Ladies' Group be formed. Valerie Elvidge chaired a meeting of interested ladies to see whether they wanted to form a new branch of the Women's Institute. The general feeling was that they did not want to be affiliated to the WI but they wanted to have a less formal group. Several friends with young families were keen to start such a group, meeting on the first Thursday of each month. Founder committee members were Hilary Lingham (Leader), Lorraine Bishop (Secretary), Sue Wellard (Treasurer), and Linda Crawley and Christine Davis. The Minutes of the hall meeting of 1st March 1984 report that the group "had got off to a flying start".

Photo: Courtesy of Jessie Bradley

A visit to Bettshanger Colliery

Standing left to right: Joan Glover, Joan Kemp, Brian Allen, Wendy Allen, Philippa Bennett, Heather Fitch, Peter Fitch
Kneeling left to right: Jessie Bradley, Nita Levine

Many of the events staged by this founding group still continue to this day but, in the early days, to reflect the needs of the members with young families, there were several events for young children, such as Teddy Bears' Picnics and Christmas parties for the young children of the village, usually with some financial help from the hall committee. Popular entertainers 'Uncle Dennis' and 'Auntie Jean' helped to make sure the party went well.

Photo: Courtesy of the Ladies Group

Children's party organized by the Ladies' Group in January 1987 with 'Uncle Dennis' and 'Auntie Jean'

Village School to Village Hall

Photo: Courtesy of the Ladies' Group
Teddy Bears' Picnic in July 1984 with Grace Davies, centre back, in her Andy Pandy costume

The December meeting was always well attended when the ladies organized a Christmas Carol Concert, open to friends, husbands and children of members. Local musicians were invited to lead the singing, which was always followed by seasonal refreshments provided by the ladies. Pianists Maurice Copus OBE and Dennis Mathew led the singing and, on several occasions, members of the Wassell family played the piano and stringed instruments. However, from 1995 the City of Canterbury Brass Band had started to hire the hall and in 1996 they were requested by the hall committee to stage a carol concert. The Ladies Group felt that two carol concerts would not be well supported and decided no longer to hold their December meeting. They agreed to the hall committee's request to provide refreshments at the band's concert and have done so ever since. Proceeds from the concert go to a charity which is chosen on alternate years by the hall committee and the Ladies' Group.

It is an impossible task to list all the meetings, talks, demonstrations and visits enjoyed once a month for the past twenty-four years! Each meeting has been faithfully recorded with photographs in a series of scrapbooks, compiled for many years by Chris Fox and, more recently, by Georgie Talbot. The following photographs show some of the activities enjoyed by the members.

Photo: Courtesy of the Ladies' Group
Dot Wassall with Ben and Emily, Christmas 1991

Photo: Courtesy of the Ladies' Group
Harold Rogers OBE talked about 'The Story of Desert Island Discs' on 4th September 1999

Village Hall Activities

Photo: Courtesy of the Ladies' Group

Wendy Allen demonstrating sugar flowers at a meeting on 6th April 1995

Photo: Courtesy of the Ladies' Group

Maurice Copus OBE on 7th September 1989 with costumes made by Audrey Stevens for Group 81.

Left and centre are the costumes for the Pharaoh Seti and his sister Anath for "The Firstborn" by Christopher Fry and right is a Roman Centurian costume used in various Biblical presentations including "Son of Man" by Dennis Potter

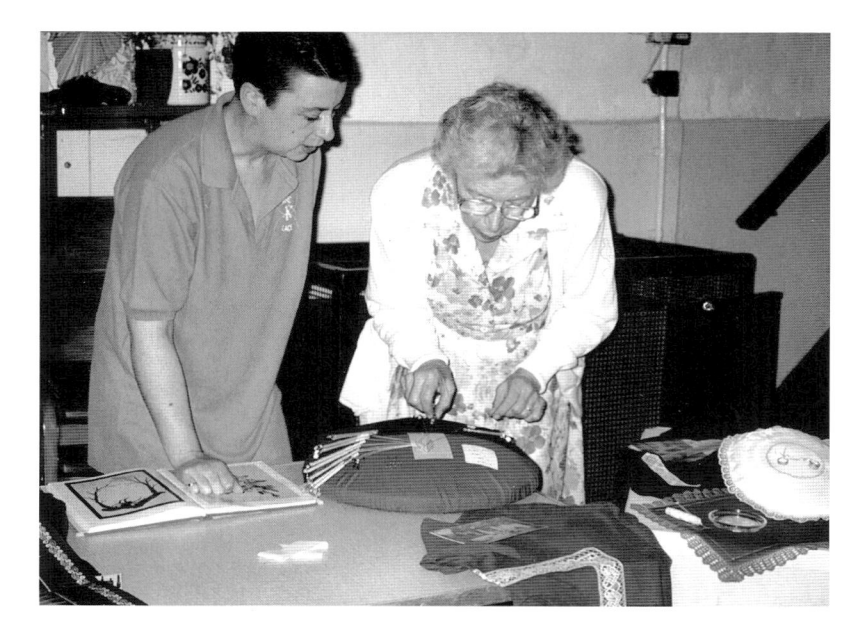

Photo: Courtesy of the Ladies' Group

Jessie Bradley trying her hand at lace making watched by the visiting speaker, Jane Scull, on 6th July 1995

In 1987, Conservation Year, the Ladies' Group planted spring bulbs around the hall.

Many of the visiting speakers are from charities and several of the events organized concern charities, often local. The following are just some that the Ladies' Group has supported.

Patty Baxter from Canterbury gave a moving talk about the children's home, Casa Hope, which she set up in Romania. Home-made articles by a member of the group were sold in aid of Patty's work. An open coffee and craft evening was held on behalf of the Georges Turle House, the child and family therapy unit based in Canterbury. Proceeds went towards buying camping equipment and large floor cushions. Donations have also been made to Amnesty International (carol singing), Kent Kids Miles of Smiles (a bring and tell and sell evening) and also to the Pilgrims Hospice. The group has also visited Footprints, the home of Kent Kids Miles of Smiles in Stodmarsh Road, just outside Canterbury.

Several of the meetings involve food and drink, including the Summer Lunch held in a member's garden and the Harvest Supper held in the hall. The catering is shared out between everyone, so there is not much work but plenty to eat!

A twenty year reunion was held in 2004 and the group welcomed previous members for an evening of reminiscence and, of course, food and drink.

Photo: Courtesy of the Ladies' Group

Members of the Ladies' Group relaxing during a visit to Footprints on 3rd May 2001

Left to right: Jill Simmons, Wendy Allen, Camilla Tuite, Georgie Talbot, Rose Mills

Photo: Courtesy of the Chartham Society

The Ladies' Group enjoying a Harvest Supper in the Hall, 2000

Left to right: Ruth Harling, Heather Fitch, Camilla Tuite, Jessie Bradley, Gill Dodds, Chris Fisk, Chris Leahy, Jill Simmons, Daphne Goldsmith, Rose Mills, Mabel Sparks, Chris Fox

Village Hall Activities

Keep Fit

There have been several attempts to 'keep fit' in the hall over the years. The first group was run by Elaine Popplewell. Philippa Bennett was the Keep Fit representative on the committee at the time (1968-69) and remembers the classes being very energetic. The Minute Book of February 1971 shows that the Keep Fit class was a regular hirer. In September 1974, Lilla Dawes took a class on Tuesday evenings. Several members passed a Grade 1 Proficiency Test in Keep Fit and received a certificate from the Northern School of Yoga and Health Activities! As well as yoga exercises, Lilla devised a routine to music and, apart from a short break around 1981, her class ran until about 1987. In 1986 the Minute Book records that they made a quilt for the Michaelmas Fair – did they stitch whilst jumping up and down?

For a short while the class was run by Barbara Hudgell before it was taken over by Pam Dron, a former dance teacher. Pam ran a class from June 1987 until September 1989. She followed the same type of routine as Lilla but put her own slant on it and used more modern music.

themselves routines and exercises. They also went running and cycling (and sometimes finished their session at the pub!). However, numbers gradually dwindled and, by 1993, the club had closed.

New classes for the ladies

It was now the turn of the ladies to start a new class, this time on a Thursday morning. In 1993, a small number of recently retired ladies started a Stretch-and-Exercise group. For a few weeks they employed a teacher but, when they realized that this was not affordable for so few members, they decided to carry on by themselves using their own tapes. Although a few more tapes have been added to the collection, the original routines are still being used. The group uses 'yoga-type' stretch exercises and also some old Eileen Fowler routines which never fail to raise a smile because, although great fun, they are very dated, with Eileen Fowler calling out from time to time to remind the ladies what fun they are having and to warn them of the risk of getting a dowager's hump if they don't do their shoulder exercises!

Photo: Courtesy of the Chartham Society

From left to right: Rose Mills, Heather Fitch, Sybil Hammond, Norma Brooker and Georgie Talbot at the Thursday morning class in

Men's Keep Fit and Weight Training

Drawing: Bret di Lu

At about the same time, in July 1987, Rob Fisk and Adrian Williams started a Men's Keep Fit and Weight Training class. Members included Peter England, Tony Dorman, Trevor Davis and Trevor Pilbeam. Equipment was donated, lent or bought from boot fairs. There was no teacher – the men set

A maximum of half a dozen ladies still attend the Thursday morning Keep Fit, including founder members Rose Mills and Jill Simmons.

Another class began at the end of the 1990s, this time on a Monday evening under the leadership of Lucy Brown from Blean. Lucy was very young and energetic and introduced a rigorous cardiovascular workout to loud dance music. She wore a small microphone so that instructions could be heard over the music.

When Lucy left in the spring of 1997, the next class was led on similar lines by Mel Lea from

Sturry, who was studying Sports Science at Canterbury College and who stepped in when she heard that the group was without a leader. Mel's enthusiasm was boundless and she frequently introduced new ideas. She even organized an aerobathon in February 1994 to raise money for the renovation of the toilets.

When Mel moved away in the autumn of 2005, Linda Regan was persuaded to continue the class. Linda, whose training was in ballet, tap and modern jazz, starts the class with traditional warm-up exercises in a much gentler fashion than the two previous teachers and then continues with a series of modern dance routines, often with actions that might seem comical to the casual on-looker! From June 2007 it is planned that the class will be taken by Francine Earl, who also hires the hall for children's dance classes.

Yoga

After some persuasion, Jim Sanders offered a light-hearted approach to Yoga in the hall on Tuesday evenings, around 1999. This attracted first-timers as well as students from the past, both from the village and the surrounding area. It ran with a few breaks up until 2006.

Gardeners' Society

One of the first things the hall committee did in April 1967 was to ask Mr. Albert Bradley if he would like to form a Gardeners' Society. He had been the Show Secretary for the Gardeners' Society which used to meet in the Social Club. It was agreed in November that, until they became sufficiently established to have an annual subscription, they should pay 6d per member per meeting. There was also a Flower Club.

However, it was reported in May 1972 that they had not met for some time and seemed unlikely to meet again. Since that time, keen gardeners from Chartham Hatch have been members of the Chartham Gardeners' Society. Recently, however, this society has been without a meeting place in Chartham and has rented the Chartham Hatch hall for its regular meetings and annual show.

Art and Craft

Painting Club

Although there was a painting club run by Canterbury artist Leslie Marsh for a brief while in 1986, there was not much artistic activity in the hall until the present painting club was started by Jill Simmons in October 1994, inspired by a series of six watercolour classes earlier in the year given by local artist, Jon Wilmot.

The club, which started with six members, has continued to grow and members now total fourteen. A sad loss to the club was Ted Hill, who died on 11th August 1999. Ted gave help and encouragement to experts and learners alike while never professing to be a teacher.

The artists' wide range of skills has been demonstrated to the public in three successful exhibitions in the hall. In 1986 the club was asked by the Parish Council to take part in the production of the Parish of Chartham Field Names Map, which can be seen in the Old School Surgery in Chartham. When funds allow, the club has a day school when a professional artist

Photo: Jim Sanders
Just after judging at the Gardeners' Society Show in 2004

Photo: Jenny Harries
The Painting Club getting ready for an exhibition in July 2005

Photo: Courtesy of the Chartham Society
Craft Club members in 2000
Left to right: Muriel Sparks, Alma Hill, Rose Mills, Joy Alexander, Jill Simmons, Harry Alexander

demonstrates the use of different media. Each member contributes to a shared lunch, always popular with the demonstrator! The club meets weekly on Thursday afternoons.

Craft Club

There have been several craft clubs over the years. In the early years Lilla Dawes held an evening session where villagers could bring their own work and, more recently, Julie Blyth of Bigbury Road held an afternoon class where villagers also brought their own work and Julie taught them new skills. The current club, started by Jill Simmons shortly after she started the painting club, meets on the second and fourth Tuesday afternoon of each month. A wide variety of craft is practised, including card-making, knitting, calendar-making and découpage. Of course, this is all accompanied by a cup of tea and a good chat!

Senior Citizens' Club, Social Club and Over 50s' Club

The Senior Citizens' Club started shortly after the school became a hall and disbanded after the May 1976 meeting when Mrs. Tomlin retired as Chairman. Representatives on the hall committee were Mr. J. Faiers in 1969, Mr. O. Bellamy in 1970 and Mrs. J. Barker from 1973 to 1976.

The Social Club was started with thirty members in January 1989 by Lesley Larrigan and was run by Lesley and Grace Davies. When Reg Whale took over from Lesley in August 1992, he took on the responsibilities of Treasurer and Secretary and worked with Grace, the Chairman.

As well as organizing many of the club's activities in the hall, Grace did an amazing amount of ingenious fund-raising for the group – from making and raffling a blanket in 1991 (which raised £60) to selling bunches of chrysanthemums grown by her husband, Bob.

The club invited a wide variety of speakers, usually local, to the meetings. Reg always gave a full report in the Parish Magazine of what they had learned from the talk. Of particular interest is his report in September 1993 when Ted Hill showed pictures of the Autumn Fayre of 1985 and Chartham Hatch throughout 1986. Reg was also always very complimentary and appreciative of the cakes provided by the members after the talks – these were an equally important part of the meeting! There were also coach outings, again with tea and cakes.

The Christmas lunch was a highlight of the year. A team consisting of Rose and Dick Mills, Rose's sister Linda Murphy, Pam Whale and Jill and Ken Simmons shopped, decorated tables, cooked, served and cleared away a traditional meal. The rector and his wife, Clive and Helen Barlow, were always invited and, between 1993 and 1997, Mrs. Muriel Laming gave a generous donation each year towards the meal. In December 1994 the Winkle Club also provided a lunch for all pensioners in the village, so that year most of them had two Christmas lunches!

In February 1997, the remaining ten members of the group who were having their Christmas lunch, this time not in the hall but in the Chapter Arms, heard the sad announcement that this was to be the last lunch as the club was to close. Numbers had dropped significantly and, more importantly, Pam and Reg Whale were due to leave the village to move to Bexleyheath.

A sad note in the history of the Social Club was the death in November 1995 of Grace Davies who had been such an active member. Reg wrote in an obituary notice in the Parish Magazine:- "Grace will be remembered for her hard work, effort and devotion to making the village a better place for its community".

The Social Club was officially dissolved at its meeting on 25th March 1997, when Pam and Reg were presented with a picture of the village hall painted that year by Ted Hill.

Over 50s' Club

The Chartham Over 60s' Club, which had been meeting since 1964, became the Chartham Over 50s' Club in April 2002. It is run by Chairman Julie Fegan, with committee members Veronica Litten and Gill Dodds, with June Owen serving as Treasurer. From January 2003 to January 2007 the group met in the Chartham Hatch village hall. Volunteer drivers brought members to the hall, where there were talks by visiting speakers, bingo sessions or trips to local garden or craft centres. To finish, volunteer hostesses provided and served tea. The club now meets at Shalmsford Court, Shalmsford Street (sheltered accommodation provided by Canterbury City Council). This is a temporary venue until the new village hall in Chartham opens.

Source: Norton Harries
Valerie Elvidge talking to the Over 50s' Club in 2006 about schooling in Victorian times

St. Mary's Church, Chartham

Another regular hirer of the hall since the early 1980s has been the parish church of St. Mary's, Chartham. The church had previously been able to hold its activities and events in the parish hall on The Green in Chartham but, when this was demolished in 1984, the Friends of St. Mary's, the social and fund-raising committee of the church, needed another venue. One of the first events held in the Chartham Hatch village hall was an Auction of Promises in the late 1980s where a large audience was able to bid for donated items or for services from room decorating to oven cleaning.

Other memorable evenings were masterminded by Pamela Hooker and a team of helpers. These evenings usually had a theme, giving the guests the chance to appear in fancy dress, to enjoy a meal suitable to the occasion and to be entertained by a topical concert. On 21st May 1993, to raise money for St. Mary's, there was a Victorian evening, when Queen Victoria, Prince Albert and their court sat at the top table and dined on Good Woman's Soup, Stargazey Pie, Boiled Beef and Carrots, followed by Prince Albert Pudding. Music hall entertainment followed, one of the performers being Clive Barlow, the rector.

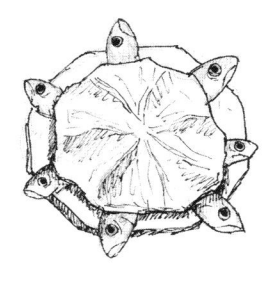

Photo: Gordon Luck
The rector, Clive Barlow, and his wife, Helen, at the Victorian Evening in 1993

Drawing: Stephen Croucher
Stargazey Pie

In 1995, the Friends held an evening entitled "As We Were", an evening of nostalgia to commemorate VE Day. Guests wore war uniforms, 1940s' style clothing or just red, white and blue. The war-time supper was Rabbit Stew, Rhubarb Crumble and Custard (made with dried milk power), war-time bread and 'mouse-trap' cheese, washed down with best bitter and white cider, for which guests had the privilege of paying four guineas. Songs and topical recitals followed the meal. The profits from this evening went to the British Legion.

Photo: Gordon Luck
Examining the menu at the "As We Were" Evening in 1995

A fund-raising jumble sale

Most of the crockery and cutlery for these evenings had to be brought in the boots of cars from the Church kitchen as at that time the hall was not well equipped for entertaining. Pamela Hooker and her team of helpers held a jumble sale in the hall in October 1996 to help equip the kitchen and raised the sum of just under £200, with which the present set of six dozen place settings of crockery and cutlery were bought.

Modern day pilgrims

1994 saw the first visit to Chartham Hatch of l'Arche, an international organization which originally started in 1964 when ex-Naval Officer Jean Vanier, helped by a Dominican priest, Père Thomas Philippe, started to set up caring homes in France for people with learning disabilities. L'Arche first arrived in the UK in 1974, with the first community opening in Kent. Another community opened in Lambeth in 1977 and it is this group which makes an annual pilgrimage, by minibus and on foot, from its London home to Canterbury Cathedral. Here they join up for worship and friendship with clients and carers of other homes who have all been making their way to the Cathedral at the same time but by different routes.

The groups stay in various parishes en route, with churches providing hospitality. Some of the Lambeth group spend the last night of its journey in Chartham Hatch village hall where a team of villagers welcomes the pilgrims, offers baths and showers in homes nearby and serves an evening meal in the hall. The pilgrims then hold a simple evening service grouped around a candle and sheet with images depicting the highlights and lowlights of their journey.

Photo: Jenny Harries
L'Arche group evening service in the hall on their visit in 2006

Villagers are invited to share their service and never fail to be moved by it, after which the pilgrims are left to entertain themselves and sleep in sleeping bags on mattresses on the floor. They are always up and ready to leave by 9 o'clock in the morning for the final stage of their journey, excitement growing at the thought of meeting up with old friends at the Cathedral. Before they set out on their way, they hold a morning service in the house or garden of Dorothy and Harold Rogers in Bigbury Road.

The present coordinator of the annual visit is Georgie Talbot. The first coordinator was Pam Whale, followed by Thora Wadhams.

Photo: Dorothy Rogers
Members of the L'Arche group in 2003 at the home of Dorothy and Harold Rogers

Lent lunches

The idea of a simple lunch during Lent was started in 1980 by Joyce Lowry, who held a lunch in her home in Chartham every Friday during Lent. Mugs of soup were served at a cost of 70p, the money going to church funds.

After ten or so years, Pamela Hooker took over the responsibility for organizing the lunches which were then held in different homes throughout the parish. When Valerie Elvidge, Georgie Talbot and Ruth Harling were asked to cater for a lunch, they decided to try the idea of using the village hall to attract a wider range of visitors. This was in 2000 and, as the venue proved popular, they have continued to use the hall for one Lent lunch a year.

Lunch consists of a choice of soups served from slow cookers in the kitchen, a roll, butter, cheese, salad, and a cup of tea or coffee. It runs from noon to 2 o'clock and costs £4.00 in aid of the Church Mission Society. Usually between 30 and 40 people sit down at tables decorated with flowers to enjoy a leisurely lunch with time to chat.

Improvements at St. Mary's

St. Mary's is now able to stage its own events in the church, thanks to an improved heating system and a new servery.

Channel Theatre

For several years, the Channel Theatre Company, a touring company specializing in performances for schools and village halls, entertained the village with the following plays:-

- The Canterbury Tales – 25th April 1987
- Hoppers Harvest – October 1987
- Twelfth Night – April 1988
- The Saga of Earl Godwin – October 1992
- A Warning to the Curious – 18th March 1994

At the performance of The Canterbury Tales, the children in the front row found the large, pink plastic bottom in the Miller's Tale particularly entertaining!

Impressed by their performances, Jenny Harries, with Tim Pomfret as driver, organized a coach trip on 4th January 1989 to the Pavilion in Broadstairs to see the company in The Glass Slipper, an adaptation of the Cinderella story. The coach was packed and a good time was had by all.

Although there are no curtains or special lights, the stage has been in much use over the years. In the early days it was hired by The Chilham Players from the neighbouring village of Chilham and by Group 81 for rehearsals and the occasional performance. Group 81 was an amateur travelling repertory company set up in 1981 by Maurice Copus OBE with the purpose of presenting drama and dance in churches in East Kent. More recently, The Chameleons, a local drama group, have put on several evenings of entertaining readings. Unfortunately, the hall committee is no longer able to accommodate performances by the many local touring theatre groups as the hall is too small to make the venture financially viable.

Photo: Courtesy of Audrey Copus
Group 81 putting the final touches to the hall before members arrive for their annual dinner in 1987

Dancing classes

Over the years the hall has been hired by several dancing classes, ranging from children's ballet to the present adult Lindy Hop classes.

For many years the Julie Kim School of Dancing hired the hall, finally leaving in September 1989. On several occasions, pupils entertained visitors to the Michaelmas Fair with dancing displays. The hall is currently hired on Saturday mornings by the Margaret Giles School of Dancing, who installed the ballet barre at its own expense. On weekdays it is hired by Linda Regan, who teaches jazz and modern dance and also gives tuition to teachers. The Francine Earl Dance School runs classes on a Monday afternoon for infant-aged dancers and on a Friday afternoon for junior-aged children. Francine has been hiring the hall since April 2004, starting with five young girls. The class now numbers twenty-eight dancers who develop their skills in freestyle, street dance and hip hop, musical theatre, lyrical and modern jazz.

The children also take exams and appear at local school fairs and other local events, and have also appeared at the Brook Theatre in Chatham.

Photo: Jim Sanders
Some of the pupils from the Margaret Giles School of Dancing, 2006

City of Canterbury Brass Band

The City of Canterbury Brass Band has been a regular hirer of the hall since December 1995, initially for twice weekly rehearsals on Wednesdays and Fridays, but now on Friday evenings only. As part of their hiring agreement, the Band stages two concerts a year. Starting with a concert on the playing field in June 1996, there has been a summer concert every year either on the field or in the hall and a Christmas carol concert early in December.

The carol concert always attracts a full house. Refreshments are provided by the Ladies' Group, and the proceeds of the concert are donated to charity. Over the years donations have been made to Kent Air Ambulance, the Odyssey Project, Demelza House, the Royal National Lifeboat Institution, Kent Kids Miles of Smiles, Kent and Canterbury Hospital Radio, L'Arche, the Pilgrims Hospice and the Young Carers' Project.

Apple Day festivities

In December 1995 the parishes of Chartham and Harbledown became the first communities to jointly own a traditional orchard in Kent. The orchard, alongside the North Downs Way and straddling the boundary of the two parishes, was launched as No Man's Orchard on 28th April 1996, with refreshments supplied in the hall by members of the hall committee. Over 400 people attended the launch. Since then, the hall has been hired annually every October when the Orchard Management Committee celebrates Apple Day with traditional, rural events both in the orchard and in the hall. More recently there has been an afternoon musical event as part of the Canterbury Festival.

The Chartham Society

The Chartham Society, an organization formed in 1970 to protect the local environment, has regularly hired the hall every other year for its Annual General Meeting, with speakers talking on topics as wide ranging as Spiders, Green Spaces, Chartham Paper Mill and Kent – Brick by Brick. The hall was also the venue for the Society's 30th birthday party on 30th July 2000.

Photos: Left – Jim Sanders
Above – Jenny Harries

The City of Canterbury Brass Band play to a capacity hall at the carol concert in December 2005 with Will Powell, the band's musical director, above

Village Hall Activities

Source: Kentish Gazette

Apple Day was celebrated in the hall in October 1999 because of bad weather

Seated left to right: Jon Shelton, Veronica Litten, Clive Barlow

Standing left to right: Sheila Webb, Jane Pepper, Babs Golding

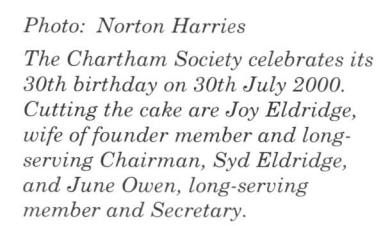

Photo: Norton Harries

The Chartham Society celebrates its 30th birthday on 30th July 2000. Cutting the cake are Joy Eldridge, wife of founder member and long-serving Chairman, Syd Eldridge, and June Owen, long-serving member and Secretary.

In 1999 the historical section of the Chartham Society was awarded a grant to create a photographic record of the houses and their inhabitants in the parish of Chartham, which became known as the Chartham 2000 Project. An exhibition of the photographs taken in Chartham Hatch was held in the hall on 22nd April 2001.

Photo: Jenny Harries

Chartham 2000 Project photographers left to right: Mike Talbot, Norton Harries, John Harling, Nick Tooth, Jim Sanders, Gill Dodds, Bernard Moat, Trevor Pilbeam

Source: Kentish Gazette

Lost Landscapes' tale tellers outside the hall, 4th July 2004

Back row left to right: Kenneth Dawes, David Hopper, Robert Palmer, Norman Dale, Jenny Harries

Front row left to right: Philip Redhead, Marjorie Purkess, Gill Dodds, Andreas Lowson, Tony Gowers (North Downs Way Project Officer)

The Lost Landscapes Project

Situated close to the North Downs Way, the village hall became a regular venue for many events associated with the Lost Landscapes Project which ran for three years from February 2004. This project was initiated by the Kent County Council North Downs Way Unit with grants from the Heritage Lottery Fund through the Local Heritage Initiative and the Rail Link Countryside Initiative. Its aim was to promote local distinctiveness in the landscape and to remember and reconstruct events of the past along and around the North Downs Way in six parishes in Kent, working with local communities. Chartham was one of the villages selected and Chartham Hatch village hall was the venue for the launch on 15th February 2004, of its part of the project, with presentations in the hall and a walk along the North Downs Way. Other events involving the hall have been a stroll around Chartham Hatch (and through its history) on Sunday, 4th July 2004 with local residents in costume recounting episodes of local events, a Sensory Workshop on 11th August 2004 and Apple Wassailing on 29th January 2005 with a torchlight procession to No Man's Orchard. Leaflets describing circular walks in each of the six parishes have now been produced.

The Rainbows

The 1st Chartham Rainbows is the most recent organization to become a regular hirer. Their Assistant Guider, Jeanette Kennett, has provided us with the following description of their activities:-

"The 1st Chartham Rainbows moved to the Chartham Hatch Village Hall in November 2006. Rainbows is part of Girlguiding UK and is for girls aged between 5 and 7. It is seen as the forerunner to Brownies, to which many of our girls move when they reach 7.

"Our meetings are weekly during term time. When we get together, we do a range of activities: some are food-based, some involve art or craft; we play games, take part in sporting activities and learn new skills; parties are an important part of Rainbow life – to celebrate new arrivals and to see 'old friends' off to Brownies. During the summer months we try to get out and about and have our sports events and explore the local area. In the past we have also visited Chilham Fire Station and Pet World.

"From our point of view, the move to Chartham Hatch village hall was imperative. We have a total of 15 girls in the unit and can have two or three activities on the go at once. The hall gives us the opportunity to spread out and be heard in our groups and to be more adventurous with our food activities.

"The photo on the next page features a recent evening when we encouraged the children to make a sandwich blindfolded. This activity provided us with a lot of laughs and the eating part was much appreciated by everyone. On a serious note, we also came to have some understanding of the difficulties experienced by blind people.

"We really are enjoying the facilities that the hall offers and are planning to have an Open Evening to allow parents to come and see what we get up to. We hope to continue a long and happy relationship over the coming years."

Photo: Ann Pomeroy
Some of the Rainbows eating a sandwich blindfolded

Royal celebrations

The Silver Jubilee

The Silver Jubilee of Queen Elizabeth II in June 1977 was celebrated in style, starting with a party in the village hall organized by a working committee of several villagers on Sunday, 12th June. A letter was sent to every household in Chartham Hatch with a request for a donation of 20p to help with food and drink. Many villagers provided food and Jessie Bradley made a Jubilee cake. Many donations were received, including a significant contribution from Joan Balfour, the licensee of the Chapter Arms. Before tea in the Village Hall, Martin Casey and Elaine Popplewell organized sports on the recreation ground with sweets in home-made paper cones provided by Martin and Mary Casey as prizes.

The hall was decorated in red, white and blue bunting with flags and balloons everywhere, and commemorative paper cups, plates and serviettes. Around 100 children sat down to tea. There was a magic show provided by Mr. G. Hatten and, as they left, each child was presented with a souvenir Jubilee book and leather bookmark.

This was followed by a carnival and fête in Chartham on 9th July, organized by a committee under the chairmanship of Mr. Tony Clark, the village policeman, with Chartham Hatch well represented by several floats.

The Village Hall Society's float depicted characters from Walt Disney®, with costumes kindly loaned by the East Kent Bus Company. The float took first prize in the Local Societies Class and came second overall.

Source: Kentish Gazette
Silver Jubilee party, 12th June 1977

Village School to Village Hall

Other entries from Chartham Hatch included the Nursery School float (Toyland), Billy Skeet with his sisters as a Pearly King and Queen and David Kemp's Mace Stores.

Photo: Jim Sanders

The Village Hall Society's float with Mandy Sanders as a baby mouse next to Minnie Mouse (Hazel Groombridge)

Photo: Margaret Tuffin

The Chartham Hatch Nursery Float with characters from Toyland

Photo: Ann Sanders

Village Hall Activities

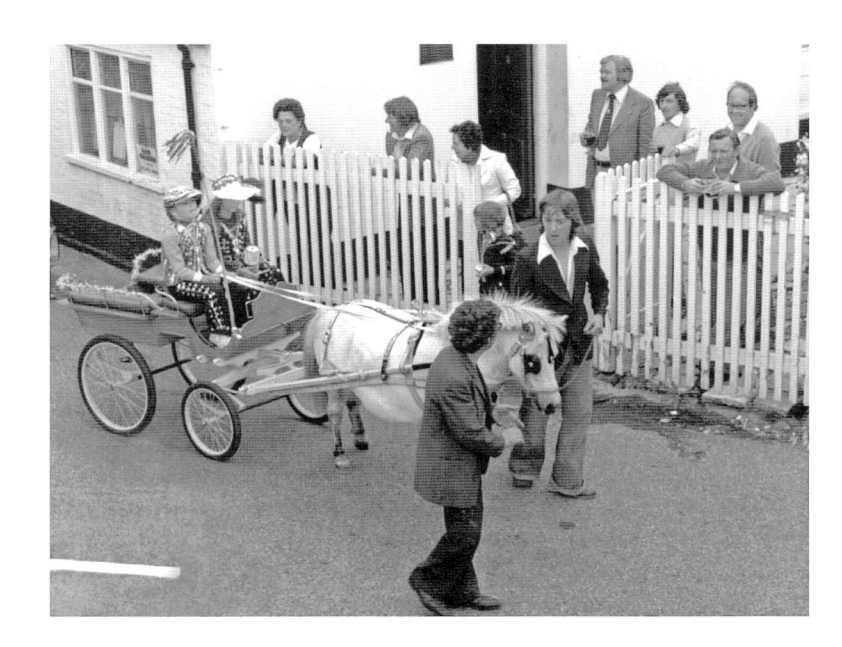

Photo: Jim Sanders
Billy Skeet leads his pony and trap with his sisters as a Pearly King and Queen

Photo: Georgie Talbot
From left to right in David Kemp's Stores float are Melanie Dawson, Philip Talbot, Dean Elvidge, Stephen Talbot and Lesley Kemp

Memories of the Jubilee were relived later that year in November when an exhibition of photos, films and slides was arranged in the hall by Jim Sanders.

The year ended with a children's Christmas party in the hall, organized by Wendy Allen and Ann Sanders with money left over from the party in June. Again, there were donations from many villagers, including one from the Village Hall Society from the sales of dresses donated by Jonathan Riceman (Director of a well known department store in Canterbury). Over 90 children, from babes in arms to teenagers, took part. There was an afternoon party for the younger children with games and a conjuror –

'Uncle George', helped by 'Auntie Jean' – followed by games and a disco for the older children in the evening arranged by Adrian Williams and David Hulks.

A Father Christmas cake was made by Jessie Bradley. Father Christmas (Pat Sheckleton) presented each child with a gift. The day is remembered by Wendy and Ann as very happy, but exhausting!

The Golden Jubilee

The Golden Jubilee of Queen Elizabeth II was celebrated in a much more restrained way on 4th June 2002. Unfortunately there were no young volunteers to step in the shoes of those who

Village School to Village Hall

Source: Kentish Gazette

Children's Silver Jubilee Christmas party in the hall, 1977

organized the Silver Jubilee and so the Golden Jubilee was celebrated in the hall with drinks and a buffet provided by the Ladies' Group. It was attended mainly by the older members of the village (and a dog!).

Photo: Derek Cage

Fun and Festivities

New Year Parties

The village hall committee was keen from the very outset to have village social get-togethers and, from 1968, a dance or social evening was organized around Christmas or New Year. The first few years saw a Tramps' Supper, a Victorian Evening (with piano music provided by Vi Cole from the Kent Music School), a Valentine's Evening with Supper and Sing-a-Long, a Barn Dance and a Fish and Chips party. Food was brought for all to share, and glasses, plates and cutlery had to be brought from home.

True New Year's Eve parties started in 1976 with a disco provided by Ray Saunders and food provided by the committee. Fifty people attended and the Minute Book records it as "an unqualified success". It was not until 1980 that the evening took on a different style with Adrian Williams' disco 'Movin' Sound', helped by Dave Hulks. As well as dancing, there were games, and each year the committee decided on a theme for the evening - 'Can Can', 'Tarzan and Jane', 'Leader of the Pack' and "Ello, 'Ello'. All too soon it was time for Auld Lang Syne with fire extinguishers representing bagpipes.

Photo: Ann Sanders

Seeking to impress 'Jane' (Pam Williams) are, from left to right, 'would-be Tarzans' Jim Sanders, Nigel Dawes and Trevor Davis

In 1983, to go with the 'Tarzan and Jane' theme, there was a 'Tarzan' competition and five would-be Tarzans (Trevor Davis, Nigel Dawes, Dave Hulks, Jim Sanders and Adrian Williams), with a rope attached to one of the hall's beams, vied with each other to impress 'Jane' – Pam Williams. Too much hilarity resulted in all five as winners. The decision was taken not to have a party in 1986 and from then on parties were held on an irregular basis.

However, in 1996, the committee felt that there should be something for villagers but on a more informal basis and decided that the hall would be open for anyone who would like to have a get-together from 9.00 pm onwards. Again, it was bring your own food, drink and games. At £1 per head towards heating and lighting, it was a bargain! Over the following years enjoyable evenings were held with team games, quizzes and singing round the piano. Many a back was stiff after limbo dancing and the odd toe black and blue from the crashing Jenga® blocks. The 1999 party saw in the Millennium with fireworks and sparklers. The party continued almost until dawn when those revellers who had committed themselves to the Dawn Walk in Chartham realized there was no time for sleep! By 2003, however, attendance numbers had dwindled again and it was decided to make this the last one. Since then the hall has been hired out for private New Year's Eve parties.

Easter Monday Activities

One of the first events to involve the whole village was the Easter Monday pram race in 1967, with an Easter bonnet competition for adults and children in the hall. Competitors for the pram race had to wear fancy dress and the following rules applied:-

> "Passenger to remain as such for duration of race"
>
> "A drink to be consumed at both the Oak and the Chapter Arms"
>
> "Token of confirmation to be issued by licensees"
>
> "Competitors to pay for own drinks"

The event attracted large crowds and the local policeman was on hand to stop the traffic. Stewards were positioned along the route to give assistance if necessary and to ensure fair play. Many still remember Roy Cooper in tunic and fez directing the traffic! At the signal 'Go!', ancient prams, pushchairs and homemade contraptions sped from the hall along Town Lane and into Hatch Lane, where a quick drink was consumed in the Royal Oak. Then it was down Hatch Lane to Hoppers' Oast and sharp left into New Town Street and into the Chapter Arms for a second drink. With the finish feeling miles away, the competitors continued into Howfield Lane where

Photo: Philippa Bennett

Waiting for the signal to go at the pram race, Easter 1967
Note the fund-raising thermometer in the car park

the cheering crowds and the village hall were a welcome sight.

The festivities continued in the afternoon on the playing field with a comic football match using a rugby ball. However, this proved to be rather dangerous and it was the first and last of its kind.

After a couple of years the route of the pram race was reversed. It gradually became shorter as the years went - maybe the stamina of the participants declined! Contestants now raced from the hall along Bigbury Road to the entrance to the gravel pit, back to the crossroads, left into Howfield Lane, round Nightingale Close and back to the hall – this time with no pubs en route! However, as it also became gradually impossible to stop the traffic through the village, it would certainly have been dangerous to have continued with the longer route. In the last few years the route became even shorter – from the hall along Bigbury Road to 'Beckets' and back. In 1993 the races were divided into separate categories for adults, primary and secondary school children.

Over the years a wonderful display of 'prams' has been seen, with participants in a variety of fancy dress costumes. Many a wife dreaded Easter Monday morning when their husband decided at the last minute to rummage through wardrobes looking for a skirt, top, dress and hat to wear! Others dressed as babies, doctors, nurses, bikers, St. Trinians schoolgirls, Hercule Poirot, Noddy and Big Ears to name but a few. Even Boy George, Kenny Everitt, Superman, Wonderwoman, Orville and Dean, and Prince Andrew and Fergie made their appearance.

The rules changed too. Pusher and passenger were allowed to swop places along the route, and bicycles, wheelbarrows, go karts and even a shopping trolley became acceptable modes of transport. The prizes were only small but the greatest fun was the taking part.

Once the pram races were over, everyone crowded into the hall for the adult and children's Easter bonnet competitions. For many contestants and their parents, this was the culmination of hours of work, possibly through the night, and some wonderful creations were on view. Newcomers to the village were generally asked to be the judges – an unenviable task as the talent was so high. Parading along a makeshift catwalk lined with crowds of people made even the most confident nervous. The winners received an Easter egg and all the children who had entered were given a small Creme® egg.

In 1969 decorated eggs were included in the competition and again the incredible talent of villagers was on show. Humpty Dumpty, rabbits, scarecrows and funny faces, together with cars, aeroplanes, dolls, Super Egg (a goose egg) and a lighthouse were some of the intriguing exhibits. Some eggs had been carefully 'blown' to allow the shell to be delicately painted and decorated.

Photo: Jenny Harries

Photo: Ann Sanders

Source: Kentish Gazette
Pram race, April 1988 with, left to right, Helen Rymill, ?, Adrian Williams, Pam Williams, Rob Fisk, Trevor Pilbeam, Trevor Davis, Nicola Fisk, Josie Harries, Lucy Kentish

Village Hall Activities

Source: Kentish Gazette
Adrian Williams, left, starting the egg and spoon race, April 1990

Competitions for posies and decorated gardens soon followed – one little girl even incorporated a tiny pond with a tadpole into her garden. Finally, small decorated cakes were added to the competition, but the number of entrants was never high.

The last few years also saw the introduction of an egg and spoon race from the hall to the entrance of the playing field and back. This event attracted many entrants, probably as it involved far less work to run with an egg than to decorate it!

Numbers gradually dwindled and the last Easter Fun Day, as it had become known, was in 1995. The Easter Monday activities will always be remembered, not just for the prams, hats and eggs, but for Jessie Bradley's 'famous' bread pudding, which was served every year by members of the hall committee with tea and coffee.

The following photographs give an idea of the ingenuity shown by entrants in both the Easter bonnet and pram race competitions.

Source: Kentish Gazette
Alex Wilmot, seated, and Adam Dearing had no difficulty in finding an alternative to a pram in April 1990

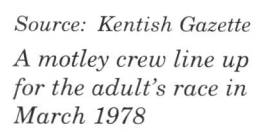

Source: Kentish Gazette
A motley crew line up for the adult's race in March 1978

Village School to Village Hall

Photo: Courtesy of Philippa Bennett

Lots of entrants for the adults' Easter bonnet competition in 1969

Left to right: unnamed, Miss M. Shoreham, Mr. T. Bradshaw, Nancy Robinson, Jean Bradley, Wendy Allen, Julie Sheckleton, three unknown

Source: Kentish Gazette

Adult and children's Easter bonnets in 1972

Source: Kentish Gazette

Children's Easter bonnets in 1983

Back row, left to right: Nicola Epps, Helen Rymill, Naomi Hill, ?, Catherine Brodie, Wendy Dron, Ryan Bishop

Middle row: Adrian Rymill, Kelly Bishop, Lucy Kentish, ?, Claire Rymill

Front row: Christopher Kentish, Josie Harries

Fêtes, Fairs and Fayres

The first fête to be organized by the hall committee was the Whitsun Fête in 1967. The hall had not yet been purchased and funds were desperately needed. A fête was seen as an ideal way of providing entertainment while at the same time raising money for the hall and, indeed, twenty-six stalls made a total profit of £105. There had obviously been a great effort on the committee's part but, from the comment in the Minute book, they felt that "more active help was needed for events of this kind" – a comment no doubt felt by many an organizing committee!

Over the next few years the committee tried various ways to encourage and entertain visitors, but with limited success. By 1969, the Whitsun Fête had become a Country Fair (raising only £90); it then became a Summer Fair but stalls and attractions only produced £66. In 1971, the first of the many Michaelmas Fairs was held. Each year the committee thought up new attractions in addition to firm favourites such as bowling for a prize, pick-a-straw, tombola, cakes, plants and produce. Children's sports were organized by Roy Cooper and Major Plowman in 1971. In 1974, the Mayor and Mayoress, Councillor and Mrs. Castle, were invited and a fancy dress theme was 'the Common Market'.

Source: Kentish Gazette
Bowling for a prize at the Whitsun fête in 1968

Source: Kentish Gazette
Left to right at the Whitsun Fête in June 1968 are Christine Guss, Pauline Sparks, Ann and Jean Bradley

Village School to Village Hall

Two beautifully knitted sweaters, made and donated by Lilla Dawes, were raffled separately and greatly enhanced the profit on the day which totalled £225. At the 1979 Fair, Grace Davies dressed up as 'Busby' and entertained the crowds. Guess the weight of 'Busby' added to the attractions.

The committee realized that, to be able to offer bigger and better attractions, more space was needed and from 1980 the fête was held on the playing field. It was now possible to include attractions as varied as pony and trap rides (provided by Mr. and Mrs. Vic Barber), model flying displays by the Herne Bay Flying Club, Morris Dancers, lawn mower races, a birds of prey demonstration, children's games and a Pets' Corner, both organized by Martin Casey, and a 'Fun Castle'. Adrian Williams supplied a public announcement system. The ATC or Sea Cadets Band would march into the playing field to herald the start of the fair. Other organizations such as the Gardeners' Club and St. Mary's Church, both from Chartham, also had stalls. Produce from Hoppers Farmhouse Bakeries was sold from the old fashioned handcart lent by David Hopper.

In 1982 a tug-o'-war was also organized for teams of eight people – the prize a 'pipkin' of beer. The tug-o'-war continued for several years, with regular entrants from the local pubs. The serious competition was always followed by a less serious one, often regretted the following day! Following Joe Auty's death in 1992, the tug-o'-war prize was the Joe Auty shield which was held by the winning team until the following year.

Source: Kentish Gazettes
Vic Barber giving a ride in his pony and trap to Naomi and Matthew Hill at the Michaelmas Fair in 1980

Source: Kentish Gazette
A display by the Kent Youth Motor Cycle team at the fair in 1988

Source: Kentish Gazette
Nickle Farm struggle at the losing end of a rope against the Royal Oak in a tug-o'-war contest at the Michaelmas fair in October 1983

Village Hall Activities

By 1988, a motor cycle display team had been added and a display by the Julie Kim School of Dancing. Lesley Larrigan, the hall's Secretary, had now taken on the organization of the fête and worked tirelessly each year to make each one better than the last. Profits soon rose and, in 1988, an all time record of £1054.92 was achieved.

Unfortunately, an outdoor event is weather dependent and in 1992 the fête had to be held in the hall and this was reflected in the profits. The committee therefore decided that, from that time on, the fête would be held in May and it became known as a May Fayre or a Summer Fête. There was both a May Fayre and a Michaelmas Bazaar in 1993. Although both had been well supported, the committee felt that it was unfair to ask for donations for prizes twice in the same year and decided to concentrate on the May Fayre.

The following years, back on the playing field, there were new attractions – a dog show, 'Madame Aurora' in her fortune telling tent and a new team competition game, 'Walking the Plank'.

It was then all change again – back to a late summer event, this time a 'Late Summer Barbecue' in 1997 and 1998 with stalls and new attractions – 'Stumpy' the Clown, welly throwing, Splat the Rat and an electric wire game.

However, the numbers of visitors gradually fell over the years and the committee felt that too much effort was involved for too little profit (an echo of 1967?). It was decided instead that the summer concert provided by the City of Canterbury Brass Band and would be the hall's summer event. For the last two years this has been on the playing field, with visitors invited to bring a picnic.

Source: Kentish Gazette

Visitors to the Michaelmas Fair in 1976
Top: Lilla Dawes hoping for a sale at her stall
Bottom: Children enjoying toffee apples

Source: Kentish Gazette

Michaelmas Fair 1992
Top: Judith Harling, Sophie George and Fay Pilbeam with home-made candles for sale
Bottom: Jon Wilmot and Jenny Harries encouraging visitors to guess the weight of the pumpkin

Photo: Jenny Harries
No time to look at the camera as the City of Canterbury Brass Band try to catch up with a village team in the "Walking the Plank" game

Photo: Jim Sanders
The City of Canterbury Brass Band providing the music on the playing field in the summer of 2005

Christmas Bazaars and Parties

Bazaars were held regularly in the hall between 1968 and 1993 and were either organized by the hall committee or by village organizations, with the profits going into the hall fund.

The Welcome Club was the first organization to volunteer its services and ran a Christmas bazaar in 1969, borrowing a Father Christmas outfit from Dunkirk School. Other memorable Father Christmases were Roy Cooper and Derek Andrews. Derek even took up the committee's suggestion to parade around the village. With lots to buy and competitions to enter, there was plenty to entice the visitor and for many years the bazaar provided a welcome boost to funds.

A new approach was tried in 1995 with a Craft Fair in late November and this has continued ever since.

Christmas parties for village children have also been held over the years and have been organized by groups including the Ladies' Group, the Senior Citizens and the Sports Club, or by individuals. Often entertainment by a conjuror was provided for the younger ones, while a disco proved popular for the older children.

The largest Christmas party for children was a 'dual' one held in 1977 with money left over from the Silver Jubilee celebrations in the summer. Separate parties for the younger and older children of the village filled the hall on both occasions.

The various playgroups over the years have also held parties but lately the hall has been hired by private hirers for their own parties.

The hall is always decorated by the committee for Christmas, with most of the decorations being donated.

Source: Kentish Gazette, January 1967

"A party for children of Chartham Hatch was held at the old school on Saturday. The Rev. R.C. Lloyd attended and, with Mrs. R. Mount, presented the 55 children with gifts. Several older children and teenagers helped with games. A buffet was prepared and served by Mesdames Barrow, Bennett, Bradley, Fitch, J. Glover, Hills, Hubbard, Martin, Mount, Thomson and Woodbridge".

Source: Kentish Gazette

The Rev. Robert Lloyd 'helping' at the bun competition at the party

Village School to Village Hall

Photo: Georgie Talbot
Derek Andrews as Father Christmas in 1971 with, from left to right: Michael Kemp, Billy Skeet, Geoff Fitch, Melanie Dawson, Mark Wickenden, Stephen Talbot and, kneeling, Tina Skeet

Source: Kentish Gazette
Christmas party in 1982 where an open-topped white Rolls-Royce delivered Santa Claus and his sack of presents to the hall in style and the children were entertained by 'Mr. Mystery'.

Current fund-raising events

Even though the committee had reluctantly agreed that the Easter and Michaelmas events were no longer viable, they have always felt that the village hall should continue to run events, both to raise funds and to provide an opportunity for villagers to get together. There have, of course, been many 'one-off' events over the years but the following have now become regular firm favourites.

The Craft Fair

A Craft Fair has been held in the hall at the end of each year since 1995, with stalls manned mainly by villagers selling their own crafts. Originally billed as an Arts and Crafts Festival, it coincided with National Tree Week and for the first few years villagers were invited to 'dress' the oak trees outside the hall with home made decorations to recognize the importance of trees. The Craft Fair is also noted for its refreshments provided by the committee, not least of which is the mulled wine!

Village Hall Activities

Photo: Jenny Harries

Preparing the refreshments for the Craft Fair in November 2005 are Barbara Armstrong, heating the mulled wine, and Ruth Harling

The Plant Sale

A more recent introduction (in 1997) has been the spring Plant Sale where villagers can either sell their own plants or donate plants to the hall stall for other villagers to buy. The committee also included a 'White Elephant' stall in 2006 which proved very popular and it looks likely that this too will become a regular event.

The Wine and Wisdom Quiz

Currently, the most profitable event run by the hall committee is the twice-yearly Wine and Wisdom Quiz, which started in December 1992 under the question-mastership of Mick Tuite. Fifteen years later, Mick is still the question master. In the early years he was both question-setter and marker, but was later helped by Graham Belfield and John Lewis. Since October 2003, Mick has been joined by Tim Flisher (to the cost of those who know nothing about steam trains and mountains in Scotland!). With prizes for both winners and losers and a Ploughman's

Photo: Jim Sanders

The Plant Sale in May 1999 was captured in watercolour by Ted Hill and was donated to the society by Alma Hill. The painting now hangs in the hall.

supper provided by Margaret Pomfret (since 1994!), it has become a regular fixture in February and October.

Photo: Jenny Harries

Mike Armstrong proposing a vote of thanks to question setters Mick Tuite and Tim Flisher at the Wine and Wisdom Quiz in October 2005

139

Committee activities

The 100 Club

The suggestion of running a 100 Club to increase hall funds was first made in May 1980 by Lilla Dawes, wife of the Chairman at the time, Kenneth Dawes. It involved collecting £1 per month, or £12 per year, from subscribers who were each allocated a number. A draw was made every month for three prizes with the remaining money going into hall funds. The draw had to be made in a public place with more than ten villagers present and the results had also to be posted in a public place. It was not until the beginning of 1982, when Grace Davies volunteered to run it, that it became reality with the first draw taking place in August, with prizes of £20, £15 and £10. Grace continued to run the 100 Club until April 1992 when it was handed over to Margaret Pomfret who runs it to this day. An article written by Reg Whale in the Chartham Parish Magazine calculated that Grace had raised "the magnificent sum of almost £5,000 for the village". At the Annual General Meeting in 1989, the Chairman, Adrian Williams, said that "without the 100 Club the village hall would have gone under". By 1997 the number of subscribers had risen to over the hundred mark and it was decided that, on two months of the year, June and December, the prizes would be increased to £60, £45 and £30 with a fourth prize of £20.

Margaret still goes round to each individual subscriber but encourages everyone to pay for the whole year in advance. She says "it's a long task because you have to have a little chat. But it is very good for the community and very good for the village hall". It has always been intended that these funds should be used to improve the hall's facilities and over the years they have made a significant contribution.

To thank the 100 Club members for their support, drinks and nibbles in the hall are provided from time to time by the committee, either as a separate occasion or combined with another event.

Clean-up days

A well-used hall must be clean for the hirer and the committee has played its part over the years, particularly when funds were not sufficient to employ a cleaner. Even with a cleaner, there are always extra jobs that need to be done and the Clean-up Day has become a regular event in the hall calendar when a loyal group of supporters joins members of the committee to help spruce up the hall – from sweeping cobwebs from the high ceiling to clearing drains.

Photos: Courtesy of the Ladies' Group

No job is too menial for Frank Fox left and Ruth Harling below

The first Clean-up Day was in April 1988 but perhaps the most memorable was on 7th May 1994 when, to celebrate the opening of the Channel Tunnel, funding was available from the Kent Rural Community Council for communities in East Kent to have a party with a French theme. The committee decided to make its party a working party and held a French-style Clean-up Day. A record number of villagers turned up in striped jerseys and black berets to clean the hall to strains of music from Edith Piaf. Lunch was French bread, pâté, Brie and grapes washed down with – what else? – a good French wine.

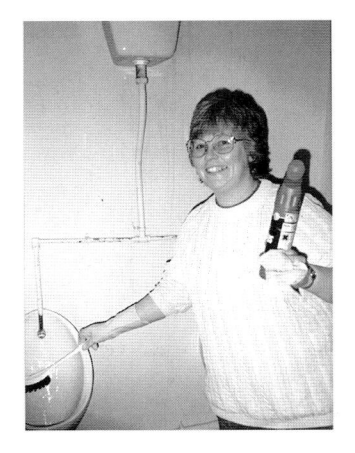

Many thanks

These are just some of the activities that have taken place in the hall over the years. There have been too many clubs and organizations to mention them all – we hope that the above selection is a good representation. The hall is, of course, also regularly hired for parties of all kinds and many other functions. We are truly grateful to all our hirers, as it is their support that ensures that the hall can continue to be used and the building preserved.

The many events over the years have provided an opportunity for villagers to get together and enjoy one another's company, as well as contributing to the hall's funds. We hope that this will continue and that there will always be villagers willing to participate in whatever way they are able.

The Tower

Photo: Veronica Litten *Photo: Ted Hill*

The damaged tower and the finished replica

Introduction

On the ridge of the village hall there is a rather ornate and possibly unique tower. It looks as if it has been there since the building was originally constructed but this is not the case. The present tower is actually a wooden replica made with painstaking care by the late Ted Hill of New Town Street.

The tower is on the part of the building extended in December 1906 and the original, made of zinc plate, was most likely fitted at this time. It is often referred to as a bell tower or a ventilation tower but what it was actually used for is still unknown. Inside the hall, aligned with the tower, is a small tube protruding through the ceiling. Passing through the tube is a short length of hooked wire, which may have had a cord attached and then secured round the cleat on the wall. The wire may have controlled a vent flap or have been used to ring a bell, but no-one knows for sure.

The great storm of October 1987

Some readers may remember TV Weather Presenter Michael Fish showing a forecast chart which was packed tight with isobars. He assured us that there would not be a hurricane, but there were certainly some very strong winds that night causing significant damage over Kent and Sussex.

In Chartham Hatch a number of buildings suffered structural damage. The Hunstead Wood Nature Reserve off Primrose Hill was devastated, access to the village was impaired by fallen trees and the tower was dislodged from the village hall roof. It took several days for the electricity supply to be restored to the village.

The only record

Luckily, local Parish Councillor Veronica Litten had the forethought to photograph the damaged tower as it stood on the ground at the back of the hall. Shortly afterwards, the tower mysteriously disappeared without trace. Veronica's photograph is the only record of the damage and without it a true replica of the tower would not have been possible.

Ted's tower

The village hall committee had originally thought of having something made to replace the tower but this had not proved possible. In March 1989, the committee approached local builder, Steve Dearing, to ask his advice. Steve remembers seeing the original tower on the ground the morning after the storm. The bottom half of the tower had been so badly damaged by the weather over the years that the zinc had almost dissolved, making the structure top heavy and very unstable. Steve contacted master craftsman Ted

Village School to Village Hall

Hill of New Town Street, who was well known for his carpentry and artistic skills, and, in August 1989, they both scaled the roof and measured the remaining stump on the ridge. It was from these measurements and Veronica's photo that Ted was able to deduce the size, shape and style of the tower. He counted the bricks in the photo to gauge the height and proportions, created working drawings and built a scale model to work out construction details and its appearance. Then the real work commenced.

Ted not only built this new tower from scratch in his garden shed but he took photos and recorded his progress on 8 mm ciné film, complete with magnetic sound track recording his comments. To quote Ted's words from the film "151 carefully crafted pieces of wood were glued and screwed together – well almost..." as a piece escaped the jaws of the vice and hit the floor.

Before it was given its protective coating, the tower was brought into Ted's sitting room at night and for a while it became part of the furniture.

Eventually the reconstruction was finished and on Sunday, 15th October 1989, while there was no-one about, the completed tower was loaded into Steve's car and taken round to the back of the hall. Steve's ladders were once again set up and Ted and Steve secured the tower back where it belonged. It was then wrapped in readiness for an unveiling and dedication ceremony on the following Sunday.

Source: Kentish Gazette
Steve (left) and Ted at the ceremony

Source: Kentish Gazette

The dedication ceremony on Sunday, 22nd October 1989

The Tower

Unveiling and dedication ceremony

The ceremony took place at 2 pm on Sunday, 22nd October 1989. It was organized by the village hall committee, officiated by the Reverend Maurice Kidd from Chartham and attended by over one hundred villagers, including many former members of the village hall committee. At the dedication Maurice led prayers and read an extract from "Choruses from 'The Rock'" by T.S. Eliot to illustrate the importance of community life. After the ceremony, high tea was served in the hall. There was coverage on TVS News and in local newspapers.

Ted's tower takes a trip to Luton

Eleven years later, the ravages of the weather had caused some rot in the pinnacle of the tower and so it was brought down for safety and closer inspection. John Bradley, visiting his mother in Bigbury Road, saw that the tower was missing and offered to renovate it. The tower then went with John to his home in Luton in the back of his car.

John used solid pine to replace the decayed pinnacle and treated the inside with bitumen paint. He was able to reuse the dormers and included a vent hole, which he protected with mesh to prevent bees from entering, under one of the dormers to reduce the risk of rot. The whole tower was cleaned and painted with Potmolen Paint®.

Photos: Ted Hill

Just three of the many stages that went into the reconstruction of the tower

Photo: Mike Armstrong
The repaired tower is replaced

On 5th March 2002, Trevor Coleman and Darryl Griffith of S&W Asphalt roof repairers carried the assembled tower up their ladders to install it in place once more.

In tribute to Ted's workmanship, John had a plaque made and fitted it underneath the top part of the tower.

MADE BY
EDWARD (TED) HILL
OCTOBER 1989

Details on the plaque made in Ted's honour by John

Still more to do

The tower is now in need of further cleaning and repair. Some of the lower parts may need to be replaced soon.

APPENDIX

Elected Officers and Committee Members of the Management Committee of the Chartham Hatch Village Hall Society, as minuted

According to the Deed of Trust the Society is entitled to eight Committee Members, plus representatives of each organization using the Hall.

1967
Mr. L.A. Mount	Chairman
Mr. J. Auty	
Mr. F.J. Smith	
Mr. J. Faiers (to 5.6.67)	
Mr. R.J. Dissington	
Mr. J.H. Bennett	
Mr. K. Thomson	
Mr. T. Lyons (from 14.4.67-5.6.67)	
Mr. R. Williams (from 20.11.67)	
Mr. B. Allen (from 20.11.67)	

1968
Mr. L.A. Mount
Mr. J. Auty
Mr. F.J. Smith
Mr. R.J. Dissington
Mr. J.H. Bennett
Mr. K. Thomson
Mr. R. Williams
Mr. B. Allen
Mr. D. Andrews (from 4.1.68)

First meeting of the Management Committee – 16.10.68
Mr. L.A. Mount	Chairman
Mr. J. Auty	Treasurer
Mr. J.H. Bennett	Secretary
Mr. D. Andrews	
Mr. B. Allen	
Mr. P. Nash	
Mrs. H. Fitch	Nursery
Mrs. P. Bennett	Keep-Fit
Mrs. J. Bailey	Whist Drive
Mrs. W. Allen	Library/ Woodcraft Folk
Mrs. Barker	Chartham Parish Council
Mr. A. Moat	Chartham Parish Council
Mrs. J. Harrison	Welcome Club
Rev. R. Lloyd (from 20.11.68)	

1969
Mr. L.A. Mount	Chairman
Mr. J.H. Bennett (to 9.6.69)	Secretary
Mr. & Mrs. R.N. Nash (from 9.6.69)	Joint Secretaries
Mr. J. Auty	Treasurer/Vice Chairman (28.4.69)
Mrs. J. Harrison	Welcome Club
Mr. J. Faiers	Senior Citizens
Mr. A.H. Moat	Gardening Club/ Parish Council
Mrs. P. Bennett	Keep Fit
Mrs. J. Bailey	Whist Drive
Mrs. W. Allen	Library/ Woodcraft Folk
Mrs. J. Barker	Church of England
Mrs. H. Fitch	Nursery
Mr. R. Barrows	
Mr. Brooks	
Mrs. Brooks	
Mr. D. Andrews	
Rev. R. Lloyd	

1970
Mr. L.A. Mount (to 16.4.70)	Chairman
Mr. A. Moat (from 16.4.70)	Chairman
Mr. J. Auty	Vice Chairman/ Treasurer
Mr. & Mrs. Nash	Joint Secretaries
Mr. D. Andrews	
Mr. Bellamy	Senior Citizens
Mrs. V. Elvidge	
Mrs. Harrison	
Mr. E. Opie	

Mr. L.A. Mount accepted the Office of President – 16.4.70

1971
Mr. A. Moat	Chairman
Mr. J. Auty	Vice Chairman/ Treasurer
Mr. D. Andrews	
Mrs. V. Elvidge	
Mr. E. Opie	

Village School to Village Hall

Mr. D. Kemp
Mrs. Tomlin

Dr. Dawes accepted the Office of Honorary Vice President – 21.6.71

1972
Mr. A. Moat	Chairman
Mr. E. Opie	Vice Chairman
Mr. J. Auty	Secretary/Treasurer
Mrs. W. Allen	County Library
Mr. D. Andrews	
Mrs. J. Bailey	Whist Drives
Mrs. K. Barker	Chartham Parish Church
Mrs. P. Bennett	Welcome Club
Mr. R. Cooper	Chartham Parish Council
Mrs. H. Fitch	Nursery
Mr. D. Kemp	
Mr. D. Leech	
Mrs. Tomlin	

1973
Mr. A. Moat	Chairman
Mr. E. Opie	Vice Chairman
Mr. J. Auty	Secretary/Treasurer
Mrs. W. Allen	County Library
Mr. D. Andrews	
Mrs. J. Bailey	Whist Drives
Mrs. J. Barker	Senior Citizens
Mrs. K. Barker	Chartham Parish Church
Mrs. P. Bennett	Welcome Club
Dr. K. Dawes (from 23.7.73)	
Mrs. H. Fitch	Nursery
Mrs. J. Knight (from 4.4.73)	
Mr. D. Leech	
Mrs. Tomlin	
Mr. C.P. Wells	

1974
Mr. A. Moat	Chairman
Mr. E. Opie	Vice Chairman
Mr. J. Auty	Secretary/Treasurer
Mrs. W. Allen	County Library
Mrs. J. Bailey (from 8.4.75)	
Mrs. J. Barker	Senior Citizens
Mrs. K. Barker	Chartham Parish Church
Mrs. P. Bennett	Welcome Club
Dr. K. Dawes	Vice Chairman from 28.10.74
Mrs. H. Fitch	Nursery
Mrs. J. Knight	
Mrs. Tomlin	
Mr. C.P. Wells	
Mr. R. Burgess (from 13.5.74)	
Miss J. Martin (from 8.7.74)	Youth Club
Mr. N. Dawes (from 8.7.74)	Youth Club
Mr. & Mrs. Woodbridge (from 9.9.74)	

1975
Dr. K. Dawes	Chairman
Mr. A. Moat	Vice Chairman/Chartham Parish Council
Mr. J. Auty	Secretary/Treasurer
Mrs. W. Allen	County Library
Mrs. J. Barker	Senior Citizens
Mrs. K. Barker	Chartham Parish Church
Mrs. P. Bennett	
Mr. R. Burgess	
Mr. N. Dawes	Youth Club
Mrs. H. Fitch	Nursery
Mrs J. Knight	
Miss J. Martin	Youth Club
Mr. C.P. Wells	
Mr. & Mrs. Woodbridge	

1976
Dr. K. Dawes	Chairman
Mr. A. Moat	Vice Chairman/Chartham Parish Council
Mr. J. Auty	Secretary/Treasurer
Mrs. W. Allen	County Library
Mrs. J. Barker	Senior Citizens
Mrs. P. Bennett	
Mr. R. Burgess	
Mr. N. Dawes (from 8.4.76)	
Mr. M. Down (from 8.4.76)	
Mrs. H. Fitch	Nursery
Mrs. H. Groombridge	Ladies Keep Fit
Mr. A. Jankowski (from 8.4.76)	
Mrs. J. Knight	
Mr. P. Webb	
Mr. & Mrs. Woodbridge	

1977
Dr. K. Dawes	Chairman
Mr. A. Moat	Vice Chairman

Mr. J. Auty	Secretary/Treasurer	Mrs. G. Walton (from 23.4.79)	
Mrs. P. Bennett		Mr. A. Williams (from 23.4.79)	
Mr. R. Burgess		Mrs. A. Woodbridge	
Mr. N. Dawes			
Mr. M. Down		**1980**	
Mrs. H. Fitch	Nursery	Dr. K. Dawes	Chairman
Mrs. H. Groombridge		Mr. P. Hill	Vice Chairman
Mr. A. Jankowski		Mr. J. Auty	Secretary/Treasurer
Mrs. J. Knight			
Mr. D. Millis	Chartham Parish Council	Mrs. J. Barker	
		Mrs. P. Bennett	
Mr. R. Philpott (from 2.5.77)		Mrs. G. Davies	
Mrs. M. Pomfret (from 2.5.77)		Mrs. W. Dyer	Nursery
		Mr. A. Jankowski	
Mr. C.P. Wells		Mrs. J. Kirby	Ladies Keep Fit
Mrs. A. Woodbridge		Mrs. J. Knight	
		Mr. D. Millis	Chartham Parish Council
1978			
Dr. K. Dawes	Chairman	Mrs. M. Pomfret	
Mr. A. Moat	Vice Chairman	Mrs. G. Walton	
Mr. J. Auty	Secretary/Treasurer	Mr. A. Williams	
		Mr. S. Wilson (from 29.4.80)	
Mrs. J. Barker		Mrs. A. Woodbridge	
Mrs. P. Bennett			
Mr. N. Dawes		**1981**	
Mrs. H. Fitch	Nursery	Dr. K. Dawes	Chairman
Mr. P. Hill (from 17.4.78)		Mr. P. Hill	Vice Chairman
Mr. A. Jankowski		Mr. J. Auty	Secretary/Treasurer
Mrs. J. Kirby	Ladies Keep Fit		
Mrs. J. Knight		Mrs. J. Barker	
Mr. D. Millis	Chartham Parish Council	Mrs. G. Davies	
		Mrs. W. Dyer	Nursery
Mrs. M. Pomfret		Mrs. K. Johnson (from 6.4.81)	
Mr. C.P. Wells		Mrs. J. Knight	
Mrs. A. Woodbridge		Mrs. H. Lingham	Ladies Keep Fit
		Mr. D. Millis	Chartham Parish Council
1979			
Dr. K. Dawes	Chairman	Mrs. M. Pomfret	
Mr. P. Hill	Vice Chairman	Mr. C. Rymill (from 6.4.81)	
Mr. J. Auty	Secretary/Treasurer	Mr. S. Walton (from 6.4.81)	
Mrs. J. Barker		Mrs. G. Walton	
Mrs. P. Bennett		Mr. A. Williams	
Mrs. G. Davies (from 23.4.79)		Mr. S. Wilson	
Mr. N. Dawes		Mrs. A. Woodbridge	
Mrs. P. Dearing	Mothers and Toddlers	**1982**	
Mrs. W. Dyer	Nursery	Dr. K. Dawes	Chairman
Mr. A. Jankowski		Mr. P. Hill	Vice Chairman
Mrs. J. Kirby	Ladies Keep Fit	Mr. J. Auty	Secretary/Treasurer
Mrs. J. Knight			
Mr. C. Laming	Table Tennis	Mrs. J. Barker	
Mr. D. Millis	Chartham Parish Council	Mr. E. Callender (from 22.4.82)	
Mrs. M. Pomfret			

Mrs. G. Davies
Mr. T. Davis
(from 22.4.82)
Mrs. W. Dyer
Mr. R. Elvidge
Mrs. D. Kentish
(from 22.4.82)
Mrs. J. Knight
Mrs. H. Lingham
Mr. D. Millis

Mrs. M. Pomfret
Mr. C. Rymill
Mrs. G. Walton
Mr. A. Williams
Mr. S. Walton
Mr. S. Wilson
Mrs. A. Woodbridge

100 Club

Nursery
Sports Club

Ladies Keep Fit
Chartham Parish
Council

1983
Dr. K. Dawes
Mr. P. Hill
Mrs. H. Lingham
Mr. S. Wilson
Mr. E. Callender

Mrs. J. Barker
Mrs. C. Davis
(from 20.4.83)
Mrs. G. Davies
Mrs. W. Dyer
Mr. R. Elvidge
Mrs. D. Kentish
Mr. D. Millis
Mrs. M. Pomfret
Mr. C. Rymill

Mrs. G. Walton
Mr. S. Walton
Mr. A. Williams

Chairman
Vice Chairman
Secretary
Treasurer
Booking Sec. &
Maintenance

100 Club
Nursery
Sports Club

Michaelmas Fayre
Organiser

1984
Mr. D. Millis
Mr. S. Walton
Mrs. H. Lingham
Mr. S. Wilson
Mr. E. Callender
Mrs. J. Barker
Mrs. L. Bishop
Mrs. C. Davis
Mrs. G. Davies
Dr. K. Dawes
Mrs. W. Dyer
Mr. R. Elvidge
Mrs. T. Goodban
Mrs. D. Kentish
Mrs. M. Pomfret
Mr. C. Rymill
Mrs. G. Walton

Chairman
Vice Chairman
Secretary
Treasurer
Booking Sec.

Ladies Keep Fit

100 Club

Nursery
Sports Club

Mr. A. Williams

1985
Mr. D. Millis
Mr. S. Walton
Mrs. H. Lingham
Mr. S. Wilson
Mr. A. Williams
Mr. C. Rymill
Mrs. J. Barker
Mrs. .L. .Bishop
Mrs. A. Bradfield
(from 17.4.85)
Mrs. C. Davis
Mrs. G. Davies
Mrs. L. Dawes
(from 17.4.85)
Dr. K. Dawes
Mr. R. Elvidge
Mrs. T. Goodban
Mrs. D. Kentish
Mrs. M. Pomfret
Mrs. G. Walton

Chairman
Vice Chairman
Secretary
Treasurer
Booking Sec.
Special Events

Ladies Club

Nursery
100 Club

Keep Fit

Sports Club

1986
Mr. D. Millis
Mr. S. Walton
Mr. B. Allen
(from 17.4.86)
Mr. T. Pilbeam
(from 17.4.86)
Mr. A. Williams
Mr. C. Rymill
Mrs. G. Davis
Dr. K. Dawes
Mrs. L. Dawes
Mr. R. Elvidge
Mrs. H. Fitch
(from 17.4.86)
Mrs. D. Pilbeam
(from 17.4.86)
Mrs. G. Walton
Mr. S. Wilson

Chairman
Vice Chairman
Secretary

Treasurer

Booking Clerk
Special Events

Keep Fit
Sports Club

1987
Mr. D. Millis
Dr. K. Dawes
Mrs. M. Bennett
(from 8.5.87)
Mr. T. Pilbeam
Mr. A. Williams
Mr. B. Allen
Mrs .G. Davies
Mrs. L. Dawes
Mrs. C. Fisk
(from 8.5.87)
Mrs. H. Fitch
Mr. H. Rogers
(from 8.5.87)

Chairman
Vice Chairman
Secretary

Treasurer
Booking Sec.

100 Club

Mr. C. Rymill
Mr. S. Wellard
(from 8.5.87)
Mr. S. Wilson

1988
Mr. A. Williams	Chairman
Mrs. H. Lingham	Secretary
Mrs. L. Robson	Treasurer
(from 8.4.88)	
Mrs. L. Larrigan	Booking Sec.
Mrs. C. Davis	
Mrs. G. Davies	100 Club
Mr. R. Elvidge	Sports Club
Mrs. C. Fisk	
Mr. P. Whistler	
(from 8.4.88)	

These members include representatives from the Ladies Group, Mens Keep Fit, Ladies Keep Fit and Nursery School.

1989
Mr. P. Whistler	Chairman
Mrs. V. Elvidge	Vice Chairman
(from 18.5.89)	
Mrs. L. Larrigan	Secretary/ Booking Clerk
Dr. M. Tuite	Treasurer
(from 18.5.89)	
Mrs. C. Davis	Advertising/ Publicity
Mrs. M. Cox	
(from 18.5.89)	
Mrs. G. Davies	100 Club
Mrs. J. Lane	
(from 30.3.89)	

1990
Mr. P. Whistler	Chairman
Mrs. V. Elvidge	Vice Chairman
Mrs. L. Larrigan	Secretary/ Booking Clerk
Dr. M. Tuite	Treasurer
Mrs. C. Davis	Publicity
Mrs. G. Davies	100 Club
Mrs. M. Cox	
Mrs. M. Sparks	
Mr. R. Whale	Chairman from 12.8.90
Mrs. M. Pomfret	
(from 12.8.90)	

1991
Mr. T. Davis	Chairman
Mrs. L. Larrigan	Secretary
Dr. M.Tuite	Treasurer
Mrs. C. Davis	Advertising
Mrs. G. Davies	100 Club
Mrs. M. Cox	
Mrs. V. Elvidge	
Mrs. M. Pomfret	
Mrs. M. Sparks	

1992
Mr. T. Davis	Chairman
Mrs. L. Larrigan	Secretary
Dr. M.Tuite	Treasurer
Mrs. C. Davis	Advertising
Mrs. M. Pomfret	100 Club
Mrs. M. Cox	
Mrs. V. Elvidge	
Mr. T. Flynn	
(from 11.6.92)	
Mrs. P. Lewis	
Mrs. M. McCormack	
Mr. V. McCormack	
Mrs. M. Sparks	
Mr. J.A. Wilmot	

1993
Mr. J. Wilmot	Chairman
Mrs. V. Elvidge	Vice Chairman
Mrs. L. Larrigan	Secretary
Dr. M. Tuite	Treasurer
Mrs. C. Davis	Advertising
(to 11.3.93)	
Mrs. M. Pomfret	100 Club
Mr. T. Flynn	
Mrs. P. Lewis	
Mr. J. Lewis	
(from 11.3.93)	
Mrs. P. Torralba	
Mr. T. Davis	
(to 11.3.93)	
Mr. V. McCormack	

1994
Mr. J. Wilmot	Chairman
Mrs. V. Elvidge	Vice Chairman
Mrs. L. Larrigan	Secretary
Mrs. J. Harries	Treasurer
(from 11.3.94)	
Mr. T. Flynn	
Mrs. R. Harling	
(from 11.3.94)	
Mrs. P. Lewis	
Mrs. M. Pomfret	100 Club
Mrs. J. Simmons	
(from 11.3.94)	
Mrs. P. Torralba	
Dr. M. Tuite	
Mr. G. Belfield	
(from 11.3.94)	

1995
Prof. M. Tuite	Chairman
Mrs. V. Elvidge	Vice Chairman

Village School to Village Hall

Mrs. L. Larrigan — Sec./Bookings
Mrs. J. Harries — Treasurer
Mrs. M. Pomfret — 100 Club
Mrs. D. Beck
(from 10.3.05)
Mr. G. Belfield
Mrs. R. Harling
Mrs. P. Lewis
Mrs. J. Simmons
Mr. J. Wilmot
Mr. M.J. Armstrong
(from 10.3.95)

1996
Prof. M. Tuite — Chairman
Mrs. V. Elvidge — Vice Chairman
Mrs. P. Lewis — Secretary
Mrs. J. Harries — Treasurer
Mrs. J. Simmons — Bookings Clerk
(from 26.9.96)
Mrs. M. Pomfret — 100 Club
Mr. M. Armstrong
Mrs. D. Beck
Mr. G. Belfield
(to 30.5.96)
Mr. D. Cage
(from 28.3.96)
Mrs. R. Harling — Publicity Officer
Mrs. L. Larrigan
Mrs. H. Stevens
(from 28.3.96)
Mr. J. Wilmot
(to 28.3.96)

1997
Mr. M.J. Armstrong — Chairman
Mrs. V. Elvidge — Vice Chairman
Mrs. P. Lewis — Secretary
Mrs. J. Harries — Treasurer
Mrs. J. Simmons — Bookings Clerk
Mrs. M. Pomfret — 100 Club
Mrs. R. Harling — Publicity Officer
Mr D. Cage
Mrs. H. Stevens
Prof. M. Tuite
Mr. J. Wilmot

1998
Mr. M. Armstrong — Chairman
Mrs. V. Elvidge — Vice Chairman (to 26.3.98)
Mrs. P. Lewis — Secretary
Mrs. J. Harries — Treasurer
Mrs. J. Simmons — Bookings Clerk
Mrs. R. Harling — Publicity
Mrs. M. Pomfret — 100 Club
Mr. D. Cage
Mrs. H. Stevens — Vice Chairman (from 26.3.98)
Prof. M. Tuite

1999
Mr. M.J. Armstrong — Chairman
Mrs. H. Stevens — Vice Chairman
Mrs. P. Lewis — Secretary
Mrs. J. Harries — Treasurer
Mrs. J. Simmons — Bookings Clerk
Mrs. R. Harling — Publicity Officer
Mrs. M. Pomfret — 100 Club
Mr. D. Cage
Mrs. V. Elvidge
Mr. E. Gaskell
(from 25.3.99)
Mrs. A. Griffiths
(from 25.3.99)
Prof. A. Griffiths
(from 25.3.99)

2000
Mr. M.J. Armstrong — Chairman
Mrs. H. Stevens — Vice Chairman
Mrs. P. Lewis — Secretary
Mrs. J. Harries — Treasurer
Mrs. J. Simmons — Bookings Clerk
Mrs. R. Harling — Publicity Officer
Mrs. M. Pomfret — 100 Club
Mr. D. Cage
Mr. E. Gaskell
Mrs. A. Griffiths
Prof. A. Griffiths
Mrs. G. Dodds
(from 13.4.00)
Mrs. N. Brooker
(from 13.4.00)

2001
Mr. M.J. Armstrong — Chairman
Mrs. H. Stevens — Vice Chairman
Mrs. P. Lewis — Secretary
Mrs. J. Harries — Treasurer
Mrs. J. Simmons — Bookings Clerk
Mrs. R. Harling — Publicity Officer
Mrs. M. Pomfret — 100 Club
Mr. D. Cage
Mr. E. Gaskell
(to 25.10.01)
Mrs. A. Griffiths
Prof. A. Griffiths
Mrs. G. Dodds
Mrs. N. Brooker

2002
Mr. M.J. Armstrong — Chairman
Mrs. H. Stevens — Vice Chairman
Mrs. P. Lewis — Secretary
Mrs. J. Harries — Treasurer
Mrs. J. Simmons — Bookings Clerk
Mrs. R. Harling — Publicity Officer

Appendix

Mrs. M. Pomfret	(to 28.2.02)	Ms K. Harrison	Painting Club
Mr. D. Cage	100 Club	Mrs. M. Wheeler	Ladies' Group
Mrs. A. Griffiths		(to 24.6.04)	
Prof. A. Griffiths		Mrs. N. Johnson	Mothers and Toddlers
Mrs. G. Dodds		Mrs. J. Bradley	Over 50s
(to 28.3.02)			
Mrs. N. Brooker	Publicity Officer	**2005**	
	(from 28.2.02)	Mrs. H. Stevens	Acting Chairman
Mrs. V. Elvidge		(to 21.4.05)	
(from 25.4.02)		Mr. M.J. Armstrong	Chairman
			(from 21.4.05)
2003		Mrs. V. Elvidge	Vice-Chairman
Prof. J. Lewis	Chairman	Mrs. R. Harling	Acting Secretary
(from 10.4.03)			(to 31.3.05), Chartham
Mrs. H. Stevens	Vice Chairman		Parish Church, Ladies
Mrs. P. Lewis	Secretary		Group
Mrs. J. Harries	Treasurer	Mrs. E. Anderson	Secretary
Mrs. J. Hitchen	Bookings Clerk		(from 31.3.05)
(from 10.4.03)		Mrs. J. Harries	Treasurer
Mrs. R. Harling		Mrs. J. Hitchen	Bookings Clerk
Mrs. M. Pomfret	100 Club	Mrs. M. Pomfret	100 Club
Mr. D. Cage		Mrs. N. Brooker	Publicity Officer
Mrs. A. Griffiths		Mr. D. Cage	
(to 27.3.03)		Mrs. J. Simmons	
Prof. A. Griffiths		Mr. T. Jordan	Gardeners' Society
(to 27.3.03)		Mr. R. Neve	City of Canterbury
Mrs. N. Brooker	Publicity Officer		Band
Mrs. V. Elvidge		Ms K. Harrison	Painting Club
Mr. M.J. Armstrong		Mrs. N. Johnson	Mothers and Toddlers
Mrs. J. Simmons		Mrs. J. Bradley	Over 50s
Mrs. G. Talbot		Mrs. A. Dawes	Chartham Parish
(from 10.4.03)			Council
		Mrs. B. Hart	
2004		(to 24.11.04)	
Prof. J. Lewis	Chairman (to 15.4.04)	**2006**	
(to 16.6.04)		Mr. M.J. Armstrong	Chairman
Mrs. P. Lewis	Secretary (to 15.4.04)	Mrs. V. Elvidge	Vice-Chairman
(to 16.6.04)		Mrs. E. Anderson	Secretary
Mrs. H. Stevens	Acting Chairman	Mrs. J. Harries	Treasurer
	(from 15.4.04)	Mrs. J. Hitchen	Bookings Clerk
Mrs. R. Harling)	Acting Secretary,	Mrs. M. Pomfret	100 Club
	Chartham Parish	Mrs. N. Brooker	Publicity Officer
	Church (from 15.4.04)	Mr. T. Jordan	Gardeners' Society
	and Ladies Group	Mr. R. Neve	City of Canterbury
	(from 24.6.04)		Band
Mrs. E. Anderson)	Acting Secretary	Mrs. J. Bradley	Over 50s
	(from 15.4.04)	Mrs. A. Dawes	Chartham Parish
Mrs. J. Harries	Treasurer		Council
Mrs. J. Hitchen	Bookings Clerk		
Mrs. M. Pomfret	100 Club	**2007**	
Mrs. N. Brooker	Publicity Officer	Mr. M.J. Armstrong	Chairman
Mrs. V. Elvidge		Mrs. V. Elvidge	Vice-Chairman
Mr. M.J. Armstrong		Mrs. E. Anderson	Secretary
Mrs. J. Simmons		Mrs. J. Harries	Treasurer
Mr. D. Cage		Mrs. J. Hitchen	Bookings Clerk
Mr. T. Jordan	Gardeners' Society	Mrs. M. Pomfret	100 Club
Mr. R. Neve	City of Canterbury	Mrs. N. Brooker	Publicity Officer
	Band	Mr. T. Jordan	Gardeners' Society

Mr. R. Neve   City of Canterbury Band
Mrs. J. Bradley   Over 50s
Mrs. A. Dawes   Chartham Parish Council

Mr. C. Anderson